THE FAMILY CAT

THE FAMILY
CAT

AN OWNER'S GUIDE TO ALL ASPECTS OF
CARING FOR YOUR CAT

CONSULTANT EDITOR:

DAVID TAYLOR BVMS, FRCVS, FZS

First published in 2001 by
HarperCollins*Publishers*
77–85 Fulham Palace Road
Hammersmith
London W6 8JB

The HarperCollins website address is www.**fire**and**water**.com
Collins is a registered trademark of HarperCollins Publishers Limited.

07 06 05 04 03 02 01
9 8 7 6 5 4 3 2 1

Text, design and illustrations © HarperCollins*Publishers* Ltd, 2000
Photographs © HarperCollins*Publishers*, Frank Lane Picture Library, The British
Museum and Marc Henrie.

David Taylor hereby asserts his moral rights to be identified as the author of
his Contribution. Sarah Heath hereby asserts her moral rights to be identified
as the author of her Contribution. Dr David Sands hereby asserts his moral
rights to be identified as the author of his Contribution. Trina Balharrie hereby
asserts her moral rights to be identified as the author of her Contribution.

A catalogue record of this book is available from the British Library

ISBN 0 00 710323 9

This book was created by
SP Creative Design
Editor: **Heather Thomas**
Art director and production: **Rolando Ugolini**
Artwork illustrations: **Rolando Ugolini**

Photography: Rolando Ugolini
Additional photography
Key: t - top, b - bottom, l - left, r - right, c - centre
British Museum: 16, 17
Charlie Colmer: 3, 5br, 10, 20, 22, 23, 26, 27b, 36, 38t, 48, 60t, 62t, 70, 85t,
88b, 91, 101, 103, 104, 107t, 113, 138b, 142, 146, 152, 169, 178, 191, 192
David Dalton: 24t, 41br, 43t, 44b, 81b, 85b, 96r, 100
Frank Lane Picture Library: 14 Philip Perry, 179 Gerard Lacz
Marc Henrie: 145, 149, 167t, 171t, 172, 179, 182, 184, 185, 187t, 188b
Richard Palmer: 77
Marion Rutherford: 155
Bruce Tanner: 32t, 33t, 45, 46br, 68, 78t, 82, 94, 134, 175b,
Rolando Ugolini: 1, 4, 5, 8, 9, 11, 15, 18, 19, 21, 24b, 25, 27t, 28, 29, 30, 31, 32b,
33b, 37, 38b, 39, 40, 41c, 41t, , 42, 43b, 44c, 44t, 46c, 46t, 47, 49, 50, 51, 52, 54,
55, 56, 57, 58, 59, 60b, 61, 62b, 63, 64, 65, 66, 67, 69, 71, 72, 73, 74, 75, 76, 77b,
78b, 79, 80, 81t, 81c, 83, 84, 86, 88t, 89, 90, 92, 93, 95, 96l, 97, 98, 99, 102, 105,
106, 107, 118, 125, 127, 129, 135, 136, 137, 138, 139, 140, 143, 144, 147, 148,
149t, 150, 151, 153, 154, 156, 157, 158, 159, 160, 161, 162, 163, 164, 165, 166,
167b, 168, 170, 171b, 172t, 173, 174, 175c, 175t, 176, 177, 180, 181, 182t, 183,
186, 187b, 188t, 189

Colour reproduction by Colourscan, Singapore
Printed and bound by Printing Express Ltd, Hong Kong

Contents

Part One

Owning a cat

Part Two

Cat behaviour

Consultant editor

David Taylor BVMS, FRCVS, FZS

David Taylor is a well-known veterinary surgeon and broadcaster and the author of over thirty books, including six volumes of autobiography, some of which formed the basis for three series of the BBC television drama *One by One*.

He has also written the *Small Pet Handbook* and *Collins Family Pet Guides: Rabbit*. The founder of the International Zoo Veterinary Group, he has exotic patients across the world, ranging from crocodiles to killer whales and giant pandas. He lives in Richmond, Surrey, with his wife, four cats and a hamster called 'Fudge'.

Contributors

Trina Balharrie

Trina Balharrie started showing and breeding cats in 1984 when she got her first Birman and is very active within the Cat Fancy. She is a committee member of two Birman breed clubs and is the joint magazine editor for one of these clubs. She often stewards for pedigree judges as well as judging in the non-pedigree section. She takes part in seminars all over Britain, where she talks about breeding and rearing cats. She has also been featured with her cats in a BBC television programme about the National Cat Club Show. Trina lives in Maidenhead, Berkshire, with her husband, son, nine Birmans, an elderly 'moggie' and a Cavalier King Charles Spaniel.

Sarah Heath BVSc MRCVS

Sarah Heath qualified as a veterinary surgeon from Bristol University in 1988 and spent four years in mixed general practice before setting up a behavioural referral practice in 1992. She sees cases at monthly behavioural clinics at Bristol and Liverpool University Veterinary Schools and at private veterinary practices in northwest England. She is currently Secretary for the BSAVA affiliated Companion Animal Behaviour Therapy Study Group and Veterinary Officer for the Association of Pet Behaviour Counsellors. She is also Secretary of the European Society of Veterinary Clinical Ethology. Sarah lectures extensively on behavioural topics and is an Honorary Lecturer in the Department of Veterinary Clinical Sciences and Animal Husbandry at the University of Liverpool. She contributes to the undergraduate veterinary curriculum at both Liverpool and Bristol Universities and the Royal Veterinary College. In addition to her clinical work, she writes regularly on behavioural topics for veterinary publications and popular magazines, has written the books *Why Does My Cat...?* and *Cat and Kitten Behaviour*, and is involved in radio and television work on the topic of animal behaviour.

Dr David Sands

Dr David Sands runs the Animal Behavioural Clinic in Chorley, England, treating pet dogs, cats, birds and horses. He is an internationally established author and photographer with a doctorate in ethology. David has been featured in several British television documentaries and programmes and has also contributed to TV and radio on related human and pet companionship subjects. He has scripted a number of animal information videos on small animals, dogs and cats and has contributed to and written many books including *Cats and Kittens*, *Dogs and Puppies* and the *To The Rescue – Dogs* and *To The Rescue – Cats* guides on providing a rescue or re-homed dog or cat with a new life.

Foreword

A harmless, necessary cat

William Shakespeare: The Merchant of Venice, Act IV Scene 1

Do you suffer from ailurophilia? If so, you're in distinguished company. Pope Gregory I, Cardinal Wolsey, Richelieu, King Louis XV, Abraham Lincoln, Theodore Roosevelt, Sir Harold Wilson, Mussolini, Lenin, Doctor Johnson all had it in common. So does my charlady. So, in chronic advanced form, do I. It is the love of miw the sacred, of the Egyptian Goddess, Bast, of the inscrutable grimalkin, of the *Felis catus L.*, the domestic cat.

There are a hundred good reasons for having a cat around. Economic to run, self-exercising, small and relatively silent, they are ideal for folk of limited means, for the old, for those who live in blocks of flats. Cats are easily acquired, unless of course your household mouser must be a Mexican Hairless or a Red Self Persian with a pedigree that reads like Doomsday Book. In the normal run of things, people just acquire cats or cats just acquire people. One walks in on the other and, if the stars are right for both the human and the feline side of the partnership, a permanent union develops.

I hesitate to use the word 'owned'. Cats, unlike dogs, do not take lightly to being 'owned'. Many cats own people. A cat's individuality, its 'self', is never up for grabs. So it is perhaps more accurate to say that a cat sojourns with its adopted *homo sapiens*.

Nevertheless, with such lodgers under one's roof, remarkably constructed athletes, not-so-distant relatives of the Lords of the Jungle, which have raised religions, toppled kings, drawn the thunders of the Vatican and the protection of princes, it is vital to look intelligently to their needs and their foibles. Care for your quest well and he or she will reward you abundantly.

David Taylor BVMS, FRCVS, FZS

Owning a cat

When you decide to welcome a cat into your home, you are taking on not only a new member of your family but also a commitment to care responsibly for your new pet. Contrary to what many people may think, cats do not fend for themselves, and there's more to owning a cat than just feeding it.

By learning about this fascinating animal's evolution and history, you can understand its behaviour better. By finding out about different breeds and humble moggies, you can choose a cat that will become your much-loved companion. And by truthfully examining your lifestyle, you can assess how much time and effort you are prepared to put into building and sustaining a rewarding relationship.

Chapter One

HISTORY OF THE CAT

In order to fully appreciate the mystery of the cat, you must understand something of its history and the way in which its relationship with mankind has survived and flourished over the centuries. Domestication is something of an anathema to the cat; domestic species are supposed to be under the control of man but most cat owners would agree that their cats are under the control of nobody but themselves. This is an independent creature, which has proved itself to be highly adaptable, and, while it enjoys a mutually beneficial relationship with humans, few of us would be so presumptuous as to assume that we were the ones who are in control.

Selecting for tolerance and affection

It is certainly true that man has manipulated the cat to some extent in order to fulfil certain functions, and in the early years of the relationship the cat

■ **Right:** *Although cats retain a high level of independence, they can also be very rewarding companions.*

was certainly a valuable asset to the communities in which it lived. Tolerance, affection and tameness were qualities that enabled cats to live closer to human settlements and therefore have access to a reliable source of food and shelter. Through a rather primitive form of selective breeding, it was individuals with these traits that managed to pass their genes on to the next

generation. However, most cats retained a level of freedom and independence that effectively kept man at arm's length, and many of the non-pedigree cats of today work on much the same principle. Humans have no effective control over their breeding programmes, and variations in size, conformation and appearance are kept to a minimum.

Pedigree cats, on the other hand, have been under far greater influence from man's desires in terms of appearance and behaviour. Some diversity in shape, size and function can be seen within the recognised breeds, but even then the level of manipulation endured by cats pales into insignificance when compared to the human control over breeding in the canine world.

■ **Opposite:** *Despite the process of selective breeding, cats show very little variation in size and shape, as is emphasised in this Egyptian Mau, which can trace its origins back to Ancient Egypt.*

The origins of the modern cat

As a result of this minimal human interference, today's cat has altered very little from its original wild type and, in terms of its behaviour, much can be learned about our modern pet by studying its ancestors. The exact ancestry of the domestic cat has been a subject of some debate over the years, but it is generally accepted that the most likely candidate for the direct ancestor of our modern domestic cat is the African wild cat (*Felis lybica*). Evidence for a link between this species and our feline friends comes from a variety of sources, including studies of anatomy, similarities in coat colour and patterns, similarity of brain size, as measured by the cranial capacity of the skull, and also a common chromosome complement of nineteen pairs.

At one time, the African wild cat was thought to be a distinct species from the European or Scottish wild cat (*Felis sylvestris*). Certainly there are some very marked differences between them in terms of appearance and of temperament, but it is now accepted that they are, in fact, two extremes within the same species. The African wild cat is a fine-boned creature with long legs, a small head and proportionately large ears, whereas its Scottish relative is of a much heavier build with short, stocky limbs and short, neat ears. Both of the cats have a striped tabby coat, but the heavy markings of the Scottish wild cat appear to have more in common with the coat of the modern-day cat than with the more flecked appearance of the African wild cat.

It is in the realm of behaviour that the links between the modern domestic cat and its African ancestor become clear, and whilst the appearance of the Scottish wild cat may make it a potential candidate for the true ancestor of our modern-day companion, its temperament illustrates how unlikely this relationship is.

Research into the behaviour of the Scottish wild cat has shown it to be a virtually untameable species and, despite intensive contact with kittens during the most influential early weeks of life, researchers have found that it is impossible to make any significant progress towards forming a real relationship with these cats. Even the offspring of successful cross-matings between one of the Scottish wild cats and a domestic feline showed noticeable problems of nervousness and poor temperament, and in every case they could not be trusted by humans by the time they were a few months old.

In contrast, the African wild cat has a strong affinity with people and, although no attempt has been made to domesticate the cats in the southern part of Sudan, these individuals show a marked willingness to live close to the settlements of the local Azande tribe.

The role of the jungle cat

One extra piece of the jigsaw that makes up the history of our modern cat comes in the form of the jungle cat (*Felis chaus*). While most authorities are happy to accept that the African wild cat is indeed the true ancestor of our feline companions, some question the involvement of the jungle cat in the mysterious process of

Below: There has been some debate over the origins of the domestic cat but it is generally accepted that the African Wild Cat (Felis lybica) is the direct ancester of our modern feline companions.

feline domestication. Certainly mummified remains of *Felis chaus* have been found alongside those of *Felis lybica*, and research has shown that cross matings between the jungle cat and the modern domestic cat can result in offspring with an increased level of tolerance towards human beings. However, there are too many questions that remain unanswered for any definite conclusions to be drawn, and the exact genetic origins of the modern domestic cat are still something of a mystery.

No doubt, we could have learnt a great deal by studying the vast numbers of feline mummies which were buried in Ancient Egypt, and when a consignment of nineteen tons of these mummies were docked at Liverpool in 1889 a unique opportunity to unravel the mystery of feline domestication was certainly on offer. However, the people of that time failed to recognise the historical significance of the cargo and, with the exception of one cat skull which is now on display in the British Museum, this precious load was sold off as fertilizer.

The love-hate relationship with man

Although we have limited information about the genetic origins of the domestic cat, we do have substantial information about its relationship with man and the most striking feature of this aspect of feline history is the variation in human attitude to the feline species over the years. No other domesticated animal has experienced such periods of overt devotion and utter revulsion and, although the practices of feline worship and persecution are no longer evident within Britain, it is still common for cats to evoke strong emotions of devotion and hatred. Indeed, the qualities that make the cat so endearing to some people make it almost abhorrent to others. This swinging interpretation of feline behaviour and appearance has been a feature of the cat's turbulent history.

Left: *The cat's hunting skills are demonstrated from an early age. They have benefited both man and cat for thousands of years.*

Cats in Ancient Egypt

The relationship between man and the cat is thought to have developed as something of a symbiotic arrangement and, although the exact date when feline domestication began is still a mystery, it is believed that the process coincided with the development of agriculture as an important part of the human economy. The large grain stores in Egypt attracted vast populations of vermin, and the small wild cats that were prepared to come close to human settlements had easy access to a ready food supply. The bold and confident individuals were rewarded with a larger share of the rodent haul, and man was given a reliable form of vermin control at minimal cost.

■ **Left:** *This mummy of a cat dates back to the first century AD. Cats were often mummified in the later periods of Eygptian history. Most cat burials were at sites that were associated with Bastet. Many of the mummified cats were less than a year old and it is thought that Temple cats may have been sacrificed to provide subjects for mummification. Burying an animal mummy was perceived as a pious act towards the deity represented by that particular animal.*

Evidence from art

Evidence for the timing of the onset of this working relationship between man and cat is largely derived from early Egyptian tomb paintings dating from 2000 B.C. The art can be divided into two main types: firstly, those pieces depicting the cat in a marshland setting hunting for birds; and, secondly, those showing cats in more obviously domestic settings.

The inclusion of the cat in a retrieving role in marshland art is obviously not an accurate representation of feline behaviour, and it is now thought that such inclusion of cats in pictures that depict people enjoying a plentiful supply of game is actually a symbolic reference to the feline representation of fertility.

This theme of fertility is also evident in art which depicts the cat in more formal domestic settings, and in most of these paintings the positioning of the cat beneath the chair of a woman is believed to be a very important form of symbolism. The cats depicted in much of the early Egyptian art show striped tabby markings, which suggests that they were still closely related to the African Wild Cat, but the increasingly domestic settings that are seen in these paintings suggest that a more formal relationship with man had begun to develop from around the start of the Eighteenth Dynasty.

Owned by a nation

All of the information relating to the early history of man's relationship with the cat comes from Egyptian history, and there is no evidence of any domestication outside Egypt at that time. This restriction of a species to one geographical location is unusual and, in the case of the cat, it is believed to have been a direct consequence of the deity status of the species within Egyptian culture.

During the period of feline devotion, large numbers of cats were kept confined to temples in order to prevent them from interbreeding with the local wildcat population and to protect them from the influences of the outside world. Other countries and cultures were considered unfit to keep cats, and if any were known to have left Egypt they were rapidly captured and returned to their 'rightful home'. This isolation of the cat is believed to have been an important factor in speeding up the process of selection for cats that were friendly and affectionate and therefore more adaptable to life in close association with human beings.

Divine powers

The belief that cats possessed divine powers lasted for more than 1300 years in Egyptian society, and while male cats were considered to be sacred to the sun god Ra it was the females that attracted most attention due to their association with Bastet, the feline fertility goddess. In early art, Bastet had the head of a lioness but her image was modified and the face of the fertility goddess became that of the domestic cat. This change is believed to have coincided with the onset of feline domestication. The Bastet statue carried an aegis, or shield, in her hand, depicting chastity, and also held a basket, which was believed to reflect the appearance of Bastet devotees. In the other hand was a four-stringed musical instrument called a sistrum, and this was believed to be linked to the fertility theme, since its sound represented the rhythm of love-making. In addition to the four strings on the sistrum, the Bastet also incorporated four kittens sitting at the feet of the statue. Since female cats usually give birth to four kittens, this was believed to be a representation of high-level fertility.

The divine status of the cat brought with it an enormous level of devotion from the Egyptian people, but it also led to a number of strange rituals which were part and parcel of the worshipping of this important deity. For example, kittens of between one and four months of age were regularly slaughtered in sessions of mass strangling and their remains were then interned in a huge feline cemetery at the Temple of Bubastis on the Nile Delta. This temple was the centrepiece of feline worship, and thousands of pilgrims would flock there for the annual festival of Bubastis in order to pay their homage to Bastet.

A species commanding respect and devotion

By 1600 B.C., cats were allowed to be kept by Egyptian people as domestic pets and, while the deity status was still retained, some cats started to live in people's homes rather than in temples. Despite the change in location, these cats still commanded an unparalleled level of devotion, and when a cat died all members of the household would shave off their eyebrows as a mark of respect and enter a period of official mourning.

In 950 B.C., when Bastet became the national deity in Egypt, the cat was at the peak of its popularity, and devotion to the feline goddess united all sections of Egyptian society. It was considered illegal to kill or maim a cat in any way, and when a cat died it would be buried with the appropriate respect and ceremony. Indeed, a range of feline mummies have been retrieved, and the noticeable differences between the elaborate linen wrappings used to mummify the cats of the rich and famous and the simple cloth mummies created for the cats of the lower classes help to illustrate the universal appeal of the cat at this point in its history.

Right: *The feline fertility goddess was an important part of Egyptian culture and the name Bastet, which literally means 'she of the ointment jar', was thought to reflect her soothing and peaceful nature.*

The spread of the cat

While the cat was being used as a divine rodent controller in Ancient Egypt, the Romans were using ferrets and polecats for the same purpose, and it was not until they began to adopt the cat as their primary control measure against rats and mice in A.D. 400 that cats began to leave Egypt in any significant numbers. Subsequently, the cat spread rapidly along the trade routes, and its appearance in countless settlements around the world appeared to mirror the expansion of the Roman Empire.

Having left the confines and security of Egypt, the cat's history took a dramatic turn and the relationship with man changed beyond recognition. The roller coaster of a love affair between man and cat had truly begun, but the links with the feline deity state were not lost overnight and when the cat first appeared in Europe it still retained a divine status. The sistrum that had been held in the hand of Bastet still accompanied it, and this stringed instrument may form the basis for many later mediaeval portrayals of the cat playing the fiddle.

One of the most well-known associations came in the form of the ancient nursery rhyme 'Hey diddle diddle', which is believed to refer to the sistrum while also bringing in elements from the cow goddess Hathor and the moon. The side arms of the sistrum were believed to symbolize the horns of Hathor, while its roundness represented the lunar sphere. Hence the cat, the fiddle, the cow and the moon are all brought together in those familiar words 'Hey diddle diddle, the cat and the fiddle, the cow jumped over the moon'.

Magic without divinity

When the establishment of Christianity as the Roman Empire's accepted religion resulted in the removal of the cat's divine status, this fascinating species was still believed to retain certain magical properties. Many stories from the mediaeval period refer to cats which brought their owners good fortune. Many of them are charming stories of feline intervention leading to wealth and glory for their owners.

However, not all tales of feline magic have such pleasant endings, and the human interpretation of feline magical powers led to some unpleasant practices, not least of which was that of interring cats in the walls of houses to ward off evil spirits.

Links with the Devil

During the thirteenth century, the magical powers of the cat, which had been so sought after in the past, took on a more sinister significance, and as man became increasingly intolerant of his fellow man the cat became embroiled in a wave of hysteria against demons and witchcraft. The cat was identified as a symbol of the devil, and simply owning a cat was sufficient evidence to convict someone of being a witch. People were persecuted in their thousands but cats were also burnt to death in a misguided attempt to rid the world of all evil. The death was designed to be prolonged, and roasting cats in wicker cages above bonfires was considered to be a justified form of torture since it would ensure that the devil was made to suffer.

One of the most ironic features of this change in feline fortune was the fact that the very aspects of the cat that had led to its divine status in Egypt were now condemning it as a symbol of evil. The cat's reflective eyes, which are the result of a special feature of their retina called the tapetum, were believed by Ancient Egyptians to hold the rays of the sun and to symbolize deity status. However, in the Middle Ages, this same feature was thought to symbolize demonic powers. Other misinterpretations of feline biology added weight to

■ Right: *Many superstitions are centred on the feline links with magic, and black cats are still believed to have magical powers even to this day!*

the campaign against the cat, and its promiscuous lifestyle, together with the scream of the queen as the male cat withdraws after mating, was taken as additional evidence of demonic possession.

As the cat's reputation began to deteriorate, so its torture and persecution became an accepted part of everyday life, and, although burnings associated with witchcraft trials may have decreased, the vicious teasing and abuse of cats was a widespread practice well into the mid-seventeenth century.

Links between the cat and the devil were to remain for some time, and during the reign of Mary Tudor of England cats were burned as embodiments of Protestantism. The same practice was justified during the reign of Elizabeth I on the grounds that cats were symbols of the Roman Catholic church.

In France, the situation was no better, and during the celebrations for the festival of St John on 24 June, captured cats would be thrown onto fires amidst the hysterical cries of the people who believed that they were liberating themselves from the devil. These bizarre practices attracted the support of the clergy and royalty and by 1400 the domestic cat was

■ **Left:** *Cats often live together in feral groups, only coming near to people in order to scavenge for their food.*

virtually extinct, but there was a very dramatic price to pay for this. With insufficient cats to kill the rats that carried the bubonic plague, two-thirds of the human population of Europe died.

A persecuted species

Although the outright religious persecution of the cat began to tail off towards the mid-eighteenth century, other forms of torture did continue, and it was not until the French Revolution that previous widely-held beliefs about cats were recognised as pure superstition and the practices of the preceding

years were seen as cruel. Even then, however, misunderstanding of the cat's natural behaviours continued, and for a long time cats were more commonly found in feral groups scavenging from human garbage than living as house pets.

The cat's independence was seen as a sign of unreliability, and many people felt that there was an element of untrustworthiness associated with the species. Indeed, this level of suspicion continued for many years, with the cat effectively living alongside man rather than with him in his home as a domestic pet.

Taking on an air of respectability

In the mid-1800s, the public attitude to disease and illness took a dramatic turn, and scientific discoveries relating to methods of disease transmission weakened the old belief that sickness was a punishment of God or the work of the Devil. This changing public perception helped to smooth the

way for reintroducing the cat as an accepted companion species. The cat's fastidious grooming habits earned it recognition as a shining example of hygiene and it was able to enter a new era in its relationship with man. The keeping of pets was becoming fashionable, and in 1871 Harrison

Weir set out to change public attitudes to his favourite species by organising the first cat show in the UK. Through that event, he sought to give the cat an air of respectability, which would allow it to take its rightful place as a much-loved human companion, and he certainly succeeded.

Chapter Two

CHOOSING A CAT

Choosing a cat suggests that the decision to keep a pet cat is always part of a carefully thought-out process which is then followed by a visit to a local breeder or rescue centre. However, in a world where cat populations are expanding fast, this is not always the case. It may not even be possible for you to choose between a cat and a kitten as sometimes one or the other will find your family!

Cats can find you

There are many cats which have 'wanderlust' and kitten litters that do not 'belong' to a particular keeper. Instead, these feline equivalents of gypsies happily adopt several families within their local neighbourhood, all of whom are offering food and sometimes a safe, warm place to sleep at night. Adopting such a cat can be a gradual, surreptitious process that goes almost unnoticed until the realisation dawns that your feline friend has decided to live at your home and has adopted you!

The first you know of a cat adopting your family may occur when it sits at your front or back door. Such cats will often be quite vocal, and there is a particular style of cry that can suggest starvation to most sympathetic people. It may be worth checking locally to ascertain if anyone has reported a cat missing; check with the local veterinary clinics and shop notice boards. It is possible that someone has just moved into or left your area and your new-found friend has simply become confused. Wandering cats may stay in the short term and then, as suddenly as they arrived, they may disappear.

Always ensure that any new cat that arrives in this way is examined by your local veterinary surgeon for signs of infections and recommendations for vaccinations.

Right: *All kittens are always cute and cuddly, so make sure that you don't rush in and acquire one without carefully considering what is in the best interests of you and the cat.*

Left: *However you acquire your cat, whether it's from a breeder, a rescue centre or a friend, make sure that it is properly vaccinated and get it checked over by a vet as soon as possible. You must also take the appropriate measures to protect it from fleas. A special flea collar may be a good idea.*

The short and the long

When choosing your cat (rather than it choosing you), there are a number of factors to be taken into consideration. Cats, regardless of their breed, do not vary too much in size but they do range widely in shape. There are a number of basic body shapes to choose from, of which two, muscular and cobby cats, are recognised by most authors. Cat breeds can also be divided into two main categories according to their coat length: shorthaired and longhaired. It is this aspect of cat physiology that can significantly affect many keepers because of the potential for allergies and the contrasting difference in grooming requirements.

■ **Right:** *A longhaired cat, like this magnificent Persian, will require intensive grooming on a regular basis, preferably every day.*

Grooming requirements

One of the most basic, yet important, decisions to make when choosing your cat is to consider owning a shorthaired cat rather than a longhaired one. The latter will definitely need extensive brushing and grooming on a daily basis if its coat is not to become matted and difficult to clean. Members of your family who suffer from dust and hair allergies may find themselves more affected by a longhaired than a shorthaired cat. This important aspect of cat ownership is certainly worth your consideration because although some people are allergic to all cats, most of them are especially allergic to longhaired ones. In contrast, shorthaired cats will normally affect only those individuals who are extremely allergic to cat hairs.

Before deciding to select a longhaired cat, it is perhaps worth first making sure that no members of your family are allergic to them. It is also important to check out allergies to skin dander. It is essential for you and all the family members who will come into contact with your new pet to attempt to handle a cat before taking on your own. This is to establish that allergic reactions are not going to occur.

■ **Left:** *If you don't have a lot of time to spare, it is better to acquire a shorthaired cat which will not need grooming more than twice weekly.*

Colour and sensitivity

The colour of cat that you select can have a rather surprising effect on individuals who are likely to show an allergy to them. In some recent research, doctors looked at mild to moderate sufferers of allergic rhinitis and compared cat owners with people who did not own a cat. The researchers looked at cat owners without allergies and studied their cats. Cats kept in or out of the bedroom proved not to influence the eventual results. However, perhaps rather surprisingly, those people keeping a dark-haired cat were seventy-five per cent more likely to display allergic symptoms than those with a light-haired cat. Although the reason for this is currently unknown, it may be linked to the thickness or composition of the hairs.

Testing for allergy

It may be necessary to arrange for those members of your family with suspect allergies to encounter cats prior to introducing one into your home. British shorthaired cats, especially the black and black-and-white varieties, are one of the most popular cat breeds in the United Kingdom. It is these types of cat that you are most likely to encounter if your budget does not allow for owning a pedigree cat.

Longhaired cats will require about twenty minutes of grooming at least three times a week, if not daily, in order to keep their coats knot-free and in good condition. If you cannot guarantee the time to provide a cat with this amount of brushing and combing attention, then it is always much better to choose a shorthaired variety which will require less grooming time.

Finally, it is very important when you are making a breed selection, to choose the variety of cat that would seem most likely to fit in with your personal lifestyle and that of your family. For example, you should never consider keeping a cat that is going to require a great deal of companionship, such as a Siamese, if you and your family work and are out of the house for most of the day.

Pedigree or moggie?

It is possible to invest large sums of money when buying a pedigree cat. Indeed, some champion 'show winners', rare breeds and top breeding stock can cost far more than expensive TVs and music systems. True pedigree cats

are bred to standards published by relevant organisations, and they will have splendid coats and distinctively beautiful eyes which are correctly coloured.

It is probably a myth that top pedigree cats might be termed 'aristocratic' with their specific tastes in home and dietary

▨ **Left and below:** *You can decide to buy an expensive pedigree cat, such as the Siamese (left), or you may opt for an ordinary moggie (below). One of the advantages of the non-pedigree is that it can have free access to your garden.*

requirements! However, once you have invested a great deal of money in an expensive pedigree kitten, your commitment to its welfare will undoubtedly increase.

One valuable aspect of opting for a pedigree cat is that it is usually possible to predict the breed quality that you have obtained, particularly once it is an adult. There are show and pet quality types, and the price range will reflect the potential show winner over the cat that simply 'shows off' on your lap.

FINDING YOUR CAT

The top breeders will be listed in breed registers or at your local veterinary surgery, or their details can be obtained through the advertisements in the leading cat magazines and newspapers. They usually attend major cat shows and you will be able to inspect their standards on attending. A cat show can also offer you a good opportunity to meet some different breeders and compare cat types, colour varieties and any peculiarities that may be relevant for a particular breed. Whilst substantial cat literature will often illustrate the most

popular breeds, it can be an advantage to see the cat types at first hand, so take time out to visit a show and see for yourself.

■ **Above:** *Beware of timid, nervous kittens, however deserving of a good home. Check that they have been well socialized before buying one.*

Where to look

Your veterinary surgeon will have local knowledge of cat breeders and will be aware of those with good standards and an interest in the well-being of the kittens they offer to members of the public.

Recommendation is often the best method of locating a respected breeder. Those breeders with the highest standards in temperament and physiology will provide their kittens at a premium price.

However, it is often best to buy from these breeders because they offer happy and healthy kittens.

Professional breeders may only sell kittens at certain times of the year, and if they produce top-quality

■ **Right:** *Responsible breeders will let you meet the kittens and their mother in the environment in which they were raised. You should always insist on seeing the mother in addition to her offspring, and make sure that she is healthy and has a good temperament.*

popular cat breeds of 'showing standard' they will often have a waiting list of potential clients.

Pet shops

It is not wise to purchase a kitten from a pet shop or a large store. Litters of kittens will have been passed on either by those people who have them as a result of an accidental mating by their pet, or by commercial breeders whose primary motivation is making a profit. Kittens in pet shops may well have suffered from an interruption in their socialization period (up to six weeks or more) and may have been disturbed by the change in environments. A number of common behavioural problems seen in cats, such as 'spraying' in the home or even aggression, sometimes stem from socialization disruption, and the pet shop environment is not ideal or healthy for developing kittens. Thus, many of the larger, more responsible pet stores will not sell kittens for these reasons.

Left: *If buying a rescue cat, don't go by appearances. Take the advice of the staff at the rescue home. Many cats are unfortunate victims of circumstance, and they can still be integrated into most families and will make affectionate, loyal companions.*

Rescued and re-homed cats

Most rescue centres usually have a wide range of cats available, both in age and type, from 'moggies' to pet-quality kittens and, sometimes, even pedigree cats.

Non-pedigree cats are often known affectionately as 'moggies'. Frequently, they can be seen advertised in local newspapers or in shop windows, or they may even be offered by a family which has experienced an accidental pregnancy with their pet cat. These 'moggies' are always much cheaper than pedigree cats and are sometimes 'free to good homes'.

There are often several cross-breeds of cats available at rescue centres. Specific breed rescue groups may even be available in your area. There are also many different colour variations within breeds, ranging from white to lilac to black. Coat markings also vary from self (one solid colour throughout the body) to tabby (striped) or spotted.

Your local area will often be home to individual cat lovers who kindly take it upon themselves to rescue and re-home any cats and kittens that have been abandoned or whose keepers cannot care for them any longer. Your veterinary surgeon will usually know of these people and will be happy to direct you to them.

A donation to help towards the upkeep of their 'home rescue' centre will usually suffice, although they will always welcome gifts of cat food, pet accessories and any items they can sell on when they have fund-raising events.

ORGANISATIONS

All charitable cat rescue organisations across the country require loving and caring homes for the thousands of abandoned kittens and cats they receive each year. Your local newspaper or Yellow Pages will usually detail these centres or individuals in reports or advertisements. The person involved with rehousing the cats and kittens at the rescue organisation should have a good idea of the temperament of each cat in their care. Firstly, tell them about the type of cat you want and they should be able to match your needs to one of their cats or kittens. It should be noted that those kittens that have been the subject of a feral mating (involving a semi-wild cat) can be extremely instinctive and throughout their lives may always be shy and nervous around people. Kittens that have been taken in by rescue organisations under the first six weeks of 'socialization' may have suffered from the absence of the litter mother. These youngsters sometimes develop faulty learning with regards to using 'toilet facilities' and can require careful handling under the guidance of a behavioural expert.

Kitten or adult?

Once you have made your initial decision to keep a cat, it is necessary to decide whether you want to get a kitten or an adult. You will need to choose which would be best suited to you and your family's lifestyle. There are some very important questions to ask at this stage and they should be answered realistically. The answers will help when deciding which is the ideal cat for you.

The arrival of a new cat in the family will undoubtedly affect each member of the household, including other pets. Therefore, it is important that before you decide to introduce a cat or kitten into your home, you should seek the opinions of all your family members about keeping a cat. It is better that everyone agrees to having a cat around the house.

Young kittens

The age of your feline friend to be can range from a kitten that is only a few weeks old to a grand old cat aged in years that can reach double figures. Of course, all healthy kittens appear to be 'cute and beautiful'. They are naturally playful, inquisitive, naughty, lively and adorable. However, kittens require a great deal of attention in their early months. During this time, they need to be fed small meals three or four times a day. This is because a kitten's stomach is

Right: Even a small kitten needs a lot of attention and money lavished on it. Kittens love to play and you must make time to play games.

Above: Children love cats but no matter how friendly and gentle the cat is, they should not be left alone together.

quite small and, as it is growing quickly during these important early months, it requires lots of nourishment. Veterinary costs, including vaccinations and neutering, are also a factor that needs to be considered. All kittens need to be inoculated against common infections. In addition, if you are to be a responsible cat keeper, it will be necessary to have your cat neutered, from about six to twelve months, to avoid any unwanted pregnancies in a female or to prevent a male cat from spraying (marking with urine).

Growing cats

In contrast to a kitten, a young adult cat will require less frequent meals and will not necessarily demand continual contact from its human companions. Mature cats will normally be toilet trained and are almost always more streetwise than kittens when it comes to the outside world beyond your home.

However, kittens can usually be trained to use a litter tray as their indoor toilet. A properly socialized kitten will have been trained by its mother to urinate and defecate beyond the nesting site.

The older kitten

At six months of age, cats do not require quite the same attention as young kittens. They now need only two or, possibly, three meals a day. Cats become fully mature when they are about one year old. However, it has been said on many occasions that happy cats just love to play and never grow up – they just grow larger!

Most adult cats will usually be house trained, and they should be accustomed to living in a home environment. They can make the best house cats for elderly people because older felines are happy to lounge around lazily. Indoor cats appear to thrive when they are kept in pairs, and some rescue

■ **Left:** *All kittens are very inquisitive and love to explore. Any new object will be treated with interest and curiosity.*

centres will have older cats that they want to keep together. Provided that their new home is warm and friendly, most mature cats will take very little time to

settle down. However, despite all the precautions that you can take, some adult cats will still be unsettled by being transferred from an 'institutional' environment to your comfortable home. It is particularly important to provide covered indoor litter trays to enable your cat to 'mark' and settle into its new territory.

One or more cats?

Homely cats certainly enjoy human companionship. Being fed and groomed on a daily basis is a feline's idea of heaven. If the lifestyle of your family means that everyone is out at work or school for most weekdays, then it is probably wise to consider choosing to keep two cats. This will provide an opportunity for both cats to play and interact with each other rather than getting bored with their own company and turning to other more destructive outlets for activity, such as damaging the furniture. If you decide that two cats would best

■ **Left:** *Many cats live quite happily together, especially those that were littermates. It is perfectly possible to successfully introduce a new cat or kitten into an established cat household.*

suit your situation, then it is much easier to introduce kittens of a similar age into your home at the same time. A breeder will more often than not argue that two

littermates are the easiest kittens to introduce together. Nevertheless, it is possible to introduce kittens of a similar age from different breeders or sources with relative ease.

Introducing adult cats

Introducing two adult cats into your home at the same time, unless they have already been housed together, is certainly the most difficult challenge of all. This is because mature cats are much more likely to display territorial aggression than are kittens. The socialization of adult cats is rarely accomplished without some behavioural problems, which may not only include aggression towards each other but also indoor marking (spraying), scratching furniture and indoor urination and defecation. Unless you are familiar with keeping cats and enjoy a 'challenge', it would therefore be inadvisable to consider purchasing two adult cats to keep in your home.

Male or female?

All cats, regardless of whether they are male or female, can make good pets. Some people prefer to keep a male cat rather than a female or visa versa! However, it is important to be a responsible cat owner and to avoid unplanned pregnancies. In order to safeguard against an unwanted litter, it will be necessary, as your cat reaches sexual maturity, to arrange for it to be neutered. Unfortunately, mature cats that are not neutered can also be quite unpopular in a home environment. Males (toms) tend to mark their territory by spraying urine, both outside and inside the house. This behaviour also has the purpose of attracting females. In addition, male cats are more likely to wander off looking for a female with which to mate.

Female cats (queens) come into 'season' periodically, and when this occurs they are more likely to become restless – during the day and night. Females that are in 'season' will frequently make long and loud caterwauling noises, especially if they have visual contact with other cats. During this period, a female cat may also become very attached to her keeper and she will require extra attention from you.

A kitten can be neutered at six months. The veterinary charge for neutering males is usually less than for females because spaying the latter requires more surgery Most rescue centres will have already neutered an adult cat.

Below: *Kittens socialize much more easily and are less competitive than adult cats.*

HEALTH CHECKS

It is important to make sure that you acquire a healthy kitten or cat. A kitten that develops infections in the early stages of its life can become disturbed and nervous later on in adulthood. Kittens are particularly susceptible to infections when their immune systems are still being established.

Quick health check

When first selecting your kitten, you must carefully and deliberately check that the coat is smooth and clean. The fur, especially on its underside, should not be knotted or wet. Closely inspect the cat's, or kitten's, coat for any signs of fleas (bites) or skin infections (bald or reddened skin patches). Watch the cat and note any excessive scratching which could indicate the presence of parasites or infections. A cat's eyes should be clean and bright and the third eyelid should not be visible. Any excess moisture or matting would indicate an eye infection.

The kitten's or cat's anal region should also be clean

■ **Above:** *Run your hand over the body. The coat should be smooth and silky.*

■ **Right:** *Check the kitten's underside for any signs of knotted or wet fur.*
■ **Below:** *Check the anal region; it should be clean and unsoiled.*

and unsoiled. Gently feel under the abdomen as this area should be slightly rounded. Watch carefully to see whether the kitten or cat walks properly and is not showing any signs of lameness.

Ears, nose and mouth

The ears should be clean inside and out. The mouth should be pink. Confirm that the teeth are clean and unbroken and that the gums are not inflamed by gently opening the kitten's mouth and inspecting the top and bottom of the inner jaws.

■ **Above:** *The kitten's gums should be pink and the teeth should be clean.*

A cat's nose should always be clean and moist. Any dryness or marks may indicate an infection. If you have any doubts whatsoever over the health of your kitten, arrange for an early health check from a professional person such as a veterinary surgeon or a senior animal nurse.

■ **Above:** *Check that the eyes are bright and free from discharge.*

If there are several kittens to choose from, identify the kitten that appears to be outgoing and in the centre of the litter activity. It would not be wise to select a kitten that is sulking in the corner away from its siblings. Do not choose a sleeping kitten unless all of the litter are sleepy and bundled up together and you have had the opportunity to watch them during an active period.

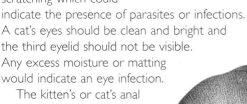

How to Select Your Kitten

The myth is that a person with an animal behaviour background can take a snapshot observation of a litter of kittens or an older cat and can make a correct decision to 'avoid the nervous individual', to decline the real extrovert and select the 'feline average' or the middle-ground cat. The usual advice to seek out the average individual is not always realistic. Without the necessary information, it would be difficult to time your visit to combine with the best likelihood of activity from the kittens. However, the breeder or individual may be able to predict the active times and suggest an optimum period for you. To make an accurate decision, based on the personality of a particular kitten, an observer would have to spend several hours, over days, to gain an insight into behaviour beyond those obvious forms that occur at 'sleep' time and 'activity' time.

Selecting from a litter

With regards to the 'group personality' of the litter, the best indicators would come from prolonged contact with the litter mother. If she is both calm and approachable, once you have entered the home and settled, and if she is sociable towards your non-intrusive handling, then it is likely that her kittens will show the same sociable personality. Following this observation of the litter mother, it is advisable to make a couple of visits to check out the litter for yourself as these will offer you the opportunity to watch and select the kitten that shines out from the rest as being lively, inquisitive and healthy.

Kittens that have been well cared for and correctly handled will all display a natural curiosity

Below: *Selecting the ideal kitten means both watching and handling individuals. One kitten will shine out from the rest of the litter.*

and playfulness. In such a litter, your preference for shape and colour would probably override any other factors for selection. The most realistic approach would then be to choose an 'average' kitten in the form of its activity and personality. There is a very simple method of selecting a kitten – just hold out your hand. Sometimes it will appear that a kitten or cat will choose you!

Introverts and extroverts

Realistically, few people have the willpower to resist a group of soft and beautiful kittens, and, more often than not, a selection will be made on the spot. In this instance, if you want to keep a playful kitten, then choose the extrovert 'explorer' over the timid introvert. This kitten is brave and wants to investigate the world beyond the nesting site. It will want to get out of your hands and escape into the excitement of the unknown, which may simply be represented by the room you are in. If you happen to be looking for the 'adventurer' in a kitten, then this one would be perfect for a busy family with an active lifestyle.

Looking for an even personality

If you wish to keep a quiet and content kitten, then it is best to choose the 'homely' one over the individual that scratches to leave your hands. This kitten may not

Right: *If you already have a cat, then check with the breeder or rescue centre that an adult cat you may wish to acquire does not display aggressive or dominant behaviour towards other cats.*

immediately offer itself up to your contact but it will be calm when you select it for handling. Neither hyperactive nor withdrawn, it has an 'even' personality.

A content cat like this would make an ideal pet for people with a quiet household who wish to keep a home-loving cat.

Selecting the adult cat

If you choose an adult cat that needs re-homing, it would be useful to visit and offer physical contact once you have been accepted. In home situations, this

Right: *A timid kitten may look for a bolt hole to hide from strangers and unfamiliar noises. Such kittens may not have been socialized properly.*

■ **Right:** *A contented, sociable cat will usually accept a cuddle happily.*

would be a realistic strategy to avoid taking on a nervous or an aggressive cat. In rescue centres, it is not usually possible to make assessments because the cats rarely show their true behaviours (beyond aggression and timidity) when they are kept in temporary accommodation. However, it may be possible for a member of staff at the rescue centre to give you a generalized assessment, which would offer some pointers for a cat's basic sociability.

If a cat can be handled (stroked and picked up), then that should provide an indicator of sociability and nervousness. Nervous cats look for bolt-holes in the smallest places, and they should not be

judged simply on a need to find sanctuary from a 'hostile world'. Such cats may stabilize eventually in a caring home and start to show a sociable personality.

Again, prolonged observations and contact on more than one occasion with a potential adoptee cat would provide a more realistic assessment of personality.

House cat or free-roaming cat?

Choosing a pedigree cat or kitten, rather than a moggie, may well influence the type of facilities that you provide for your pet and the environment access you wish to offer it. Pedigree kittens, if they are properly socialized and possess good temperaments, are known to make excellent house-bound cats. To prevent them from being exposed to infections from outdoor cats and the dangers of roads, pedigree cats are often restricted to the house. They can be supervised while exercising within the garden, provided that this area is secure.

■ **Left:** *An outdoor cat is more likely to be suitable for a busy family with an active lifestyle, or a person who works and who is often out during the day.*

Cat runs

In order to offer your house cat some access to an outdoor area, it would be necessary to create a special run, which is similar to an outdoor aviary cage. The expense of an extensive, well-constructed run can actually represent quite an investment in terms of cost unless there is a practical DIY proficient member in your family. A cat run may be accessed by your pet from an open window or a cat flap at the back or side of your home. This system, which permits controlled outdoor access, offers your pet the best of both worlds – your home and the garden – whilst protecting it from a number of potential dangers.

Allowing your pedigree kitten or pet cat to wander freely in your garden can result in several problems. Feral, or free-roaming, cats will enter your garden daily and bring with them infections and the risk of dangerous diseases. Most cats are lost to their keepers either when they are permitted to leave the home through door flaps or if they are let out into the garden to roam at night.

Risks to free-roaming cats

Cats that are unfamiliar with busy roads which carry large-scale industrial traffic can often find themselves 'frozen in headlights' and are then struck by vehicles. The greatest number of feline fatalities are the result of night-time road traffic accidents.

Other fatalities can be linked directly to serious infections, such as 'cat flu' and cat leukaemia, which may be passed on by free-roaming cats. Poisons, which are

■ **Left:** *Many house cats love looking out of the window and watching the world go by outside.*

laid down to kill unwanted pests, are another of the potential hazards for free-roaming cats.

Although some people believe that it is cruel to keep a cat inside permanently, pedigree cats that have been born and raised indoors appear quite happy and

contented to live within the protection and the comfort of their keepers' homes. And with the increased number of motor vehicles on the roads today, an indoor cat is much more likely to live a longer, healthier life than the outdoor 'free-roaming' pet.

■ **Left:** *A securely enclosed cat run in the garden can give indoor cats access to fresh air and also provide opportunities for climbing and play.*

QUESTIONS TO ASK YOURSELF WHEN SELECTING A KITTEN OR A CAT

Primary factor questions to ask yourself:

Age	Do you want a kitten or a cat?	Kittens will require more attention than adult cats and greater frequency of feeds. They are also more adaptable than adult cats. Kittens may explore without care and attention in dangerous situations unlike an adult cat which will usually have learned, through bitter experience, to avoid dangers.
		Mature individuals are often difficult to socialize because of the territorial nature of cats. More than one kitten can be socialized at the same time which means that they will interact with each other during daytime hours when most adults and young non-infant children are away from home.
Gender	Do you want a male or a female cat?	Male cats (Toms) may mark their territory by spraying urine, both outside and inside the house, to mark territory and to attract females. Males tend to explore over larger territories looking for females. They are also more likely to go missing for long periods as they attempt to 'urine mark' in order to maintain a territory.
		Female cats (Queens) come into 'season' periodically and may become restless day and night. Cats in 'season' may be extremely vocal and can make long and loud noises especially towards other cats. They may become attached to a keeper and require extra attention.
Size	Do you want a small or large cat?	This is not really a consideration as there is only a slight difference in all domesticated breed sizes. British cats can grow large by cat standards. However, individuals of many cat breeds can grow large.
Coat and breed	Do you want a shorthaired or longhaired cat?	**Longhaired breeds** tend to be Orientals ('angora'), Persians, Birmans, Turkish and Maine Coons but can also be seen in the common moggie. You must be prepared to groom such breeds on a daily basis to prevent the coat matting and to reduce loose hairs.
		Shorthaired breeds include British Shorthairs, Burmese, Siamese and Abyssinians but they can also be of Persian origins, such as the Exotic. They are easier to groom than longhairs and will produce more acceptable hair loss. Some breeds are generally said to be more 'sensitive' or nervous than others. However, a cat's temperament can be dictated as much by breeding and socialization.
	What about hair allergies?	**Shorthaired cats** are easier to groom, produce less hair and may be accommodated by people with slight allergies.
		Longhaired cats produce more loose hairs, require regular grooming and may cause acute health problems for family members with allergies.
		Note: A dark-haired cat is more likely to trigger allergic symptoms in people with allergies than a light-haired cat.

Secondary factors that can influence selection:

Presence of existing cat(s)	Do you have a cat already?	If you are already keeping an adult cat it is usually simpler to introduce a new kitten into the household than a mature individual. Adult cats, when first introduced, may fight; they may also begin scratching and marking (spraying) furniture with urine.
		Even an adult cat may initially object to the presence of a kitten but careful socialization (introduction during daytime resting periods in a neutral room with 'controlled' handling) should prevent aggression. Always have a pen or a cat carrying box available to restrict the movements of the kitten or an aggressive cat.
Lifestyle (your time and space available)	What home and lifestyle do you have?	**A small to medium urban home** with a modest garden or yard inhabited by family members sharing a busy lifestyle can be suitable to an outgoing cat or kitten. Although a number of cats with access to the outside environment can be socialized together, some competition is likely between growing cats in reduced space.
		A small to large rural home with an enclosed garden and a family that has a more retiring lifestyle may be ideal for both long or shorthaired cats or kittens.
		Cat runs can be installed to restrict the movements of a home cat yet allow access to an outside environment. It is possible to socialize more than one kitten in spacious conditions.
		A shorthaired cat may suit families with little spare time to spend on grooming. A longhaired cat will require regular grooming every day.
Home location	Where do you live?	**Urban:** In an urban location, your cat is more likely to encounter other cats once it has access to your garden or the surrounding area. This means your cat has a higher risk of infection and potential aggression. It is also more likely to be exposed to a continual traffic flow and the dangers that road vehicles will present. Urban cats can 'learn' to be wary of traffic because of continual exposure.
		Rural: In a rural location, once your cat has outside access it could encounter feral cats. Feral cats are usually nervous of human activity and they can be aggressive towards house cats, but the likelihood of an encounter is greatly reduced. Thus the risks of cross-infection from exposure to other cats is also reduced. There is usually less traffic in a rural area. However, rural cats can be naive with regards to fast-moving vehicles and are more susceptible to road traffic.

Chapter Three

THE PERFECT KITTEN

Bringing your new kitten home can be slightly nerve-wracking for both of you. However, with a little care and attention, from the moment you pick him up until you introduce him into your home, you can start your relationship successfully. Your kitten won't know why he has been removed from his litter siblings and mother; he will soon learn that a big, new world lies beyond his former home. Everything will be unfamiliar and strange to him, and it is up to you to settle him into his new surroundings and reassure him that he is in safe hands. This will be his home for the rest of his life.

Collecting your kitten

There cannot be many aspects of pet-keeping that are more exciting than bringing home your chosen companion for the first time. To make sure that bringing your cat or kitten home is a successful and stress-free occasion for everyone concerned, it would be wise to make in advance a list of all the items you require and to devise a strategy to follow. You will need the following:

◆ Transport unit (crate or carrier) or temporary carrying box
◆ Kitchen roll, newspaper or an old towel to line the bottom of the box/crate in case of mishaps
◆ Notebook to list your cat's or kitten's existing diet and any nutritional recommendations that are made by the breeder or rescue centre
◆ A friend to drive the car or to carry the cat box/carrier/crate.

Heading home

When bringing a kitten home for the first time or transporting your pet to the veterinary centre or cattery, it is important to keep your kitten secure. There are many kinds of pet carriers and travel crates available. Some temporary boxes are just made out of cardboard and are suitable for short-term use and emergencies, whereas others are made from hard-wearing plastic or plastic-coated wire, which are suitable for long-term regular use.

When transporting your cat or kitten, be sure to place a clean towel, kitchen roll or a newspaper on the bottom of the carrier to soak up any accidents that may occur. Pick up the cat gently but firmly, supporting its bottom with one hand, and place it in the carrier. Close the door quickly and secure the fastener. Carry the box on your knees to prevent any excessive sudden movements as you make your journey home.

Do not leave a cat unattended when it is inside the carrier. When transporting a cat or kitten, take care that it cannot become overheated or too cold.

Right: *Cats and kittens are great escape artists, and they need to be securely transported.*

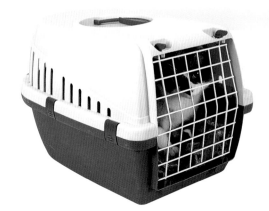

SAFETY FIRST

It is important to have a 'carry box' or travel crate for your kitten. This is because he may panic when introduced to the prospect of being with someone unfamiliar and being exposed to strange environments in your car and home. It is best to travel with a family member or a friend to enable you to concentrate on the needs of the kitten. The journey will usually be the first occasion on which he has travelled in a car, and the experience is likely to be extremely difficult for the youngster. It will also be the first time that he has been separated from his litter siblings and this can induce fearfulness in even the happiest pet. It is important to make this first journey as stress-free as possible.

Introducing your kitten to his new home

Once you arrive home, transport the carry box and your kitten into the room you have chosen for his first night. Take care to close any doors that may offer a frightened cat an opportunity to take flight. Trying to find a cat or a kitten once it has sought out a refuge can be incredibly difficult – they tend to find a bolt hole under a car or a shed or in some thick undergrowth. A little care at this early stage can prevent a great deal of heartache.

Below: *In a quiet moment, allow your new friend, or friends, to exit the carrier without any encouragement.*

A cosy home

To help your new feline friend settle into your home and family quickly, do not try to expose your kitten to everyone at once. It is not necessary to introduce all the family members and any other pets you may keep to your new kitten on the first day. Ideally, in the initial twenty-four hours, he should be allowed to explore one room which should be made secure from other animals. There should be water, a small amount of food, a litter tray (a covered one in the case of an adult cat) and peace and quiet. If you have adopted an adult cat, it may be advisable to ask your rescue centre for a small amount of his soiled litter material. This 'waste' can then be transferred to your new tray. This will ensure that your cat will 'associate' faster with his new surroundings – through scent – and will often stimulate almost immediate usage of the tray. The added benefit of this strategy is that it will also encourage an aspect of 'feline territorial security' which 'marking' with urine or with faeces stimulates.

Introducing your family

Once you have the confidence of your kitten (or cat), encourage individual members of your family to enter the room and ask them to wait for your new pet to approach them. This 'controlled' method will make any introductions gentle and less nerve-racking for all concerned. After a couple of days, or on the evidence of the kitten's sociability, all other 'introductions' can be as informal as necessary.

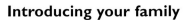

Handling your kitten

There is always a great temptation to continually pick up your new kitten (or cat). However, although it is important to have a positive physical contact with your pet, this contact should be undertaken confidently and correctly if your relationship is to develop with trust. Try to resist the temptation to pick up your kitten at every available opportunity. Sometimes it is better to watch him explore or curl up for a cat nap.

It's important that infants and small children should always be supervised during new cat or kitten encounters. This will prevent the possibility of any rough handling and accidental aggression or undue attention by either party.

While your kitten will be fairly easy to scoop up, it is important that you support his bottom with one hand while holding his body gently and firmly with the other. Hold him close to you if you have

■ **Above and right:** *To pick up your kitten, gently slip your hand under his tummy. Gripping gently but firmly, scoop him up with your other hand under his bottom for support.*

to carry him anywhere. A cuddle while you are sitting down and relaxing in a chair may even turn into a cat nap. However, on other occasions, your kitten may want to play (chew and scratch, climb and jump) and you must be very careful not to drop him from a

standing height. Make your contact positive by being brief and offering firm but gentle strokes. You may want to dangle a piece of wool after placing your kitten back on the ground, or offer a small food treat as an extra reward for good contact.

Introducing other pets

If you have a dog or another cat, controlled procedures are always recommended. If the dog is friendly towards cats and kittens, you can play a 'click and treat' retrieval game with the dog whilst the newcomer is exploring in the same room. A 'clicker' is a thumb-sized unit that can be used over a period of time to signal a food treat is to be given. This can be used to promote good behaviour, such as sitting and recall.

Use distraction if your dog becomes boisterous. If he shows aggression, use a reward to draw

him away from the cat or kitten and then separate them for the time being until a socialization programme can be undertaken.

■ **Left:** *Many dogs and cats learn to live quite happily together.*

If your dog acts aggressively towards your new kitten or cat, it is important not to make any events 'exciting' by giving them your attention; this may reinforce the dog's behaviour. Use special training discs to signal non-reward and end-behaviour rather than shout at your dog. These are small brass discs on a small cord that can be shown to your dog at the moment that a food treat is removed. After a period of use,

■ Left: *Cats can live in harmony with other small pets, such as rabbits and guinea pigs, which they would normally regard as prey.*

they will be accidentally brought together with potential aggression. For this reason, it is important that 'controlled socialization', with food rewards to both parties for good behaviour, is undertaken over a settling-in period.

Smaller pets

If you also keep small pets, such as mice, gerbils, hamsters, guinea pigs and rabbits, it is essential that they are securely housed so that your cat cannot gain access to them. Cats are natural hunters and may regard these animals as legitimate prey. However, some can learn to live together.

they will automatically signal to your dog that a reward will be removed. This is usually enough to encourage a dog to stop any antisocial behaviour.

Rewarding good friends

Reward your dog with special treats when good behaviour is

shown around the new kitten or cat. However, if you don't feel confident that you can control his aggression, then you should muzzle him when attempting to socialize him with your kitten.

It is not a good idea to keep a dog and a kitten or cat separated permanently in the home – there will always come a time when

Safety in the home – exploring safely

Cats and kittens are naturally inquisitive creatures, and they are likely to explore every nook and

■ Right: *A cat's natural curiosity can sometimes get it into trouble. Make sure that any chemicals, even diluted in water, and other toxic substances are kept securely sealed and out of reach.*

cranny of their home. Therefore, it is very important to make your home 'cat safe'. Making a home safe for a cat is similar to taking safety precautions for a child.

Household chemicals

If there is a possibility of your cat coming into direct contact with any detergents and other dangerous household cleaning solutions, then the potential for a fatality exists. Although a cat is unlikely to lick up a solution, it could easily knock over a bottle and walk through the spilt liquid. The chemical on its paws could irritate its sensitive skin or, even worse, be digested when the cat attempts to clean itself.

Electric cables

Any exposed electric cables are another potential hazard for a playful kitten. Make sure they are not frayed because if your kitten begins to play with an unsafe lead he can easily be electrocuted. Take care that no long leads are hanging down from electric kettles and any other electrical appliances.

Windows

It is also very important that all windows are secure unless your cat has safe access through a ground-floor window to the outside. There is always the possibility that a kitten could escape through an open window on an upper floor or even over a balcony and could sustain a serious injury in such a fall.

Sharp implements

It is vital that sharp implements, such as knives, drawing pins and needles, are kept safely out of reach of your kitten or cat. Most of these kitchen items should be stored safely away in drawers or hung on hooks on the wall.

Fireplaces

Fireplaces provide access to chimneys, and these entrances can become traps for inquisitive kittens. Be sure to block them off for the first six to twelve months.

Hidden dangers indoors

Some dangers to a cat or kitten may not be immediately apparent. Hot baths could prove not only difficult for a cat to climb out of but could be fatal should it fall into the water accidentally. Open doors offer access to the outside

world to an inquisitive cat. If your cat is to be an 'indoors pet', it is essential to close the front and back doors carefully on every occasion that you enter or leave the house. It is also important to shut other less obvious doors inside your home.

It is advisable not to leave the washing machine door open (or any other household appliances that could imprison a kitten) as your kitten could easily explore inside when you are unaware or distracted. It is also a sensible idea to keep wardrobe and cupboard doors closed to prevent him from mistakenly becoming trapped inside. It may surprise pet owners to know that rubbish bins can also be a potential hazard to a young and curious kitten. If he can gain access to the contents of a waste bin, he may encounter a wide range of dangerously sharp items, such as open cans, which could easily cause nasty cuts.

There are many other dangers to a small kitten in the home, ranging from an open fire (always

■ **Left:** *Cats will seek refurge in all sorts of nooks and crannies, and nervous individuals may start chewing on wires or live electric cables. Take care!*

use a fire guard) to a simple curtain sash cord (make sure that it is not accessible to your kitten). Whilst it is impossible to foresee every danger in your home, it is always wise to try and reduce any potentially risky opportunities that exist for a young cat.

You should also be aware that some house plants are potentially dangerous to a kitten. Many cats like to play with plants and chew them. Among the many common plants that are potentially toxic are Fuchsia, Ivy, Poinsettia and Philodendron.

■ **Left:** *Windows that are left open can be dangerous for cats and kittens, especially if you own a house cat or if the open window is on an upper storey.*

SAFE COLLARS

Even basic collars can be dangerous for kittens if they are loose fitting. Kittens can easily become hooked on things and trapped, and the results can be fatal. The Cats Protection offer and recommend a special circlet collar which is said to be extremely safe.

Outdoor safety

If your kitten is to be allowed out into the garden, it will also be necessary to pay some attention to certain safety aspects outdoors. Some common garden plants, such as Rhododendron, Azalea, Sweet Pea and Clematis, are poisonous to cats. Although a cat is unlikely to eat such flora, it is advisable not to stock your garden too heavily with these plants. It is best to observe your kitten or young cat closely when he is allowed into the garden to ensure that he does not come into contact with them. You should be aware also that some trees, such as the yellow-flowering Laburnum, produce poisonous seeds, and these should be avoided or access to them should be restricted.

To avoid distressing accidents, always ensure that any toxic substances, such as pesticides, together with sharp gardening equipment, are safely locked away.

Garden ponds, although an attractive water feature, are potential disaster areas for kittens and young cats. They should not have steep sides which would make it difficult for a cat to climb out if it accidentally fell into the water. Some pondkeepers place a net over the water whilst others construct a low fence around the pond to prevent access to cats. Formal ponds can be shielded with a netted frame; this would also have a secondary benefit in so far as a cover will reduce the number of leaves entering and polluting the water. By taking a few simple precautions in your garden, you can prevent potential accidents and your cat should live a long and happy life with you.

■ **Above:** *This Norwegian Forest Cat surveys the world from up a tree. Although they rarely get stuck, cats can climb too high and need rescuing.*

■ Right: *Garden ponds are potentially dangerous to young kittens and should always be netted. This fourteen-week-old Korat kitten is walking on a frozen pond but the ice could easily crack.*

CARING FOR YOUR KITTEN

Your kitten will want to explore his exciting, new world. In order to make this exploration fun as well as safe and interesting it is worth establishing training and appropriate territorial marking. A kitten will instinctively want to establish its new territory and this can be achieved easily by following the simple guidelines outlined below.

Scratching posts

A kitten will learn best by example. To encourage your kitten to scratch on a post, rather than on your best furniture, gently place his front paws on the post until the idea is accepted – a healthy kitten will soon get the message. It is normal, healthy behaviour for all cats and kittens to scratch. This enables them not only to mark via glands in the paws but also may keep their claws in tip-top condition. If you do not provide your pet with a scratching post, he will probably use the furniture as an alternative. When training your cat to use a scratching post, it is best to place it in a really prominent position where the cat has shown an inclination to stand, stretch and open up its claws.

Start scratching

During the early training of young cats it is always best to keep the scratching post in the same place. However, if there is one particular piece of furniture that your cat likes to scratch, then it could be worthwhile putting the scratching post in front of it. If your kitten is very active and you observe him scratching on the furniture, it is best to interrupt his behaviour with a reward signal (a bell or clicker sound that has become linked to a food treat) and then gently carry him to the scratching post, placing his front paws on the upright.

A great variety of scratching posts are now available from pet shops. Some are an integral part of interesting platforms or raised beds. Scratching posts can be scented with catnip and become a place where cat treats can be left in order to encourage your cat to approach and use them.

■ **Above:** *Scratching posts can be quite elaborate and can incorporate climbing stations and high platforms. They will provide many hours of entertainment for an indoor cat.*

■ **Above:** *This mini activity centre doubles as an attractive scratching post.*

TRAINING YOUR CAT

Cats cannot be trained quite as easily as dogs. In general, dogs want to please their owners and be part of a perceived 'human-canine' pack whereas cats like to please themselves! In fact, it is impossible to compel a cat or kitten to do anything that it does not want to do. However, felines are relatively intelligent creatures and it is possible to train them with a gentle, coaxing technique using a mixture of sound and reward – a 'clicker' or sound and reward signals for positive reinforcement of good behaviour by the cat.

Using the litter tray

Cats should always have access to outdoors (through a cat flap) or to a litter tray at all times. Litter trays are 'indoor toilets' for cats. They are usually made from moulded plastic and are available in various designs and sizes from pet stores and smaller pet shops. The litter trays that are designed with hoods are probably the most hygienic as any 'smells' are

■ **Right:** *Kittens learn by example, and they will watch their mother using the litter tray.*

contained and are prevented from spilling out. Covered litter trays also offer the cat or kitten privacy when going to the toilet.

The litter tray is an essential item for all indoor cats and those that are confined during the day or evening. To maintain the health of your cat or kitten, you must clean out the tray on a daily or, at least, on a regular basis. It should be relatively easy to train your

new kitten to use a litter tray as he will probably have used one already. Indeed, kittens will usually have observed their mother using a litter tray.

For the first few days after you bring your new kitten home, you should regularly place him in the tray. Position the tray where it is easily accessible and always keep it in the same place. A new kitten will quickly learn where the litter tray is situated and will become toilet-trained.

Problems in the toilet

If your kitten or cat begins toileting or spraying ('marking') in your home following the successful use of a litter tray, it is likely that he has developed a behavioural condition that would require treatment (see page 73).

Going to the 'toilet' for felines is not simply about urinating and defecating. Cats leave 'scent' signals, or messages, which are intended to offer 'marker' information to other cats. These messages include information about territory boundaries, sex, oestrus cycles, testosterone and oestrogen levels and, possibly, dominance. Fresh 'foreign' scents made by cats and other animals

■ **Above:** *Even young kittens can soon learn to use a litter tray and will become toilet-trained. Make sure that you change the litter regularly.*

within your cat's territory can cause alarm whereas old scents can be ignored and over-marked with the cat's own scent.

In cases of insecurity (marking

PUNISHMENT

It is important that you never smack or hit a cat or kitten in response to any problem behaviours. If a cat or kitten does something that is not allowed, in most instances, a sharp tone of voice and the word 'No!' are sufficient. If this fails, then a loud clap of the hands should do the trick. (It is worth recalling that cats have very sensitive hearing and they respond to loud or high-pitched noises.) For more obstinate cats, an aversion method, such as a quick squirt of water from a plant spray or water pistol, might be necessary. Alternatively, a signal for non-reward (training discs) can also work. These methods are particularly effective in curing a cat from walking on kitchen surfaces where food is to be prepared.

■ **Right:** *The small, shallow litter tray on the right is suitable for a kitten. Adult cats require a larger, deeper tray (left). Use a plastic scoop to remove any soiled litter.*

within the house), you should reduce your cat's territory within your home by restricting him to one room – ideally, one with a cat flap exit to the outside world.

Kittens and cats that are confident (however basic) should have the run of your house. If there is a refusal to use the litter tray provided it is probably because of 'insecurity' or, in adult cats, it can sometimes be linked to an earlier 'bad experience'.

To combat this problem, offer extra litter trays in different locations throughout the house. Covered litter trays can offer a nervous cat an element of secrecy, and 'clumping litter' has been found to be more 'attractive' to most cats in this situation.

The cat flap

If you allow your pet to be an outdoor cat that can roam freely, it is advisable to fit a door cat-flap. This will give your cat the freedom to come and go as he pleases. There are many different door flaps available but it is important that the type chosen is not positioned too high or too low for a cat. Cats are quick to understand how to use a cat flap. Just encourage them to pass through gently a few times and they will soon learn what to do.

Magnetized or key-collar coded cat flaps are best because they will permit only your cat to exit and enter the flap. This feature can be paramount for insecure 'rescue' cats which may find competition with other outdoor cats, especially those exhibiting territorial aggression, rather frightening. The nervousness that can follow these stressful incidents can encourage a cat to mark, or spray, indoors. Cat flaps for indoor cats can be installed to create a connection between your home and a secure outdoor run in the garden.

Collars, harnesses and leads

If your kitten is to be allowed to roam freely out of doors, it is essential that he wears a collar and a tag containing your address or, better still, that he is micro-chipped. These methods enable the owner to be traced if a cat becomes lost and is recovered. There are many types of collars on the market today although Cats Protection provides the safest with its circlet type.

Collars with bells are useful as they help you to hear if your cat is nearby. Bells can also help to warn birds if your cat is stalking them. Train a kitten to wear a collar from as early an age as possible.

Sometimes it is possible to teach a cat or kitten to walk on a lead, and some breeds are much happier lead walking than others. A cat that regularly walks on a lead will need to wear a harness.

■ **Left:** *Some cats, such as this regal Burmese, will quite happily wear a harness and can be trained to walk on a lead.*

If you decide to lead-train your cat, it is advisable for him to become accustomed to wearing a harness while he is a kitten. Lead-training a cat is a gradual process and you must be patient. Start by placing the harness on your cat for short periods of time while he is moving around the house. You must not try to 'walk' a cat at this stage. After a while, when he's used to the harness, try walking him around the garden. With time and patience, you should be successful.

Exercise and mental stimulation

All cats need exercise. However, the amount they require depends on the particular breed, as some felines seem to be more exuberant than others. Cats love to climb and their strong hind legs enable them to be excellent at jumping. If a cat is allowed outdoors, there is no doubt that it will enjoy climbing trees. Sitting on walls, fences and other elevated objects gives a cat the ideal vantage point to watch over its territory. Being high up, a cat will also be more successful at spotting any potential dangers, such as other cats or dogs. In order to maintain its territory, it is necessary for a cat to patrol and scent its boundaries regularly. Most outdoor cats get sufficient exercise to keep them fit and healthy.

Below: *Nearly all cats love to climb, and outdoor ones will enjoy shinning up trees and watching the world from a high vantage point.*

Preventing boredom

Cats that are kept solely indoors can become lethargic and bored. If your cat is a house cat, it might be advantageous to have two cats as they will provide each other with essential animal contact and play. Cats that are the best of friends will enjoy chasing each other around the house. Cats that are kept indoors will also benefit from scratching posts. Platforms are very useful as they enable a cat to climb and sit in an elevated position as it would outdoors.

Suitable toys

It is necessary to provide the indoor cat with a varied selection of toys. There are many elaborate toys on the market, but large cardboard boxes are very cheap and usually a successful way of entertaining your pet. Cats and kittens love jumping, hiding and peeping into boxes. Small balls, with or without bells, are another favourite toy which cats enjoy playing with. Absolutely anything bobbing about on the end of a string is also another irresistible attraction for an inquisitive kitten. However, don't leave a kitten unsupervised to play with this type of toy. It has been known for a cat to become entangled in a

Right: *All sorts of unlikely objects can become amusing toys for cats, such as this unprepossessing ball of foil.*

Above: *Owning two indoor cats can help prevent boredom and behavioural problems. They will amuse each other and enjoy playing together.*

long piece of string and even to strangle itself. Track toys, where a ball is 'pawed' by the cat around a circular track, have proved to be extremely successful during testing by animal behaviourists.

Cat runs

Cats that are allowed access to an outdoor run will benefit from the safety that comes of being an indoor cat while experiencing the diversity of outdoor life. Ideally,

Left: *Kittens love to play and explore their environment. These four-week-old Singapuras already like to climb and will happily play with a ball.*

Left: *An outdoor run can be equipped with high shelves, scratching posts and toys to keep a cat busy and amused. This Tonkinese, even when left alone, has plenty to do and will not become bored.*

Below: *All cats need a warm, snug bed they can feel safe in. This radiator hammock gives them some degree of protection from other pets as well as being warm and cosy.*

cat runs should be as large as possible and fitted with different platform shelves, which are placed at varying heights. You can also position a tree stump or a post in the run for the cat to use for scratching. A suitable waterproof shelter should also be provided in case it starts to rain.

Home alone

Many cats sleep for long periods during the day. Leaving a cat alone in the house during the day should not create any major problems provided that it has the necessary food, litter tray and toys. It is acceptable to confine a cat to one room, such as the kitchen, while you are away from home provided that you take the necessary safety precautions.

Beds and hygiene

There is a wide variety of beds available for your kitten to sleep in. This range includes wicker baskets, bean bags and even hammocks, which can be hung on heated radiators. A cat bed should always be warm and snug, easy to clean and positioned in a quiet, draught-free place in your home, preferably out of everyone's way.

Cats are very clean animals, and to maintain your kitten in optimum health, it is important to ensure that his bedding is always kept clean. Feeding and drinking bowls should also be cleaned daily. Wash your hands before and after handling your kitten.

KITTEN HEALTH

Giving the correct diet, care and attention to your pet is just one aspect of maintaining it in good health. It is also advisable to take your kitten to the local vet for its vaccinations and regular check-ups. When you acquire a new cat or kitten it is advisable to register your pet with a veterinary clinic and to make an appointment to take it along to the vet as soon as possible for a full check-up and to discuss a suitable worming regime. There are times when a cat could become ill and it will help if your local veterinary clinic is already familiar with your pet.

Checking a kitten for ill health

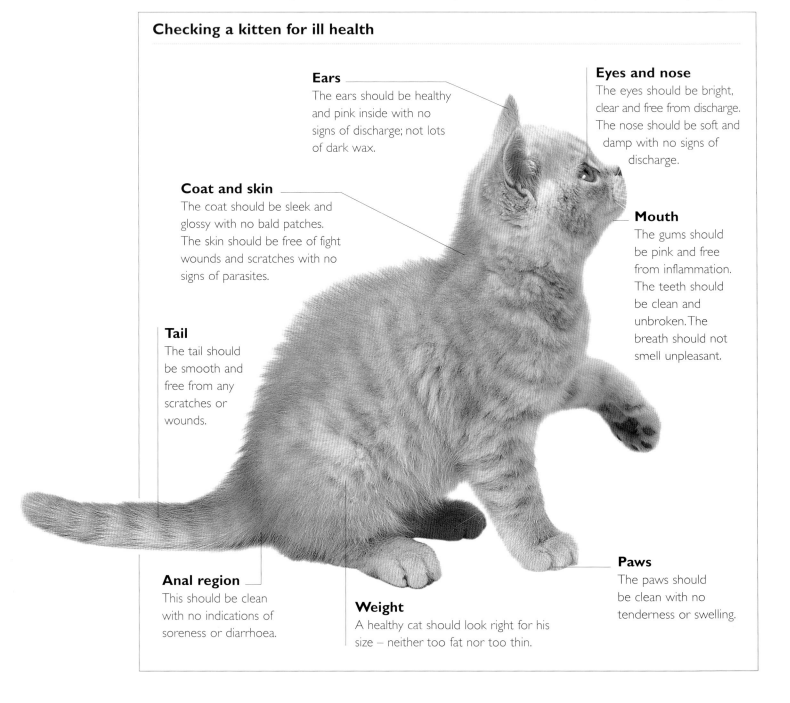

Ears
The ears should be healthy and pink inside with no signs of discharge; not lots of dark wax.

Eyes and nose
The eyes should be bright, clear and free from discharge. The nose should be soft and damp with no signs of discharge.

Coat and skin
The coat should be sleek and glossy with no bald patches. The skin should be free of fight wounds and scratches with no signs of parasites.

Mouth
The gums should be pink and free from inflammation. The teeth should be clean and unbroken. The breath should not smell unpleasant.

Tail
The tail should be smooth and free from any scratches or wounds.

Anal region
This should be clean with no indications of soreness or diarrhoea.

Weight
A healthy cat should look right for his size – neither too fat nor too thin.

Paws
The paws should be clean with no tenderness or swelling.

Signs of ill health

Always examine your kitten or cat regularly, and keep watch for the tell-tale signs of ill health. These include the following symptoms:

◆ Prolonged sleeping, lethargy or hiding can be characteristics of an unhealthy cat.

◆ Dietary changes, such as loss of appetite or excessive drinking, can also indicate a health problem.

◆ Frequent vomiting, diarrhoea and/or blood in the cat's faeces are always a cause for concern.

◆ A cat can quickly become very dehydrated, and if this condition persists, it is essential that you seek the advice of your veterinary surgeon as quickly as possible.

◆ Frequent sneezing and/or coughing, and laboured breathing are signs that a cat could possibly have a respiratory disorder.

◆ Weight loss, worms passed in the faeces and diarrhoea could indicate internal parasites. Your veterinary surgeon will be able to give you a suitable worming medication. To prevent worm infestations, it is advisable to worm your kitten or cat regularly. The recommended de-worming programme is every four months against tapeworms, and every six months against roundworms.

◆ If your cat has difficulty when walking or is in pain, it is possible that he could have been involved in a road traffic accident and could be bleeding internally. Contact your vet immediately.

◆ Runny eyes could be a sign that your kitten has an eye infection. Your veterinary surgeon will be

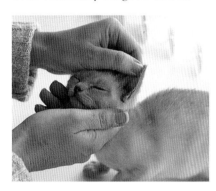

■ **Above:** *Check that the ears are pink and healthy with no signs of discharge.*

■ **Left:** *Check the kitten's coat carefully for tell-tale signs of fleas. The droppings look like fine black powder in the fur.*

able to supply you with eye drops to treat this problem.

◆ Inflammation of the ears could mean that your kitten has an ear infection. You should seek the advice of your veterinary surgeon.

◆ Excessive scratching or frantic licking could be a sign that your kitten or cat has fleas. Check the coat carefully for flea droppings, which look like a fine black powder at the base of a cat's fur. If you suspect them, seek out the advice of your veterinary surgeon as soon as possible for treatment. However, it is possible to buy flea collars as a preventative measure.

EMERGENCY TREATMENT

If your kitten or cat is involved in a road traffic accident, you will need to act quickly.

1 Remove him from danger by gently sliding a sheet underneath him, and then carefully lift and transfer him to a safe place.

2 Check his pulse, which is found on the inside of the thigh where it joins the body.

3 Check for breathing by placing your hand on his chest. If it is irregular or nonexistent, open the cat's mouth and bring the tongue forwards. Check that the airway is clear.

4 Check the cat's heartbeat. This can be felt on the chest behind the front legs.

5 Heavy bleeding should be stopped by applying pressure to the wound (see page 138).

6 Examine your kitten or cat for broken bones. He may go into shock so keep him warm with blankets. Always contact the veterinary clinic immediately. For more detailed information on first aid procedures, turn to page 136.

Your basic first aid kit

It is always a good idea to keep a basic first aid kit at home should your kitten have an accident or mishap. This should contain the following items:

◆ Safe disinfectant   ◆ Eyewash
◆ Milk of magnesia   ◆ Antiseptic cream
◆ Adhesive dressing   ◆ Cotton wool
◆ An appointment card with details of your vet's telephone numbers.

Diet

Kittens, like all juvenile animals, require small, regular feeds as they have very tiny stomachs and can only digest modest amounts of food. They also display growth spurts and these need to be fuelled with food to prevent weight loss.

There is now a wide variety of food types available, from which cat owners can choose. They range from canned and semi-moist foods to dry, 'complete' products. Better-quality foods will inevitably cost more but they will reflect a higher standard of content and also, usually, the considerable nutritional research that has been undertaken by the manufacturers. Each type of food has its own benefits and disadvantages.

◆ **Canned food:** Although there is a great amount of moisture in canned foods, some vitamins and minerals can be lost in the fluid.

◆ **Dried foods** have the advantage of being 'balanced' with a special formula for protein, amino acids, vitamins and minerals, but sometimes cats find this type of food unappetizing. Although they are 'complete' foods, it is possible to offer food alternatives.

◆ **Semi-moist foods** are popular with some cat owners.

Note: There may be situations, especially with queens in kitten or older cats, when a vet will recommend higher- or reduced-protein foods. You should always

■ **Above:** *Occasionally you may need to hand-rear a kitten. This four-week-old Singapura needs to be fed with a milk substitute through a syringe.*

follow these recommendations because they are based on clinical research. Note that many of the larger cat food manufacturers do provide feeding guides.

KITTEN FEEDING GUIDE

Under 3 weeks*	Consult a veterinary surgeon, breeder or a rescue centre expert. The kitten would require a substitute for mother's milk and may also need a vitamin and mineral supplement.
4–6 weeks	Feed 1 teaspoon, or slightly more, of liquid-consistency kitten food mixed with baby milk substitute 4–5 times per day.
6–12 weeks	Kittens should now be gradually weaned from moist food. Feed 2–3 teaspoons of solid kitten food (canned, moist and semi-moist or dried) 4–5 times per day.
3–6 months	Increase the amounts of solid foods, scaling down from 5 times to 2–3 times per day.

* Kittens should not be removed from the litter at this age because interruption to normal socialization can lead to nutritional deficiencies and behavioural problems in an adult cat.

Outdoor cats and kittens will often bring prey, as a trophy or offering, into the home. Prey targets can range from small birds, rodents and insects to even juvenile rabbits. This instinctive hunting behaviour, which occurs even in well-fed cats, can be extremely difficult to eradicate. Some cats are natural hunters and thrive when they are stalking prey. A warning bell on the collar or a 'sonic unit' can alert potential prey and reduce successful strike rates.

■ **Left:** *This ten-week-old Bengal kitten is eating its meal with relish.*

Indoor/outdoor cats

Another consideration when you are deciding on how much food to offer and the frequency of meals is dependent on whether you have an indoor or outdoor cat. The nutritional requirements of an active outdoor cat would be slightly greater than those of an inactive indoor cat because of the greater energy expenditure. Bear in mind also that cats need access to grass. They nibble grass to aid regurgitation of fur, and thus they may benefit from small amounts in their diet. For indoor cats or those given an outdoor run, it is possible to grow troughs of grass that can be rotated after use.

Kitten food

Between four and six weeks, a kitten will need four to five feeds of moist food per day. This should be followed up (from six weeks onwards) with a combination of solids, including fresh, canned or dried foods, although one feed can be a paste based on special cat milk and baby kitten food. By the time a kitten is eight weeks of age, it should be eating solid foods. The progressive weeks (months two to six) should see a gradual reduction in the number of feeds to two or three per day. The amount of food should be increased accordingly.

Going to the veterinary clinic

In an ideal world, your kitten or cat would have made several car journeys before visiting the vet for the first time. However, all kittens and new cats will require immunization and a general check-up by your vet, and this will necessitate travel, sometimes for only the second time in their lives.

It is best to randomly crate your kitten or put him in a carrier before going to the vet. This will condition him to the carrier and should help to prevent a difficult association being made. If he only goes in a carrier or crate for trips to the vet, then the unit will become associated with difficult rather than pleasant experiences.

In that 'ideal world' already mentioned, your cat or kitten would have made the journey to the vet and would have been taken inside and handled without the use of an hypodermic needle. However, this is not the case, and therefore your visit to the vet may have a negative association (the journey, scents, sounds and injections) so it is best to make the experience both swift and rewarding. An appointment can usually be made for a quiet time if you discuss the matter with the head veterinary nurse.

Only take your cat or kitten out of the carrier or crate when you are safely inside the examination room and the door has been closed safely behind you. Write down any queries you have beforehand so that, hopefully, these can be dealt with speedily. Give your cat a food treat when you return home.

Cat behaviour

Cats have proved themselves to be one of the most adaptable domestic species, and the success of their relationship with man is proof of their ability to manipulate almost any situation to their own advantage. Over the years, the cat has successfully resisted the process of domestication and has struck a deal with mankind. It agrees to share its life with people and offers us companionship in return for shelter and food, but at no time does it surrender its independence or allow its owner to take control. In order to understand the cat and appreciate its interpretation of the world around it, we need to take time to study the behaviour of its ancestors and recognise the inherent behavioural needs of our most popular companion animal.

Chapter Four

COMMUNICATING WITH YOUR CAT

One of the main factors in establishing and also maintaining a successful relationship is being able to communicate, but when the two participants in a relationship speak two completely different languages this may prove to be somewhat problematic. This is certainly the case in the relationship between man and cat, and one very important step in improving relationships between cats and their owners is teaching the owners to understand the subtle signals that make up feline communication.

Communication systems

Cats use three major systems of communication in order to get their message across; by studying these systems and by learning to interpret feline signals accurately, owners can begin to see the world from a more feline perspective. Vocalization, visual signalling and olfactory communication all combine to make the cat a very effective communicator, and the development of each of these systems can be better understood when feline communication is considered within the context of its behavioural needs.

Avoiding confrontation

For many years the cat was regarded as an asocial animal, but in recent years this solitary image has been questioned. Research has shown that cats do engage in affiliative social interactions with other members of their own species and can form worthwhile social relationships with the humans in their world. However, independence is still an important feature of feline life and, when it comes to hunting, cats do work very much on their own. One of the consequences of being a solitary hunter is that cats are highly motivated to avoid physical conflict and potential injury and keep themselves fit enough to seek out prey. As a result, they have developed a varied and fascinating language, which is designed to diffuse tension, and, in feline terms, confrontation is most definitely a last resort.

Keeping your distance

Feline communication, in general terms, is primarily adapted to maintain distance between cats and limit face-to-face interaction. Obviously, there may be times when cats come into close contact and at these times a combination of vocal and visual communication may be appropriate, but in those situations where cats have no need to have direct interaction, olfactory communication can be very important as a means of conveying specific information over time.

MARKING

Scent signals are specific to the individual, stable over time and can be deposited in the environment and detected and decoded by another cat at a later date, in the absence of the individual who deposited them. This has distinct advantages for a species that works hard to maintain distance from its conspecifics, and scent signalling plays a vital role in avoiding confrontation and maintaining distance. However, the major disadvantage of odour communication is that alteration of the signal is difficult to achieve and once the message has been left it is not possible to rapidly remove it, should that become necessary. This means that cats need to be accurate in their olfactory signalling, and it is believed that most of the information contained in scent deposits is of a factual rather than an emotional nature. The cat is highly adapted to deposit scent signals, and there are various parts of the cat's body where

Below: *When cats urinate in the open and make no attempt to cover their deposits, it is likely that they are using the urine to communicate.*

special scent-producing glands are found. The major areas of scent production are the face, the flanks and tail base, but cats also have glands on the paws, which deposit scent signals during the process of scratching, and they will utilize the scent of urine and faeces as a form of communication.

The scent signals that the individual deposits help to identify it to other cats, both within its social group and in the wider community, and also give important information about how long ago the individual was in the area. Time-scheduling is a very important feature of feline life, especially in areas of high population density, such as housing estates.

Cats that are forced to share relatively small territories will use scent signals to communicate with fellow felines and inform them of how long ago they used any specific passage track within the territory, thereby avoiding the need for any face-to-face encounters.

Above: *When cats encounter scent signals they spend time sniffing at the marks and interpreting the message.*

Reading scent signals

In order to interpret scent signals, cats rely not only on their sense of smell but also on a unique chemical sense, which has been described as a combination of taste and smell. This sense is mediated by a special organ called the Jacobson's organ, which is situated in the hard palate and accessed via two small openings in the mouth behind the upper incisor teeth. These ducts lead to two fluid-filled, blind-ending sacs which are lined with olfactory cells. Scent is forced up into the ducts by pressing the tongue against the roof of the mouth.

In order to achieve this, the cat engages in a specific behaviour, which is known, as the flehmen reaction. Cats performing a flehmen response have a very characteristic appearance, and they will stretch their neck, open their mouth, wrinkle their nose and curl back their lip in what almost resembles a snarl.

Depositing scent signals

It is almost impossible for human beings to appreciate the value of olfaction in social interactions since we rely heavily on visual and vocal communication, and our sense of smell is so limited that we cannot appreciate the subtleties of the odours around us. This causes problems in communication between cat and man since many of the signals that cats use to try to get their message across fall on deaf noses, and the behaviours that they use to deposit those signals are open to considerable misinterpretation.

The depositing of scent signals is called marking, and there are four basic forms of this behaviour in the domestic cat – these are rubbing, scratching, urine marking and middening.

Rubbing

Owners will often have seen their cat using the specialized scent glands of the face and flanks to deposit signals on inanimate objects in the house and garden, on other cats in the household and even on their owners themselves. Of all the marking behaviours of the cat, rubbing is probably the most acceptable, and many owners actively encourage their pets to rub around their legs. This full-body rubbing is a form of greeting behaviour, and it is usually accompanied by an erect tail, which signals a desire to interact. Rubbing is recognised as one of the important affiliative behaviours which work to maintain stability within a feline community.

However, within the pet-owner relationship, this behaviour is often reinforced as a greeting ritual by the owner's response. The most striking thing about rubbing behaviour between cats is that it is usually initiated by the weaker individual, and although cats do not live in a structured hierarchy rubbing does appear to be important as a means of acknowledging status as well as a method of exchanging scent. When domestic cats rub against their owners' legs, they are acknowledging status and confirming the stability of the relationship, but they are also picking up and depositing scent in order to establish a common signal, which can then be used to identify members of the same social group and reassure individuals that they belong.

■ **Left:** *Rubbing is an important method of communication between a cat and its owner. It acknowledges status and confirms the relationship.*

■ **Left:** *Cats use the scent glands on their face to leave messages for other cats in the neighbourhood, and to reassure themselves that their territory is secure.*

Scratching

The sight of a cat stropping its claws on a fence panel in the garden is a familiar one to most people, but the apparent simplicity of this behaviour masks its true complexity in terms of feline communication. Misinterpretation of this particular form of marking can even lead to real tension between a pet cat and its owner.

Healthy claws

Most people interpret scratching as purely functional behaviour and believe the cat is sharpening its claws. Certainly scratching is an important form of manicure for cats, and it is important to keep their claws in trim in order to hunt successfully. However, rather than sharpening the existing claw, the cat is actually removing the blunted outer claw sheath in order to reveal a glistening new weapon and the discarded outer claw coverings are often to be found at the bottom of favourite scratching locations.

Another functional role of scratching is to exercise and to strengthen the muscles and the tendons that are important in protracting the claws. It is very important to practise this action regularly in order to keep the claws ready for action, not only during the kill but also when the cat is climbing trees and fence panels or defending itself in a confrontation with another cat.

Marking

The third function of scratching and the one that is most often overlooked is that of marking. Scratch posts can act as a visual marker, and the vertical scratch marks are believed to be important in communicating with other cats in the neighbourhood. However, they also act as scent signposts, which play a role in the feline time-share system.

On the underside of the cat's paws are small scent glands, and the rhythmic stropping of the front feet along the scratching post activates these glands to deposit their signal. At the same time, the sweat glands on the pads release their secretion, and the combined cocktail results in a scent mark that is unique to that individual.

■ Above: *When cats scratch on trees in the garden, they are not only taking care of their claws but are also leaving clear visual and olfactory messages.*

Urine marking

The spraying of urine as a signal of communication is a deliberate behaviour, and this must be distinguished from the evacuation of urine from a full bladder during urination. It has been shown that cats can deposit urine marks regardless of the state of their bladder, and that they perform this behaviour in a set routine, during which the area they spray and also the number of squirts that they perform remains constant, despite some fluctuation in the amount of liquid that they deposit.

Urine marking is usually associated with a characteristic posture, and cats will back up against the scent post and squirt very small amounts of urine in a horizontal stream onto the vertical surface. Usually the tip of the cat's tail will quiver as it sprays, the back will be arched, the hind feet will tread and the cat will wear a look of extreme concentration on its face.

One of the reasons why cats perform urine spraying from a standing position is to deposit the urine at nose height where it will be readily noticed by other cats. However, cats may also mark with urine which they deposit from a squatting position. The exact role of squat marking in feline communication is still something of a mystery, and it is not as common as the spraying behaviour. However, it certainly occurs, and some cats will use a combination of both forms of marking in order to get their message across.

Despite a popular belief that this behaviour is limited to tom cats, it is now well recognised that most cats deposit urine around the periphery of their outdoor territory on a regular basis and that cats of either sex will use this urine marking as an important communication tool, regardless of whether they have been neutered.

Left: *When any new object enters a cat's territory, it will be subjected to a very comprehensive nose scan!*

Functions of urine marking

One of the primary purposes of urine marking in the outdoor territory is to operate a time-share system. This not only ensures that the available territory is not over-hunted but also minimizes the risk of unfamiliar individuals coming into contact. However, this spacing function is not the only application of this form of scent communication, and when urine marking is performed by sexually active male and female cats, it is used to signal the receptivity of the female and draw these cats closer together.

Tom cats pay a great deal of attention to the marks of any in-oestrus females since they contain important information about the stage of oestrus and the likelihood of mating. One important distinguishing feature of sexually-related urine spraying is that cats engaging in this behaviour will often vocalize as they deposit their signal. Obviously, this form of marking is only encountered in entire cats, and it can be readily controlled by neutering.

For quite a long time, it was suggested that urine spraying was the mark of an over-confident cat and that the scent was being used as a threatening signal to those around. However, observation refutes this. The reactions of other cats to the spray marks do not appear to be fear-related and, in fact, cats will often be positively drawn to the marks and will sniff at them with great interest. Many cats will sniff at the sprayed area and simply walk away, apparently unaffected by the message they have received, while others will spray over the mark with their own urine, presumably responding to the information by confirming that they are also in the area. In addition to this role of urine marking in communicating with other cats, insecure individuals will also use the behaviour to reassure themselves, and by spreading around their own distinctive odour these cats appear to become more confident.

Middening

The deliberate deposition of faeces as a form of marking is called middening, and this behaviour is usually seen at the boundaries of the cat's territory.

Its full significance is yet to be discovered, but there is no attempt by the cat to cover up the faeces, as there is during elimination. It appears that middens convey a very clear signal to other cats that the territory is occupied. Common locations for these unsubtle signals are the middle of a neighbour's lawn, the tops of fence posts and the roofs of garden sheds. One thing is certain – these distinctive markings are hard to ignore.

BODY LANGUAGE

Cat watching is a fascinating occupation but in order to get the most out of the cat-owner relationship it is helpful to know a little more about the messages that the cat is giving when it changes its body position and facial expression. Accurate interpretation of these signals not only makes the relationship more rewarding but it also reduces the potential for misunderstandings and enables owners to predict their cat's behaviour and avoid unnecessary conflict. Understanding cats takes practice, and interpreting body language is made even more challenging by the high degree of individuality involved. However, developing the skill of recognising and translating basic feline expressions helps enormously in cat-human communication.

■ **Right:** *The averted eyes and crouched posture suggest that this cat is trying to avoid interaction.*

■ **Below:** *Body language is an important method of communication in feline encounters. The cat on the right is preparing to escape whilst maintaining its ability to defend itself if necessary.*

From a distance

It is the overall posture of the cat that gives the first indication as to its intentions and relates how confident or insecure the animal is feeling. Readiness to run is a good indicator of intentions, since flight is the cat's primary defence strategy, and whenever there is a hint of danger or confrontation the feline instinct is to flee.

Cats try to avoid conflict, and a certain amount of bluffing is allowed if it increases the cat's chances of survival. However, this can only be done safely from a distance where the truth is unlikely to be discovered. Arching the back, raising the hair on the back and over the tail, and also standing at an angle to the perceived threat are all acceptable ways for cats to lie about their size and thereby make their potential opponent think twice about taking them on. In many cases, this bluff can be very successful, and cats retreat before they get close enough to discover the truth. Sometimes, however, the potential threat continues to advance and the cat needs to reconsider its position. If a change of plan is required during an interaction, the sideways posture enables a cat to keep its opponent in view whilst retreating very slowly so as to avoid inducing a chase response!

Honesty is the best policy

For some cats, honesty is still considered to be the best policy, and when these individuals feel threatened they take avoiding action and will retreat. If the opportunity arises, this retreat will involve physically leaving the conflict situation and getting far away, but if this is not an option the cat will shrink to its smallest possible size and try to hide. In some cases, this hiding may be complete and the cat may get under or behind some physical barrier. However, cats truly believe that if they can't see you, you can't see them – simply avoiding eye contact and turning their back on the potential threat can be enough of a withdrawal to be effective for some cats.

Facial signals

Although the overall body posture of a cat can be very important in assessing its intentions in any form of interaction, it is the facial expressions that give a much more accurate impression of its emotional state and provide the fine tuning in feline visual communication. Anyone who has worked with cats in situations where they are potentially stressed and under pressure will know how important it is to keep an eye on a cat's face in order to determine what it is likely to do next! Some feline expressions of fear and anger can be very similar and before starting to make interpretations of signals from individual components, such as the eyes, ears or tail, it is essential to put each of them into the context of a cat's total body language. Looking at one feature in isolation can be very misleading.

What do the ears tell you?

Cats can change the positions of their ears with remarkable speed. Although this is obviously advantageous from a predatory point of view in order to aid the detection of moving prey, it is also important in communication.

Cats will use small movements of their ears to assess the potential reaction of any opponent, and during any single encounter the ear position of each cat may alter several times.

A cat with ears facing forwards is alert and confident, and even when the ears are tilted slightly

■ **Above:** *The mobility of feline ears enables the cat to assess auditory information from different directions at the same time.*

■ **Above:** *Although ear positions can be important indicators of a cat's emotional state, it is important to consider them in the context of other signals to ensure that they are interpreted accurately.*

■ **Left:** *When a cat is alert and interested, its ears are usually erect and forward facing.*

■ **Above:** *Flight is the preferred defence strategy of the cat, and this individual is ready to spring out of the way if the perceived threat gets too close.*

back most individuals would still be classed as being happy and relaxed. However, when the ears are flattened, the interpretation of ear position is not quite so easy and there is a lot of potential for misinterpretation. As the potential for confrontation increases, the ears are gradually moved back and flattened against the head, but it's important to avoid jumping to any conclusions about motivation at this stage. Flattening the ears is an important precaution in any form of confrontation, regardless of whether the individual is the aggressor or the victim, since the ears are vital instruments of communication and need to be protected from potential damage in the ensuing fight.

The exact way in which the ears are positioned can provide important information about motivation. Ears that are folded sideways and downwards indicate that the cat is trying to avoid confrontation and is preparing to defend itself from an approaching threat. A cat whose ears are flattened against the head with a backwards rotation is getting ready to attack.

What big eyes you have!

Feline eyes are very expressive and the size of the pupils is a good indicator as to the emotional state of the cat. However, once again, it is important to take into account all of the available information when trying to interpret eye signals. Dilated pupils are commonly associated with fear, whereas narrowed apertures may be seen as a sign of contentment. However, large pupils can also arise from any form of non-fearful arousal, such as excitement, and observing the overall behaviour of the cat is important in putting the pupil size in context. The level of lighting is always an important factor when you are observing pupil size, and the behavioural significance of large pupils in situations of low-light intensity or narrow pupils in bright light needs to be questioned.

What are you looking at?

Another important feature of eye communication comes in the form of eye contact. When cats deliberately seek or avoid eye contact there is a message in their behaviour. Slow blinking is usually the sign of a relaxed and happy cat, but when blinking is used in communication between cats and their owners and between cats themselves it is interpreted as a way of seeking reassurance and avoiding confrontation. Staring, on the other hand, is the sign of a very assertive individual, and prolonged eye contact can be used to intimidate an opponent.

It has often been reported that cats will seek out people who do not like them, and when owners

■ **Below:** *Dilated pupils are often associated with fear, but they can be seen in combination with any form of arousal or low-light intensity situations.*

have company they often find their pet making a beeline for the one person in the room who finds cats unappealing. The reason for this apparently perverse behaviour is to be found in the eye contact that people make with the cat.

The people who do not like cats will usually avoid any direct eye contact and narrow their eyes, whereas those who want to initiate interaction with the cat will actively make eye contact with them. In feline terms, the cat

lover appears to be staring in a confrontational manner and is likely to be avoided whereas the person trying to avoid any eye contact is giving clear signals that they are not a threat and can therefore be trusted!

The tail end of communication

The role of the cat's tail in feline communication has often been overlooked. However, it is now recognised that it is an important factor in social communication as well as an expression of the cat's emotional state. The speed of movement of the tail can give us some important clues as to a cat's intention in any interaction. Rapid, thrashing movement is generally associated with arousal while graceful, slow sweeping is seen as a sign of contentment. There is an established belief that a wagging tail is a sign of extreme annoyance and anger but this is not necessarily the case, and rapid movement of the tail simply indicates that the cat is agitated and in a state of emotional conflict. If people ignore this signal and continue to advance towards the cat, this may well result in confrontation but does not necessarily prove that the cat is bad tempered or aggressive.

Saying hello

The tail is a very expressive part of the cat's body, since not only is it capable of a whole range of movements, both up and down and from side to side, but also the tip can be moved independently of the base. During greeting, cats will use their tail position to test

out the potential reaction of the other individual and to avoid rejection. An upright tail position is a friendly gesture that signals non-threatening approach, and when it is used as a prelude to rubbing it is interpreted as a request for permission to interact. Rubbing is a behaviour associated with relative status; if a cat just waded in and rubbed without asking permission it may find itself in trouble, so the raised tail is an important way of ensuring that the interaction that follows is friendly. In addition, the raised tail signals an intention to find out more about the other cat as it allows the genital region to be exposed and invites the other individual to sniff under the raised tail and find out all about that cat! As well as holding the tail high, cats will also alter the position of the tail tip during greeting, and the way in which the tip is bent over appears to be very specific to the individual.

Displaying emotion

Tail position is not only important during social greeting, and a lot can be learnt by observing the tail during other feline activities, including sexual encounters and aggressive displays. Queens will move the tail to allow toms to

receive the full impact of their scent communication and inform them that they are ready for mating, whereas aggressive cats may use concave and lowered tail positions in order to indicate their intentions during a conflict. Sometimes the signals from the tail can be very subtle and quite difficult to interpret, but one exception is the bottle brush tail, which is a clear signal associated with fear and defence.

■ **Above:** *When a cat approaches with an erect tail and a bent tail tip, then it is indicating its intention to engage in friendly interaction.*

SOCIAL BEHAVIOUR

In order to understand more about the ways in which cats interact with their owners, it is not only necessary to know about their methods of communication but also about their social behaviour and the ways in which they will naturally interact with members of

their own species. Cats live in a female-dominated society and have even been described as the first true feminists! Their social behaviour in the wild is based on co-operation between mothers, daughters, grandmothers, sisters and aunts who all live together in

family units. Within these groups, the cats share the rearing of each other's kittens, and they assist one another in defending their territory from any potential intruders. Behaviour between group members is based on affection and tolerance, but outsiders are not welcome and the hostility shown towards individuals who do not belong can be very intense.

This has serious implications in multi-cat households where cats are often expected to live with unrelated individuals. It is mainly due to the effect of neutering that such unnatural feline groupings live together in relative harmony.

It has been clearly demonstrated that littermates make the best housemates, and when owners are setting up a new feline household it is advisable to keep related individuals together. Integration of newcomers is possible, provided that adequate attention is paid to natural feline social behaviour and that the introductions are made only in a gradual and non-threatening manner.

Right: *Littermates provide important lessons in social communication, and the bonds between siblings can last a lifetime.*

Keeping the family together

Maintaining harmony within any social group can be a challenge, and family unity cannot be taken for granted in feline society any more than it can in our own.

Cats have specific behavioural patterns that are designed to minimize the potential for conflict and disruption. The two most important affiliative behaviours are rubbing and grooming, and

when they are directed towards members of the same social group they are known as allorubbing and allogrooming.

Rubbing along together

Allorubbing is a behaviour that has become well established in the cat-owner relationship, as well as in communication between cats.

In addition to being used as a sign of affection, which is encouraged by most owners, rubbing appears to have some sort of role in the demonstration of respect.

Although cats do not live in a structured hierarchy as we do, they do appear, however, to acknowledge status. Rubbing is an asymmetrical behaviour pattern which is usually initiated by the weaker individual, and it is thought that the exchange of scent that occurs during this process actually helps to build up a communal scent pattern for the social group and reassures less confident individuals that they belong. In the case of cat to owner communication, rubbing appears to have a number of different functions, including acknowledging owner status and also confirming the pet-owner relationship. However, it can also take on a learned significance when the owner consistently responds to this interaction by opening a can of cat food!

Mutual grooming

Unlike rubbing, grooming appears to be a more reciprocal social behaviour, which is not only used to cement relationships between cats but also to exchange some important social information in the form of tastes and smells.

In many successful multi-cat households, owners take great pleasure in the sight of two felines cuddled up close to one another, and it is at these moments of relaxation that the onset of this allogrooming behaviour is often seen. This grooming is not restricted to the head and neck, which are areas of the body that a cat may find difficult to keep clean, and, although it may be beneficial in terms of keeping housemates clean, it is the social significance of this mutual grooming that is of most interest. As well as grooming one another, most cats will sniff the head and the tail region of their close companions, especially when they

have been apart. It is believed that by doing so they check up on the activities of their housemates while they have been away. By detecting the scents with which the returning cat has come into contact, it is possible to discover what the individual has been eating as well as where he has been and who he has been with.

■ **Above:** *When cats develop close, mutually rewarding relationships, owners can gain a great deal of pleasure from watching them together.*

What makes a good owner?

The most important quality in a cat owner is an understanding of cats, and although this may sound obvious an appreciation of this independent and mysterious species is not something that owners should take for granted. Learning to see life from a feline perspective can take time, and it is important to recognise that the fundamental differences in our social behaviour and our communication systems can sometimes cause confusion. The feline senses are finely tuned to function in a world that is dominated by scent signals and is driven by a desire for survival. Many of the signals that are of profound significance to the cat simply pass over the heads of the novice cat owner. Priorities differ

significantly between our two species, and while we may have a real need for a loving and nurturing relationship with our cats the feline perspective of the cat-human relationship is very different. Cats can learn to enjoy human company and can make very rewarding companions, but they have no fundamental need for social interaction and this has significant implications in terms of owner expectation. Of course, the cat welcomes the provision of food and shelter and, in most cases, the pet cat will derive some pleasure and reward from being in the company of its owner, but when tension begins to develop the cat has very little in-built instinct to remedy the situation. Unlike the dog, which

■ **Left:** *Although cats can learn to enjoy interaction with their owners, they do not perceive it as being a necessity.*

actually needs social contact for its emotional survival, the cat can function as an independent unit, and if the price of social interaction becomes too high it will simply retreat from contact or, in extreme cases, move house!

The need to display normal behaviours

Although the cat is classed as a domesticated animal, it is widely believed that the process of domestication is still not complete, and this view is supported by the fact that cats retain so much of their wild behaviour.

Some aspects of this behaviour are less compatible with life as a domestic pet than others, and in an attempt to bring the cat into our own world we have tried to alter feline expectations to fit in with our own. Unfortunately, this has not been successful, and in situations where cats are being expected to forfeit their natural behaviours because the owner finds them unacceptable, it is not uncommon for stress-related behaviours to become apparent.

How could he do that?

For many owners the prospect of their cat contributing to the mass destruction of wildlife is very

■ **Below:** *Dawn and dusk are important times for hunting, and many cats become more active at these times.*

The debate over the relative intelligence of different species looks set to rumble on through the generations, and a question that is often asked in the context of companion animal species is whether the cat is more or less intelligent than the dog. The honest answer to this question would have to be 'it depends' since intelligence can be measured in such a variety of ways. One of the most common reasons for people to assume that the dog wins in the intelligence stakes is that it is noticeably more trainable and will learn obvious connections between commands and actions and then be very compliant in responding to those commands. This certainly illustrates an ability to learn but whether it should be interpreted as intelligence is a matter of some debate, and many would argue that the cat demonstrates extreme intelligence through its ability to adapt to the ever-changing relationship that it has had with mankind and its ability to take control of situations and encounters in a role of leadership rather than blind obedience.

distressing, and it is an ironic fact that many cat lovers are also interested in bird life and are very concerned about the issues of wildlife conservation! However, the reality of the situation is that all cats need to hunt, and when they are kept within a domestic environment they are no less motivated to hunt and dispatch prey than when they are living in feral conditions.

The motivation to hunt has absolutely nothing to do with hunger, and attempts to limit the level of destruction by feeding cats more proprietary cat food are only successful when the cat becomes so overweight that it can no longer run fast enough to catch its prey! Even then the cat will still be tuned for the kill, and when movement and sound combine to trigger the natural instinct, it will go through the motions of the hunt even if it cannot bring the process to a successful conclusion!

For owners who wish to curtail their pet's hunting activities, the options for enabling them to live with a clear conscience while still allowing their cat to be true to its heritage are numerous. However, in every case they require some degree of compromise. The bottom line is that all cats have an innate requirement to respond to the call of nature by hunting and dispatching prey of one sort or another, but there is plenty of opportunity for owners to control the source of that 'prey'. Cats can easily learn to hunt toys and owner-controlled food sources rather than wildlife.

Playing is not simply for pleasure

Play is vital for all cats, and every day they need to be offered the opportunity to act out their natural behavioural sequences and practise the survival skills that make them such a successful species. Indeed, hunting is one of the skills that lends itself to the situation of play, and it is by recognising the way in which rapid movement and high-pitched sound trigger the natural hunting instinct that owners can select the toys that are most likely to stimulate the same responses.

It is important for cats to have the chance to catch and dispatch some of these prey items, and toys must therefore be suitable for this purpose. In addition to triggering the hunt response, they must be able to withstand the outcome of that response and not run any risk of fragmenting or breaking when the cat attempts to kill them. In the wild, cats will spend up to six hours a day hunting, and owners need to be prepared to spend some time every day engaging in play with their pet.

Cats also need these playtimes

■ **Left:** *Owners can help maximize the benefits of play by choosing toys that trigger their cat's natural behaviours.*

to perfect other skills, especially those associated with agility and movement. This means that play sessions should be varied, both in content and location, and owners need to be imaginative in the way in which they interact with their cat. Using toys to encourage cats to move freely, climb and explore is important. Cat activity centres can be a useful way of providing for your pet's recreational needs. Toys that encourage independent play, while still enabling the owner to be involved, are also very beneficial, and the fishing rod toy design is excellent for this purpose.

Learning through reward

It is often assumed that training is simply not an option within the cat-owner relationship, and many owners will resign themselves to all sorts of behaviours from their pets in the belief that there is simply nothing that they can do

■ **Left:** *Cat activity centres come in all shapes and sizes, providing opportunities for both locomotory and object play.*

to teach them to behave in a more appropriate way. Actually this is not the case, and cats can be trained to behave appropriately and to perform behaviours on command. However, the difficulty comes in identifying a reward that the cat will consider valuable enough to work for! Determining the best reward for an individual cat will involve watching its reactions and finding those things that appear to motivate it most. Some cats will work for games and for social interaction, but their independent social behaviour does not make human praise a very strong motivator. In most cases, the successful feline rewards are food based. Very few cats will find their daily food ration rewarding, and in cat training it is more common to use treat-based foods, such as cheese, tuna and prawns. One important element of reward in cat terms is novelty, and whatever reward is selected, it is important to vary it from time to time in order to maintain the cat's interest in training and its motivation to comply.

TRAINING YOUR CAT

In common with training in all other species, successful feline education relies on the correct application of reinforcement, and timing is one of the vital factors in teaching cats new tricks. In order to be successful, the reward needs to arrive while the cat is actually performing the desired behaviour. Obviously this can be quite difficult to achieve, and it is made even more challenging by the cat's real desire to feel in control. Forcing cats to perform behaviours so that they can be rewarded is usually unsuccessful, and it is better to be prepared to wait for the desired response to occur spontaneously and then reward it. However, this can lead to long time delays and also a corresponding drop in owner enthusiasm. Another approach is to break the desired behaviour down into smaller components. This can be very successful since the individual tasks are slightly easier to perform than the ultimate goal and there is an increased probability that there will be an opportunity to reward. As each little step becomes established, the owner can then work to put them all together and eventually achieve their goal. Patience is the key to success.

Using the cat flap

An excellent example of the application of incremental learning is teaching a cat to use a cat flap. This process requires time and patience, especially in the early stages. Few cats instinctively know how to react when they first encounter a cat flap, and they will need to learn that getting through the flap will bring them access to something worthwhile. Once the behaviour has been established, the act of entering the house will be rewarded by the comfort of home, and the act of going out will be rewarded by access to outside, but in the early stages, an owner needs to provide much higher-value rewards, such as toys or food.

Keeping things positive

One of the most common approaches to cat flap training is to push the cat through the flap. However, for a creature that likes to be in control, this method runs the risk of inducing negative associations with the flap and teaching the cat to avoid it rather than use it. A more successful approach is to prop the flap open so that the cat can see the great outdoors and move through the flap with minimal resistance.

In the early stages, it is best to teach the cat to come in rather than to go out, and the prospect of warmth and shelter can be used to encourage the cat to come inside. However, entry into the home is unlikely to be sufficiently

Right: *Cat flaps are regarded by most owners as a very useful invention. However, cats need to learn how to use them and some will perceive them as a threat rather than as a luxury.*

rewarding, and the presence of a food reward or an exciting toy on the inside of the flap will usually be needed to persuade the cat that coming through the hole is really a sensible thing to do. Once movement through the open flap has been established, the next stage is to gradually lower the flap so that the cat needs to apply some pressure to open it. This part of the procedure can be very slow and, as with all training, owners will need to be patient, remembering that losing their temper or becoming exasperated will only serve to make the process even longer in the end.

Keeping your cat safe

Although the concept of training cats has often been associated with teaching them to perform certain tricks for their owner's convenience, this is not the only possible application of learning in the feline world. The development of behaviours that have a definite purpose and will add to the cat's quality of life is a worthwhile application of the theory, and the introduction of road safety training to young kittens can be very beneficial.

In this case, the aim of training is to make positive associations with outdoor territory that is not adjacent to the highway and to form negative associations with the sight and sound of traffic. If your house is facing onto a road, the best approach is to focus all worthwhile owner interaction in the back garden and to use the back door to provide access to the great outdoors. In this way, leaving from the rear of the house is always rewarded.

■ **Left:** *For some owners, the option of keeping their cat indoors seems far preferable to the risk of losing him in a road traffic accident. However, such a decision brings with it a responsibility to provide for the cat's behavioural needs.*

If you totally ignore your pet when you see him at the front of the property and never allow him access to the house through the front door, the cat's activities should be directed away from the road and into the more secure environment of the back garden.

■ **Left:** *Despite having being injured in a road traffic accident, this cat shows no fear of cars or indeed the environment in which they operate. This only serves to show how difficult it can be to train cats to be streetwise.*

Chapter Five

CURING BEHAVIOUR PROBLEMS

The investigation and the treatment of behaviour problems have traditionally been associated with our canine companions, and when cats have exhibited inappropriate behaviours in the past their owners felt that they must either put up with the behaviour, rehome their pet or, in very severe circumstances, even make the ultimate decision and take their cat on a one-way trip to the veterinary surgery. Thankfully, times are changing and it is now recognised that behavioural therapy is just as relevant to the cat as it is to other species, and

Below: Paying attention to kitten development can have a profound effect on the incidence of behavioural problems in adulthood.

owners of problem cats now have better access to an increasing amount of expertise in the field of feline behaviour.

It's only natural

Many of the so-called problem behaviours that cats display are in fact perfectly normal, but they create a problem for owners when they are performed within the home. Examples include urine spraying, scratching and hunting, all of which are part of the cat's natural behavioural repertoire. Simply stopping cats from

displaying these behaviours is not the answer, and it is important to look at the problem from a feline angle and try to understand why the behaviour is being performed in an abnormal context. Teaching people to understand the ways in which cats communicate and behave in the wild can often be the first step to dealing with many of these behaviour problems.

Ensuring the cat's environment gives it the maximum opportunity to display its normal behaviours is often another very important consideration when making behavioural treatment plans.

Anxiety and stress

While many of the common feline behaviour problems are the result of misunderstandings between our species, it is also possible for cats to exhibit behavioural difficulties resulting from factors such as genetics, inappropriate rearing and subsequent emotional trauma. Problems in each of these areas can leave cats with an inability to deal with any novelty and challenges in the

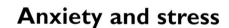

world around them, and this makes them prone to the negative effects of stress. In order to prevent these problems, it is important to appreciate the relevance of both genetic input and life experience to the behavioural development of the domestic cat and to work to ensure that all kittens are given the very best start in life in terms of socialization and habituation. Unfortunately, this is not always achieved, and anxiety and stress are common factors in the onset of feline behavioural disorders.

Cats can learn, too

Problem behaviours can also develop through inappropriate learning, and this is an area that is often overlooked in feline circles because of a mistaken belief that cats are untrainable. Not only are they capable of learning new associations through training but they are also very adept at training their owners. Unintentional provision of reward when a cat is behaving in an inappropriate manner can rapidly lead to a learned response that is difficult to remove.

Take a trip to the vet

Obviously not all cat behaviour problems are straightforward, and it is also important to remember that there is a very strong link between behaviour and physical health. A veterinary examination should always be performed when a cat behaves in an unacceptable or unexpected manner, and this is particularly important in those situations where cats begin to deposit either urine or faeces in the household. Urinary tract disease is a common factor in many cases of indoor toileting, and focusing on the behavioural issues before investigating the medical causes can lead to an unacceptable time delay and a potentially life-threatening deterioration in the cat's health.

■ **Above:** *Kittens need to be handled frequently if they are to grow up to be sociable cats.*

Investigating behaviour problems

Dealing with feline behaviour problems is a time-consuming process, and it is important to determine the motivation for any inappropriate behaviour before attempting to draw up treatment plans for cats and their owners. This will require not only a large amount of empathy and patience but also a sound level of scientific knowledge. The theory behind the development, investigation and treatment of feline behaviour problems is outside the remit of this book. However, it is possible to give a brief overview of some of the common feline behaviour problems and provide some insight into how these problems can be treated. Any owners who have behavioural concerns about their pet should make an appointment to see their veterinary surgeon and seek one-to-one advice which can be tailored to their individual animal.

■ **Right:** *Cats and dogs are traditionally regarded as enemies, but introduction at an early age can enable the two species to develop a close and lasting relationship.*

Indoor spraying and other forms of territory marking

Cats mark their territory in several ways, and whereas some of these marking behaviours are considered perfectly acceptable within human society, others are viewed as being anti-social in the extreme. Few owners will be offended by the sight of their cat rubbing its cheek against the corner of the stereo unit and, indeed, many will actively encourage this form of scent exchange as part of the greeting ritual, but when the cat starts to leave its scent in the form of urine or faeces or scratches its message on the back of the brand new sofa it is a different story. From a feline perspective, there is little difference between any of these behaviours, but the reaction they invoke from the humans in the household sends a clear signal that something is not quite right!

When dealing with marking problems, it is always important to remember that treatment will depend on understanding why these messages are being misplaced. When the onset of the marking behaviour has been sudden, it may be fairly straightforward to pinpoint the trigger for the response. However, in many cases the behaviour has been long standing before owners attempt to remedy it, and in these situations the original trigger may be difficult to determine. Identifying the locations for marking behaviour in chronological order will often reveal a pattern of behaviour, which helps in the identification of the original trigger even if that stimulus is no longer present. Once the cause has been identified, treatment is aimed at breaking the

■ **Left:** *Urine marking is a normal behaviour, but when it occurs in the kitchen it is not acceptable. The important question is why does the cat feel the need to mark at home.*

■ **Above:** *Scratching is a very important behaviour and leads to both visual and olfactory signals being deposited.*

habit of indoor marking, controlling the cat's exposure to the challenge and also working to increase its overall feeling of security.

Breaking the habit

Whatever the form of the marking behaviour, the cat will always be attracted to the signals that it has deposited, and when it detects that the scent is decaying it will be compelled to top up its signal.

This means that effective cleaning of marking locations is essential if the treatment is to be successful. Unfortunately, many favourite household cleaners contain some ammonia and/or chlorine, and since these are constituents of cat urine, it is easy to see how confusion may arise in cases of

Above: *Scratching is a complex behaviour, but it can also develop as a learned response. For this cat, scratching at the carpet is rewarded if the door is opened.*

indoor spraying. The method that has been found to be the most efficient for cleaning any sites of feline marking behaviour is that of washing the area with a warm solution of a biological detergent and then, once the area is dry, scrubbing it down with surgical spirit or other alcohol! Obviously it is important to check the fabric involved for colour fastness before using this regime – applying the treatment to a small test area

before cleaning vast expanses of carpet is a sensible approach.

Once the area has been cleaned, it may be necessary to place some deterrents in the places where marking has previously occurred. In general, the most effective deterrents are ones that are based on natural ways of redefining the function of the territory, increasing the cat's confidence and removing the need to mark.

The presence of food is a tried and tested method of identifying the home as a core territory which is safe and secure. Items of a cat's bedding or a variety of toys have been shown to have a similar effect. Likewise, the naturally occurring scent signals from the face of the cat can be beneficial in reassuring an individual of the security of its home. Owners can either use a facial cloth, which they rub across the face of their cat and then apply to previously marked areas of the house, or they can invest in a synthetic analogue of this scent signal, called Feliway, and apply this directly from the bottle. One very important thing

to realise is that the cleaning regime already outlined can affect the activity of Feliway, and a period of twenty-four hours should elapse between cleaning and its application if you are to maximize your chances of success.

Obviously there is often a lot more to dealing with marking problems than cleaning and redefining the territory, and if these simple measures are not effective you will need to contact your veterinary surgeon for more advice.

Dealing with the cause

If treatment is going to offer hope of a long-term resolution of the problem, then the approach to any form of marking problems must involve dealing with the cause of the behaviour. If it is possible to identify a specific stimulus which is acting as a trigger, then treatment should involve taking steps to isolate the cat from that challenge, at least in the short term.

The longer-term aim will be to teach the cat to cope with any challenges in its environment, be they physical or emotional, but isolating the cat from the source of its anxiety can be useful while other behaviour therapy is instituted to increase confidence. For example, the entry of another cat into the home via a cat flap, whether actual or threatened, can be avoided by blocking the cat flap. Restricting the cat's access to those areas of the home that are particularly challenging (areas of renovation, etc.) will also help.

The actual definition of what constitutes unreasonable challenge is, of course, dependent on the individual cat, and things that the majority of cats may take in their

Right: *Cat flaps can lead to a decrease in home security, especially if neighbouring cats use them too!*

stride may act as the trigger for a marking problem in a particularly sensitive individual.

Never punish

One very important rule in the approach to treating any cat with a marking problem is that punishment should always be avoided. Often the cat is not actually caught in the act, and retrospective punishment has no effect on the behaviour but merely serves to confuse the cat. Even when the owner does see the cat actually marking, then punishment is not advised. The cat is behaving perfectly naturally in feline terms and, since stress and anxiety are often causes of these problems in the first place, punishment can increase the cat's stress level and may even make the behaviour worse.

■ **Below:** *Hiding is an important strategy for cats, and this five-month-old Bengal kitten has retreated under a chair so that it can observe the world from a place of safety.*

Fear and timidity

One of the main welfare issues for cats, when we are considering the level of fear within the domestic population, is that they have two very distinct methods of dealing with situations in which they feel threatened. While one of these strategies is difficult to ignore, the other is open to misinterpretation and leaves the cat open to neglect.

◆ **Active responders,** as they are known, will make their feelings very obvious and will respond to the presence of the people they fear with vocalization and obvious distress. If the escape route is blocked, these cats are likely to resort to aggressive displays in order to repel the perceived threat, and the risk of injury from these individuals is very real.

◆ **Passive responders,** however, respond to their fear by withdrawing both socially and emotionally from the world around them. These cats will seek high-up resting places and will shut themselves off from any interaction. They internalize their fear and are

more at risk from developing behavioural problems, such as over-grooming, rather than showing any form of overt aggression.

Developing inappropriate fear responses

When considering the onset of inappropriate fearful behaviour, it is important to look at the input from the environment, from the owners and, of course, from the individual cat. Lack of appropriate socialization and habituation has been found to be the most common cause of these problems, but other factors, such as genetic input from the father, observational and genetic input from the mother and learning as the result of insufficient, inappropriate or even hostile interaction with the environment and with people, all need to be considered.

■ **Above:** *When a new kitten is introduced, the resident cat will benefit from the provision of high-up resting places where it can retreat if the youngster is too overpowering.*

Unintentional learning

One of the effects of the efficient flight response in cats is that fearful escape behaviour is highly rewarding. Thus if a cat feels threatened by someone and it manages to run away, it will learn that retreat is an effective means of limiting unwanted contact and will run sooner rather than later when the next encounter occurs. Altering this learning process is not easy since, unlike dogs, cats are not highly motivated by alternative rewards, such as food or play. Indeed, finding reinforcers for the appropriate behaviour towards people is probably one of the major limiting factors in treating feline fears.

The most effective way of dealing with this dilemma is to work to encourage the cat to be the one to take the initiative. In this way the social interaction can become inherently rewarding, and food and play can be introduced as additional reinforcers.

Treatment

Preventing fear and timidity in cats, through adequate socialization and habituation and appropriate selection of breeding stock, is obviously the ideal approach, but we also have to recognise that problems do arise and that a significant number of domestic cats are already suffering from inappropriate fear in reaction to their environment, to strangers or their owners. Whatever the actual manifestation of their fear, these cats need to be helped to overcome their problems by altering their perceptions and working to form positive associations with the world around them. Punishment is never appropriate for them and over-reassurance should also be avoided. In some cases where the level of fear prevents the cat from learning new behaviours, short-term drug therapy may be needed, but such treatment should never be used in isolation and behavioural therapy methods will also be necessary.

Teaching owners to back off and to allow their cat to take control is an essential part of the treatment approach, and although it is perfectly understandable that most owners would want to help their cat to overcome its fear, this approach is likely to be counter-productive. It is far better to work at making the world attractive in feline terms and to encourage the cat to actively seek interaction, since only once the cat actually wants to interact with its environment will it be ready and able to overcome its fear.

Left: *Fighting between cats in the same household can be very distressing for their owners.*

Aggression towards other cats

Cats are not confrontational by nature, and they have a very elaborate communication system, which is designed both to diffuse conflict and to avoid physical violence. Territorial disputes between cats in the same household are the exception rather than the rule, but problems are often encountered during the initial introduction. In some cases, the cats never learn to co-habit peacefully, and the aggression between them can be extremely distressing for their owners. In contrast, territorial disputes that occur between neighbouring cats are relatively common, and sometimes a single cat can inflict a reign of terror over a whole neighbourhood. In these cases, the consequences of the behaviour are not only measured in terms of injury to neighbouring cats but also in terms of the breakdown in friendly relations between human neighbours. Feline confrontation can easily escalate into full-scale neighbour disputes in which threats and counter-threats can eventually lead to an unpleasant atmosphere for everyone concerned.

Neighbourhood problems

The basic principles of treatment for despotic cats are to increase the perception of their own home as a secure den so that they spend more time there, and to teach them that other houses are out of bounds. Setting up a time-share system within the neighbourhood whereby the 'problem' cat has access to the outdoor territory at times when the 'victims' are safely tucked up at home may seem like a cop-out, but it is an effective way of buying time and enabling the owners to get together in a less distraught frame of mind to discuss what to do next. Making the home of the 'victim' secure by fitting a coded cat flap is a simple step to consider, but it is not always successful and some of the more experienced bullies are very adept at beating these devices and entering the home on the tail of a legitimate resident. Obviously making the home of the victim unwelcoming to the intruder is important, but it is sometimes difficult to do this in a way that does not make the house somewhat unappealing to the resident as well. Invading cats can quickly learn that the hostility is coming from the humans in the household, and when owner-driven deterrents, such as water pistols, are used, the despot will soon limit its break-ins to times when the owners are not about. Booby traps or deterrents that cannot be directly traced to the owners are therefore more effective, and if the timing of their delivery is accurate noise deterrents and water deterrents delivered with an element of surprise can have dramatic effects.

■ **Left:** *Fitting a coded cat flap can give cats an added sense of security. However, despotic cats can be very effective at breaking and entering despite the technology!*

Multi-cat households

In the majority of cases, aggression between cats in the same household occurs when a newcomer arrives. However, there are times when cats that have lived together for years suddenly fall out and the fur flies. The chances of conflict increase if one or more of the cats in the social group is poorly socialized or there is a high level of competition over resources. If there is a high density of cats in a small house and a shortage of high-up resting places, if the owner has limited time to give attention to all cats or if food supply is restricted, tension can quickly rise and cats can become very intolerant of their housemates. Other stressors within the environment can cause a breakdown in relationships, and when one of the resident cats has been absent from the home for a period, because it has gone missing, has been at the veterinary surgery or has been at a cattery, it is not uncommon for fur to fly when it comes back into the social group.

Preventing aggression

In order to minimize the risk of confrontation between cats when introducing a new feline member into the home, it is important to consider the best combination of cats for a multi-cat household and also to pay some attention to the introduction process.

It is generally accepted that littermates give the best chance of harmony, and many kittens will be inseparable playmates if they stay

■ **Below:** *When cats encounter a stranger in their territory, scent communication is very important in the introduction process.*

with each other from birth. Remember that there is a high degree of individual variation and, to some extent, it is believed that sociability, i.e. the desire to form social interactions with other cats, is genetically determined. Certainly some adult cats are more sociable than others and are more tolerant of other cats within a relatively small territory, whilst some are singularly intolerant and give a terrible prognosis for integration.

■ **Above:** *The bond between littermates can be extremely strong and they can be life-long companions.*

Gently does it

■ **Below:** *Kittens are naturally inquisitive, and they will be able to create their own safe havens from the objects they find in their environment.*

When some strangers infiltrate an established feline group in the wild, the acceptance of the newcomers' scent is the first stage in the process of integration. If the scent is familiar and is not associated with threat or danger, then there is far more chance of acceptance. This is why it often helps to have the newcomer in another room of the house for the first few days, where it is out of visual contact but is still able to infiltrate scent signals into the family. The process of infiltration can be aided by using communal bedding, toys and feeding bowls, which are alternated between the resident cat and the newcomer on a daily basis. In some cases, it helps to associate the smell of the newcomer with that of the owner, and using pieces of the owner's clothing, such as sweatshirts, can help in the integration process.

When it comes to the first face-to-face introductions, protection is the name of the game. Cats have a very strong sense of self preservation, and when danger looms the first response is to run. This results in a tendency to put to flight when confronted with a strange feline, and if another cat runs, most individuals will give chase! Such scenarios can permanently destroy any hopes of integration, and yet all of this could be avoided by the use of an indoor pen.

Providing safe havens

Escape routes and safe havens for both of the cats must be provided, and it is useful to remember that cats use vertical as well as horizontal space. Providing shelves and other high-up resting places can lead to the provision of extra living space for the cats and give them more opportunity to escape from one another. If conflict does occur, it is best to distract the quarrelling cats (with chase objects, stroking or possibly titbits) since intervention from owners can be counter-productive and increase tension rather than decrease it.

Biting the hand that strokes you

Aggression from cats towards their owners is obviously an area of concern and, as with any feline behaviour problem, it's important to uncover the cat's motivation for the aggression before you attempt to deal with it.

Aggression can commonly occur as a defence strategy in a cat that is fearful of people, or it may develop as a misdirected form of predatory behaviour in cats that have limited access to outdoors or are incompetent hunters in search of more readily targeted prey.

Another form of aggression from cats towards their owners is the so-called 'petting and biting syndrome' – perhaps one of the most difficult behaviour problems for cat owners to come to terms with. Not only are the attacks unexpected and unprovoked but they are also deeply distressing since they happen when the owner is actually petting the cat and showing it love and affection. Often the cat has been sitting quite happily with the owner for some time when it suddenly turns and bites the hand that strokes it.

For most owners, such behaviour is totally incomprehensible and they find themselves feeling uneasy when their pet comes for a cuddle. The trust between pet and owner can be severely threatened and, as the owner begins to reduce the periods of interaction for fear of being attacked, the problem actually becomes self-perpetuating.

Inner conflict

Various possible theories have been put forward to explain this behaviour, but it is now generally accepted that the root of the problem is a conflict between the relaxed and somewhat juvenile cat, who is willing to accept intimate interaction from its owner, and the independent self-determining adult, who feels threatened by the confinement of close contact. This conflict is perfectly normal and most cat owners will recognise that there is a limit to the amount of handling that their pet will accept.

However, for some cats, the threshold of tolerance is very low, and although the cat starts off by being comforted by the physical interaction from the owner, there comes a point where it suddenly develops from a kitten to an adult cat and becomes aware of the implications of such a vulnerable position on its potential for survival as a solitary hunter.

The cat's ultimate goal is escape rather than injury. However, the aggression can be very intense; typically the cat will lash out with its teeth and claws. As soon as any restraint is removed, the cat will usually run a short distance away before pausing to groom.

Many owners find this part of the process somewhat bizarre. The explanation is that the cat first gets away from the potentially threatening situation and establishes a safe flight distance, but then reacts to this state of inner conflict and confusion by displacement grooming in an attempt to relax and calm down.

Control rather than cure

The aim of behavioural therapy for these cats is to increase the threshold of reaction at which the inner conflict occurs, and this is achieved by a gradual process of

■ **Above:** *Kittens need plenty of opportunities to interact with people, but play needs to be appropriate and kittens should not be encouraged to hurt human flesh.*

■ **Left:** *The way in which young kittens are handled can have a profound effect on their future behaviour – gentle handling and mild restraint should be introduced from an early age.*

■ **Right:** *By feeding a cat at table height, the owner has the opportunity to associate very gentle handling with the pleasurable experience of eating.*

desensitization. Owners should start by restricting their physical interaction with their pet to a level that the cat finds totally unchallenging. This starting point will vary between individual cats and also according to the severity of the problem.

Those cats who will sit on their owner's lap for a relatively long time before reaching their point of conflict can begin treatment at the stage where they are fussed on the

lap. Individuals for whom the threshold of conflict is particularly low need to go one step back, and owners are advised to abandon any attempts to get them on their lap but concentrate instead on accustoming the cat to physical attention in the form of a surreptitious stroke along the back while standing on the ground.

Any stroking at this stage must be extremely gentle and should be concentrated around the least

sensitive parts of the body, such as the back and head. Areas such as the stomach and legs should be left until last, and it is important that the owner does not physically restrain the cat as it needs to know that it can escape at any time. Once physical interaction is accepted, the owner can begin to take their cat onto their lap, but the secret is to gradually increase the length of time that the cat stays there whilst keeping one step ahead of it and learning to predict when the point of conflict is getting close. The owner can then terminate any sessions of interaction before the cat has the opportunity to flip into the aggressive response.

Most cats give some warning signals if an attack is imminent. Some of these may be obvious, such as restlessness, tail lashing and pupil dilation. However, others are more obscure and you will need a lot of practice in learning how to recognise them.

Indoor toileting

Cats are fastidious creatures, and their desire to keep their core territory clean has been one of the driving forces in the increasing popularity of the species as a companion animal. Depositing urine and faeces in the household is a very common feline behaviour problem, and while some cats may be using these deposits as markers, others are simply going to the toilet in inappropriate locations.

In some cases the cat may not have learned an appropriate association between the garden or the litter tray and the act of

elimination, but in the majority of cases, house-training has been successfully completed and has subsequently broken down.

The exact reason why a cat should feel the need to toilet away from its litter tray needs to be determined before behavioural treatment is implemented. Compiling an accurate history is often the first step to unravelling the mystery of indoor toileters. It is important to determine whether the cat is using the tray at all or whether it is going outside into the garden in order to relieve itself, since this may

give an indication as to the level of aversion to the provided facilities versus the level of attraction to the new location.

Reasons for this behaviour

In order to determine why the usual litter facilities have suddenly become unacceptable to the cat, it is necessary to look not only at what the litter tray has to offer but also to consider the specific features of the inappropriate location which make it more attractive to the cat as a suitable latrine than the tray.

Surface

The surface on which the cat is expected to eliminate is very important in selecting a latrine, and it is well documented that cats prefer soft, rakeable materials when they are digging their hole for elimination. However, owners often find these fine litter types heavy to carry and opt for the much lighter wooden pellets or newspaper blocks, and these can cause problems for some cats.

■ **Above:** *Kittens need opportunities to play with appropriate litter substrates from a very early age.*

Unfortunately, these litters are often uncomfortable underfoot, and for indoor cats with soft, sensitive pads, a hard litter can lead to avoidance of the litter tray and selection of the carpet as an alternative substrate. The carpet is soft and comfortable and before long the cat develops a strong association with this surface and will toilet on carpet in preference to any other substrate.

Location

The position of toileting facilities is very important to the cat, and when people position litter trays in unacceptable locations it has no choice but to move away to a more suitable spot. Cats are renowned for their hygienic nature and yet many owners still position litter trays next to feed bowls and expect their cats to use the facilities. Since it is the owner who determines where the food is given, the cat can only increase the distance between its kitchen and its bathroom by

■ **Left:** *Cats need privacy, and owners need to be careful to ensure that efforts to encourage the kitten to use a tray do not backfire.*

■ **Above:** *Covered litter trays can offer more security to some cats, but individual preferences should be taken into consideration.*

changing its toileting site. However, when it does so, it is labelled as a dirty and disgusting creature!

As well as keeping food and excreta separate, cats will usually select the most quiet and secluded locations to go to the toilet. Owners need to do their best to mimic the locations that cats would naturally choose for their litter tray. Trays that are positioned next to the dog's bed, right beside the cat flap, under the stairs and in busy traffic areas within the house are unlikely to be considered acceptable by a species that naturally turns its back on the world at this most private of moments.

Treating the problem

Simple alterations to litter type and tray location can often be sufficient to make the tray attractive once more, but in view of the long-standing nature of most of these problems it is also necessary to consider the attractiveness of the unsuitable latrine location and work to make it less appealing. One of the attractions in terms of latrines for cats is smell; cats are encouraged back to areas by the residual smell of previous deposits, It is therefore very important to ensure that the soiled areas are cleaned effectively, using the same regime as the one described for marking deposits (see page 74), and to redefine the function of location as one that is incompatible with toileting. Cats will divide their territory into zones, and the inner core territory is the place where a cat will eat, sleep and play. For the domestic cat, our aim is for the house to be interpreted as the core territory. Ensuring that the appropriate activities are available on a regular and a predictable basis within the home will help in this interpretation. Toileting usually occurs at the boundary between the core and the home areas, and therefore placing litter facilities at the periphery of the home should be beneficial.

Improving the litter facilities and discouraging the use of any alternative sites are the main aims of treatment for feline toileting problems. In many cases, a purely behavioural approach may be entirely successful in reforming the behaviour. However, life is not always simple and some cases of inappropriate toileting can be frustratingly difficult to resolve. Ruling out any potential medical causes of the accidents is an essential part of the workup for these cases, and if the cat is found to be in good physical health a behavioural consultation will offer the best opportunity of getting to the bottom of the problem through taking an accurate and detailed history.

Below: *Scratching is a normal feline behaviour, but when the target for this happens to be an expensive sofa, owners can become very distressed.*

Scratching the furniture

Scratching is a complex behaviour in the cat and has both functional and marking components. The marking of territory involves both the deposition of a visual and a scent signal, and treatment for this has already been discussed (see page 73). However, there are times when cats scratch within the home in a purely functional manner – scratching the furniture to keep their claws in shape rather than to reassure – and in these cases, the treatment is aimed at redirecting the normal behaviour onto an acceptable surface.

The new material should be placed directly onto or in front of the affected area and, once the cat has begun to use it, it can be moved gradually to a much more acceptable location.

Commercially available scratching posts provide a very convenient way of catering for the cat's scratching needs, but it is important to ensure that they are of sufficient height, since the cat needs to be able to scratch at full stretch in order to adequately exercise its clawing apparatus.

Trimming the claws regularly may be considered, especially if the cat is kept totally indoors and is reluctant to use a scratching

Above: *It is important to determine whether indoor scratching is a functional or a marking behaviour.*

post, but it does not affect the actual scratching behaviour and merely serves to limit the damage. In North America, removing the claws by a surgical procedure called declawing is advocated by some veterinary surgeons, but it is not considered acceptable practice by British veterinary surgeons and therefore it is not used as a treatment approach in the United Kingdom.

Over-grooming

Grooming is a very important behaviour for cats. Not only is it used to keep the coat in condition but it also has a role to play in cat-to-cat communication and in maintaining the stability of feline social groups as well as acting as a means of regulating stress and conflict by stimulating the release of internal calming chemicals. When grooming is used as a calming technique, it is classed as a displacement activity and it is this form of grooming that can become excessive and may lead to problems of hair loss, skin damage and even self-mutilation.

Cats can remove quite large quantities of hair, often from their flanks, medial thighs and tail head area, in a relatively short space of time. In some cases, their owners are shocked by the speed of onset of the hair loss. Obviously any cat that loses hair over its body or shows signs of skin damage needs to be investigated from a medical viewpoint before concentrating on potential behavioural causes for the problem. Close co-operation between the fields of dermatology and behavioural medicine are necessary in order to investigate these cases fully.

As with any stress-related feline behaviour problem, the treatment involves increasing the cat's general confidence as well as trying to identify the specific trigger for the behaviour and limiting or even preventing exposure to it. Stress is an inescapable fact of life and, in some cases, the cause may not be something that can be readily removed from a cat's environment, such as a newborn baby or a dog living next door.

In these situations, the cat needs to learn to develop other ways of relieving its stress. By providing opportunities for the cat to use other less damaging coping strategies, such as hiding on high-up resting places, the owner can

■ **Left:** *A range of stress factors in the environment can lead to problems of over-grooming.*

limit the level of over-grooming and minimize the risks of the behaviour developing into self-mutilation.

One of the potential side effects of over-grooming is the formation of hair balls in the digestive tract, and in longhaired individuals this risk is obviously increased. In extreme cases, surgery is needed to remove the hair balls, and therefore grooming of an anxious or fearful longhaired cat is an absolute priority for owners.

Abnormal feline appetites

The existence of a depraved appetite leading to the ingestion of non-nutritional substances is called 'Pica', and although the most commonly mentioned form of this condition in the cat is that of wool eating, this is certainly not the only example. Indeed, cats have been reported to eat a wide variety of non-nutritional items, including cotton, synthetics, paper, card and rubber. Cats can either chew or eat their target material and, interestingly, those cats that target fabric are divided into two distinct populations of chewers and eaters, while those that target paper or card may do either. In some cases, the ingestion of these unsuitable materials can lead to an obstruction of the intestinal tract, and in extreme situations surgery may be required to remove the offending material. However, in the majority of cases, these cats can take in phenomenal volumes of fabric over their lifetime without experiencing any obvious problems.

The behaviour of wool eating was first identified in the 1950s and it was thought to be restricted to the Siamese breed at that time, but research since then has shown that it exists in the Burmese and other oriental breeds as well as in the traditional moggie.

The most common age for cats to start to display this bizarre behaviour is between two and four months, and it is thought that the stress of moving from the breeder's premises to the new home at this age could be a factor in the onset of the behaviour.

Certainly it would appear that kittens are born with a genetic predisposition to exhibit these abnormal appetites, and this may be linked to a faulty wiring within the part of the brain that controls prey detection. However, it is now believed that some form of stressor, such as rehoming, is needed to trigger the expression of the behaviour.

Treating the condition

The mystery surrounding the actual cause of the condition makes pinpointing treatment strategies quite difficult in most cases, and treatment therefore involves a number of different approaches. Preventing access to inappropriate material may seem like a very logical approach, and indeed it appears to be the ideal solution, but this can be extremely difficult. When a cat targets man-made fabrics, it is impossible to restrict its access to all fabrics in the household without housing it in an indoor pen at all times. Useful approaches and components of a treatment programme include the following:

◆ Increasing the opportunity for hunting-related play by providing the appropriate toys and food substances
◆ Increasing the amount of time that cats spend in locating and preparing their food
◆ Providing food that requires the cat to chew, such as cooked meat-covered bones
◆ Hiding food around the home,

in order to increase the amount of time that the cat has to spend searching for its food
◆ Decreasing the attraction of the target material by applying taste deterrents. This may help, but it is very important to ensure that the unpleasant experience is only associated with the material and not with the owner.

Eating houseplants

One form of unusual appetite that is very commonly reported in cats is that of plant or grass eating, and while the ingestion of plant material may not be natural for an obligate carnivore there are a number of theories as to why this behaviour might develop. It may be that this vegetable matter is consumed as a source of roughage or that it provides certain minerals and vitamins that are not available in other foods. However, this seems less likely nowadays in the age of good-quality proprietary pet foods. Another possible explanation is that the plant material has some emetic proprieties and assists the cat in bringing up hairballs from the digestive tract; this is quite a feasible option.

Whatever the motivation for this behaviour, many owners find it frustrating to find their precious plants nibbled at the edges, and in order to avoid this it is sensible to provide indoor cats with tubs of seedling grass sprouts which can be grown specifically for this purpose. Most cats find them much more attractive than the average houseplant, and even when they do have access to outdoors, they have been known to wait until they get back into the house to have a nibble on their own special grass.

Right: *It is common for inquisitive kittens to show an interest in houseplants but for some this interest will develop into an appetite for plant material.*

Straying and leaving home

It is often said that we do not own our cats, and when they have free access to the great outdoors there is no guarantee that they will stay with us. Cats are far more in charge of their own existence than our canine companions, and when pressure gets too great within a household, then moving out can become a viable option. Common situations that sometimes cause cats to move on include the following:

◆ The arrival of a new cat, dog or human in the household
◆ Problems of integration in the neighbourhood
◆ Attraction back to a previous home following a house move by the owners.

Obviously most owners wish to minimize the risks of losing their pets, and some people go to the extreme of always keeping their pet indoors in order to avoid problems of straying and leaving home. However, this is not the only approach that is available. Cats are strongly bonded to territory, and while they may not have a great motivation to be loyal to their owners, they will usually stay close to their territory. It is possible to increase this bond to the house and garden by ensuring that only positive associations are made in the form of provision of valuable resources, and working to ensure that food, shelter, affection and privacy are available in abundant supply will help to maintain the cat's interest in its home.

It is very important not to be too over-powering when you're interacting with cats. Too much human intervention in the form of oppressive affection and high levels of owner-initiated contact are likely to increase the likelihood of cats moving out. Adopting a far more offhand attitude, which leaves the cat asking for more company, will be far more effective.

When moving house, remember that cats are likely to want to return to their old territory, and when the two properties are close together it is not unusual for the cat to regularly return to its previous garden. The risks of this can be reduced by ensuring that the cat has a high concentration

■ **Left:** *Owners who adopt an off-hand attitude to interaction with their cat are likely to enjoy more contact with their pet.*

of its own scent within the new home. You can maximize this by confining the cat to barracks for the first couple of weeks. When the time comes to open the door there is a limit to how much you can do to minimize the risks of your cat making a bolt for freedom, but by releasing him just before feed time you can increase his motivation to stay close to home. With repeated excursions into the garden and returns to the house for feeding, he should rapidly learn that this new house is now home.

■ **Left:** *Providing a good supply of palatable food, together with warmth, play and human interaction, should help to identify the house as home.*

Caring for your cat

Care and consideration for your pet is much more than an expression of love or altruism; it is a rewarding investment bringing many tangible benefits to a cat and its owner. Regular inspection, maintenance and simple preventive measures will ensure a longer life, more happiness, better condition and improved performance for the animal. Dote on it, even spoil it by all means, but don't neglect to keep it well 'serviced'. Veterinary bills will be significantly reduced, and the chances of cat to human transmission of ailments, always a minute possibility, diminished. Nevertheless, sickness and accidents do occur, even in the most fussy of households. The following chapters are a guide to keeping your cat fit and to quick and effective intervention should it become unwell.

Chapter Six

DAILY CARE

An important aspect of daily care and how you look after your kitten or cat will depend on the kind of personality it has. Different feline personalities demand different attention levels. Independent, outgoing cats are 'outdoor' types and they may only be around you when it suits them: at feeding, relaxation and sleeping times. When it comes to feeding and grooming, you may find yourself committed to those times when the cat is at home indoors. By contrast, the indoor house cat may constantly follow you around, brushing up against your shins (marking and 'possessing' you) and calling out for food and your attention.

Active cats will want more food than less active ones. They may also need more extensive grooming sessions because they are more likely to be 'out and about'. Their journeys across grass and fields, through undergrowth, up trees, along dusty footpaths and walls, hedgerows and fence runs will bring them into contact with cobwebs, dirt and all manner of organic elements. A tangled coat can soon become matted if you do not give your cat a daily grooming session. Less active indoor cats will need less food than their outdoor cousins and should require less grooming against industrial grime and organic encounters.

Perhaps a shorthaired breed makes the best outdoor cat – there is less coat to groom and less dirt to accumulate. A longhaired breed may be better suited to indoor life because it is less likely to encounter outdoor grime! However, some longhairs, such as Norwegian Forest Cats, positively need the freedom to roam freely and explore outside and do not settle well indoors.

■ **Above:** *Most moggies love to be outside, exploring in the garden.*

The quiet cat

Sometimes the early period in a kitten's life has seen too many changes or even an interruption to normal socialization with the litter mother and siblings. Kittens that suffer too many changes or difficulties during the first six weeks of life are often introverted and may appear to be shy and non-sociable. These kittens can often be more nervous 'around' people and other animals, and they tend to hide away from anyone or anything which they perceive to be a threat.

Rather than force yourself onto an introverted cat, it is far better to gently draw your pet out of its

■ *Right: Shorthairs are easy to look after as they do not require a great deal of grooming. They often make good outdoor cats.*

nervousness. A quiet or, in some cases, an 'introverted' kitten or cat can be made to feel more secure by controlled handling (not too much fussing and stroking). It is also a good idea to create some positive interaction around feeding, play and grooming. If the cat is too clingy and it is given too much attention, its nervousness will be reinforced. Your absence, at work, college, school or during holidays, would then have a greater impact.

The contrast between your presence (lots of fuss and attention) and your absence (no contact) can be too great for the nervous cat. It is better to control your contact to reduce the contrast between your presence and absence. The quiet cat is often contented with 'home life' and may find the outside world of the 'concrete jungle' a little too nerve-wracking.

The outgoing cat

The outgoing, or sometimes 'extroverted', kitten may have also experienced difficulties in its early socialization. Instead of becoming withdrawn, this cat becomes outgoing and lively, aggressive and, in extreme cases, too demanding. If its attention-seeking behaviours are pandered to, this kitten can take over a family. It will be demanding over food, cuddles and playtimes, for ever demanding your interaction.

The outgoing cat will often jump onto your knee as soon as you sit down. It is best to groom or stroke it for a few minutes or so and then break off contact before any aggression (biting or scratching) can occur.

An extroverted kitten or cat can also be made to feel more secure

and less demanding by controlled handling with positive interaction, again created around the routine procedures of feeding, play and grooming. It is more often than not a 'hunter' or adventurer and therefore these kittens make better outdoor cats than indoor pets.

HANDLING AN ADULT CAT

Some adult cats can weigh more than first impressions may suggest. It is vital that all physical contact with an adult cat is based on confidence and firm handling on your part.

1 Start by encouraging the cat to climb onto your knee. A firm stroke and a food treat will make sure that this contact is very positive.

2 Once this has been repeated over a few days, it is time for you to pick up the cat from a floor position and then to carry him to a chair or sofa to offer him a cuddle. First, call the cat to you and tickle his chin or stroke his coat.

3 Then crouch down and begin the process of lifting him up. Be sure to support him under his bottom with one hand while using the other hand to cradle your pet to your chest. Do not stand up immediately, especially

if there is any possibility that the cat will 'protest' (scratch and/or bite) about being handled.

4 If the cat struggles, you may need to put him down gently. This is much safer and easier to achieve from your crouched position. This method means your cat will not be dropped. A cat will almost always land safely after being dropped from the height of a family member. However, a badly-handled cat will immediately become wary of being picked up following a difficult encounter.

If you are not confident about handling an adult cat, ask a member of the family who is used to picking up a cat to do so and place the cat on your knee. Have a small food treat ready and stroke him firmly. Rewards and positive handling ensure the cat makes a good association with you.

■ **Above:** *When picking up a cat, be sure to support him under his bottom while cradling him to your chest.*

GROOMING YOUR CAT

Cats are continually licking their fur and paws to keep themselves in good condition. They will often groom each other (known as allogrooming), and social groups use this behaviour to promote relationships. You can help your cat in this task and ensure that flea infestations, skin infections and knotted coats do not develop. Remember that when you groom your cat, you are also promoting your relationship and helping to confirm a bond between you both.

Shorthaired cats are relatively easy to groom, especially if a twice-weekly session has already been established from kittenhood. However, longhaired cats require daily grooming to prevent any tangling, knotting and problems with loose hairs.

Healthy coats

Regular grooming will prevent the build-up of loose hairs which can be ingested by your cat when it is self-grooming. The ingestion of too many hairs can result in fur balls developing in your cat's stomach which, in turn, can lead to the regurgitation of hair and of food. In acute cases, the fur ball can lead to an obstruction in the bowel which would require veterinary attention. By grooming your cat on a daily basis, there will also be less hairs on your clothing and furniture.

To rid your cat's coat of any loose hairs and to maintain the coat in first-class condition, you should use the combination of a comb and a glove brush or soft brush. It is important to use the correct tools so consider investing in the grooming accessories that are listed in the box below.

Ready, steady, groom!

Have your accessories ready in the early days and then wait for your cat to sit on your lap. Immediately your cat arrives for contact with you, begin gently brushing the coat. If your cat is nervous, offer a small food treat in order to turn the grooming experience into a 'positive event'. You may have to gently restrain him with your free non-grooming hand. Be prepared to be gentle but firm when you begin grooming your cat. Eventually, it is best to call him to you for a grooming session so that it occurs on your instruction rather than on his whim. Once your cat has accepted the basic concept of grooming, you can become more thorough in your technique.

■ **Above:** *Longhairs, such as this Persian, will need regular and intensive grooming to keep their coats silky and free of tangles.*

■ **Left:** *Grooming itself is a natural behaviour for a cat, but excessive grooming can lead to the development of fur balls in the cat's stomach.*

GROOMING ACCESSORIES

You will need the following essential items of grooming equipment to keep your cat's coat healthy and in good condition, plus some of the optional tools listed below.

Essential tools
- Fine or wide-toothed comb
- Soft and hard brushes
- Hand glove brushes
- Soft cloth or chamois

Optional items
- Claw clippers
- Bowl or baby bath of lukewarm water
- Cotton balls for cleaning

Shorthaired cats

1 Use a soft brush or glove brush to draw off any of the outer loose hairs from the cat's coat.

2 Take a fine-toothed comb and groom the back and head of your cat, initially combing the fur in the direction of the coat hairs.

Left: *There are several types of glove brushes with varying degrees of 'grip' to strip loose hairs from a shorthaired or a longhaired cat. They also work well on fabrics, carpets and furniture!*

3 Following this careful brushing and combing, change direction to comb against the fur, which will remove any deep-lying hairs that are loose.

4 Once the 'top grooming' has been achieved, turn the cat over. Support him with his head on your stomach and his bottom on your lap. Now the underside can be groomed in much the same way as his back and head.

5 Some owners finish their grooming session by rubbing their cat's coat with a damp cloth (or even a chamois leather) to put a shine on the fur.

A happy cat will often be in 'seventh heaven' by the time you have finished this grooming

exercise, and you should not be surprised if he complains when you halt the process – he may not want you to stop.

Longhaired cats

Most longhaired cats will require grooming every day if their coats are to be kept free of loose hairs, tangles and matting. You should use a combination of soft and stiff brushes, wide- and fine-toothed combs and a hand glove or cloth.

Head and back

1 Brush your cat gently with a hand glove or a grooming brush. Follow the hair line on the back, softly brushing away from the head towards the tail. Repeat this procedure several times.

2 Brush in the opposite direction, from the tail to the head, loosening as much hair as possible.

3 If you encounter any knots, try to unravel them by hand or with a wide-toothed comb. If there is a

stubborn knot of hair, which is rarely encountered if regular, daily grooming is undertaken, it may be necessary to carefully snip away the strands with a pair of round-tipped nail scissors.

4 Follow up with the stiff brush, repeating the whole procedure until the coat brushes easily.

Down under

Once the head and back have been groomed, gently but firmly turn your cat over and then repeat this grooming procedure on the underside until all the coat has been teased, brushed and back-brushed. Not all cats are thrilled by this part of the grooming session – an indignant cat will often attempt a fast exit. So try to

anticipate this and reassure your cat.

1 Gently brush the underside of your cat, teasing out any knots by hand or carefully cutting them out.

2 Follow the brushing stage with a thorough combing session, first combing with the hair along the lie and then back-combing.

3 Use a hand glove brush at the end or a damp cloth, chamois or soft brush to 'polish' off the coat.

GROOMING A LONGHAIRED CAT

Grooming is usually a daily requirement if you have a longhaired cat. Without a regular 'brushing and combing' session, your cat's coat will quickly become matted and knotted and it will be difficult to groom. A healthy cat will benefit greatly from 'care grooming' because this task can reduce the development of fur balls from ingested hair and also reduce the potential for parasite infestations. Reward your cat with a treat.

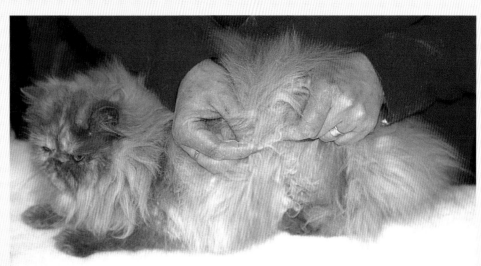

1 │ Feel your way through your cat's coat, and use your fingers to gently unravel any loose knots and tangles.

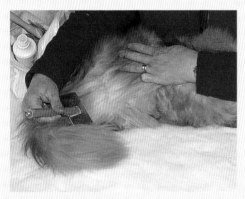

2 │ Brush or comb the fur away from the head towards the tail, holding your cat firmly but gently and talking to him.

3 │ Comb or brush the fur in the opposite direction. Be gentle and do not drag the brush or comb through the cat's coat.

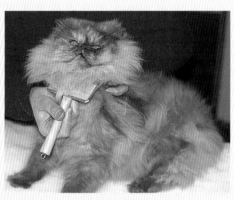

4 │ Gently brush the ruff around the neck and the head. Remember to remove the collar if the cat wears one.

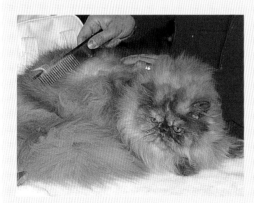

5 │ Carefully comb or cut out any knots that remain. The coat should be very soft, silky and free of tangles.

6 │ Turn the cat over and brush the fur underneath, teasing out any knots with your fingers or a comb.

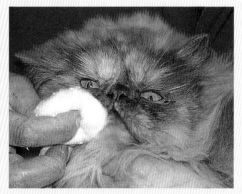

7 │ Before you finish grooming, take this opportunity to check your cat's ears, nose and eyes, wiping away any mucus.

Claw trimming

You should attempt to examine your cat's claws once every month. It may be necessary to trim them once or twice a year if they are over-long and if your cat does not wear them down naturally outdoors or on indoor scratching sites.

Trimming a cat's claws should only be undertaken by a confident owner with the appropriate claw cutter. Never be too severe when trimming them – only the very tips of claws should be trimmed. Never cut to the 'quick'. The pinkish area of each claw or quick is linked to a nerve ending and blood supply and should never be cut. If the claws are overgrown, then it is best to consult your vet to prevent the risk of pain and suffering from over-cutting. An indoor cat should always be provided with several scratching post sites to prevent, or re-direct, scratching on pieces of furniture.

Eyes and ears

A cat's eyes should always be bright and healthy. Any clouding, excessive moisture or revealing of the third eyelid would suggest signs of infection or damage, and your cat should be referred immediately to your vet. It should not be necessary to clean your cat's eyes unless an infection has developed and your vet has prescribed a specific treatment.

It is useful to wipe the inside of your cat's ears on a weekly basis to prevent a build-up of dirt that could provide a home to ear mites. Only the immediate inner area of the ear should be wiped; do this in an outwards motion with a moist cotton wool ball. Do not ever insert sticks of cotton into the ear as this can cause serious damage to the inner ear.

There should never be any discharge from the ears. If this happens, consult your vet. Look out for signs of a mite infection; the tell-tale signs are when a cat is continually scratching its head.

■ **Above:** *Always clean away from a cat's eye – never over it – as you could damage the third eyelid by mistake.*

Oral hygiene

■ **Right:** *Even cats need to have their teeth cleaned to prevent tooth decay. You can buy special 'brushes' to make this process easier.*

Cats in the wild keep their gums and teeth clean by eating prey, which needs to be chewed and crunched. However, in a domestic environment, many cats are only offered processed, moist food. This 'soft option' diet offered over a cat's lifetime can lead to gum and teeth infections. Eventually teeth can be lost, and secondary infections in the bloodstream can even lead to major organ failure and an early demise.

It is possible to prevent tooth decay in your cat by introducing an element of non-soft food into his diet. Some dried foods are promoted as being good for cat's teeth because they have to be crunched. This action will help to keep the gums and teeth clean.

There are also special cat toothpastes and toothbrushes available which can be used on a daily basis to reduce bacterial build-up, tartar and plaque forming. Regular brushing will help prevent tooth decay and gum disease just as it does in humans.

A weekly brush will ensure that your cat's teeth sparkle and that his breath does not prevent you from 'talking' directly to him. Dire-smelling breath in your cat is a result of mouth infections, in particular gingivitis which can result in bleeding of the gums.

YOUR CAT'S WELFARE

Feeding and drinking

Cats are notoriously fussy about their food, and they can be obsessively attentive about the cleanliness of dishes. All food, especially frozen or refrigerated, should be prepared in advance and offered at room temperature. This warming of food replicates the temperature of prey in the wild, and cats have been known to regurgitate cold food.

Food dishes should be cleaned thoroughly on a daily basis and fresh water added to the water bowl once or twice per day, depending on the number of visits your cat makes for water. Cats that are fed mainly dried foods will usually require more water than those that are offered canned or semi-moist foods. This is because the latter food types contain a high percentage of moisture and/or water, and thus a cat that is fed them would not need to drink as frequently.

Food serving

A cat that is older than six months can have food offered morning, afternoon and evening. To reduce fussiness towards food, it is best to put the food dish down in the usual place and ring a bell to signal feeding time. Lift the dish up after fifteen minutes; if the food has not be touched, cover it with cling film to preserve freshness and offer it again later. A healthy cat will soon begin to respond subconsciously to a sound signal for food. Some hungry cats will be at your feet as soon as the food is opened. The combination of smell and the behavioural cue of a rustling bag or packet can be enough of a signal for many cats to arrive in your kitchen. A cat's impatience will often result in it calling enthusiastically for you to serve up the evening meal.

Diet

Cats are true carnivores and, as avid meat eaters, they will rarely relish a diet that is not based on their needs. Indeed, kittens will not develop the ideal growth if they are fed on a diet based on vegetarian ingredients.

Cats instinctively search out variations in their diet. All their hunting and balancing skills have been evolved for them to be successful in their search for a meaty dinner. In nature, this meat diet would range from small birds and small mammals to a wide range of insects and invertebrates and scavenged

WATER STORE

Some owners find it best to store tap water in a plastic container in order to bring it to room temperature and to reduce chlorine levels. Water is accepted better by cats if it has been allowed to stand for a day or so before use. Storage will allow the chlorine in tap water to dissipate with the oxygen that leaves the water as it warms to room temperature. Do not be surprised if your cat actively seeks out other sources of water. Cats are often attracted to running tap water, toilet water, ponds or puddles of dirty water.

■ **Below:** *Cats will often drink from what looks like dirty water but they will only drink it if the top layer is clean.*

■ **Right:** *Healthy cats need a balanced diet to keep them in good condition.*

carcasses. By eating such prey, cats obtain many variations of food, including blood, bones, feathers, fur and even crunchy exoskeletons.

By contrast, in domestication, a diet can be rigid and repetitive, although good manufacturers do attempt to replicate a natural diet in their choice of ingredients. Although eating and feeding times do become habitualized in most domesticated pets, cats do not lose their natural instinct to seek out a variation in their diet. This aspect of behaviour will be displayed in an apparent fussiness or a dislike of food that was taken greedily and once seen to be satisfying.

Only the best

Cats will home in on any fresh food. They would eat only the 'best-quality' steak and fish if that was offered. With such a protein-rich diet, however, they would be missing essential vitamins and minerals and roughage. Having

■ **Left:** *Offer your cat a variation in his diet by giving small morsels of partially cooked fresh fish or meat sometimes.*

the equivalent of 'chocolate' at every meal may sound appealing at first but this food will not offer a healthy, balanced diet. It is important to rotate food types to offer a wide range and to help prevent potential fussiness over food. Sometimes the variation can be created with 'complete' dried foods, canned food, semi-moist food and titbits of fresh fish,

prawns and shreds of meat. These 'treats' should be partially cooked or blanched to offer your cat the opportunity to 'chew' his food.

Activity and eating

Kittens require small regular feeds (see page 50). They have very small stomachs and can only digest modest amounts of food. It

FEEDING GUIDE FOR SEMI-ADULT TO ADULT CATS (9 MONTHS +)

Age	Type of cat	'Solid food' requirements
9–12 months	Kitten	Feed 2–3 times daily (first titbit, one dry, the other moist)
12–36 months	Active cat	Feed 2–3 times daily (first titbit, one dry, the other moist)
	Indoor, less active cat	Twice daily (one dry, one semi-moist/titbit)
3–5 years	Active cat	Twice daily (one dry, one semi-moist or treats – strips of natural titbits, fish/fatty minced meat)
	House cat	Once daily (complete dry food with small amounts of natural titbit treats)
5 years +	Active cat	Twice daily (one complete dry or semi-moist – small amounts, twice daily; one complete dry or semi-moist plus small amounts of natural titbits, and one titbit meal)
	Indoor cat	Once daily (complete dry 'mature cat' food) plus occasional treats

Note: The amount of food given and the frequency of meals given will depend, to some extent, on whether you own an indoor or outdoor cat. The nutritional requirements of an active outdoor cat would be slightly greater than those of an inactive cat because of the larger energy expenditure.

■ **Right:** *Outdoor cats enjoy hunting and prowling about outside at night. Most cats hunt at dawn and at dusk.*

substantial than the other meals. Cats are naturally 'crepuscular' (animals that are active at dawn and at dusk), although some 'hunter personalities' will prefer to be active in darkness in the same way as a nocturnal animal.

Cats that are extremely active and travel over large distances within their territory are more likely to require large meals than those that are less active and live mainly indoors.

It is better to judge the quantity of food needed on the basis of consumption. If an amount is taken readily and immediately, then you can gradually increase the quantity until the cat leaves some in the dish. This method is preferred to that of placing a large meal down for your cat only to find that much of it is left (and then often spoiled).

is always best to avoid cow's milk and to seek out lactose-free milk instead; some kittens can become loose when offered dairy milk.

For adult and semi-adult cats, the feeding patterns should be scheduled evenly over the day period. Night-time sleeping patterns can be encouraged by making the last meal more

Using a litter tray

After all the eating and variation in your cat's diet, there will be rather 'smelly' by-products in the form of urine and faeces. Both indoor and outdoor cats will need a litter tray. Certainly, for indoor cats, it is essential, and although the outdoor cat will often urinate and defecate in the great beyond, there may be instances, such as when it gets accidentally trapped in the house or at night-time, when outdoor pursuits are restricted. On these occasions, a litter tray is more preferable as a site to deposit waste than your dining room carpet.

Cleaning the litter tray

It is necessary to keep a cat's or kitten's litter tray clean. Cats are meticulously clean creatures and prefer their toilet to be spotless! There are many different kinds of litter for you to choose from and they all vary slightly in texture, composition and weight.

Clumping litter is lightweight and economical to use as only the soiled litter needs to be removed and replaced. Once a day, using a scoop, you can sift through the litter and remove any soiled material. You can then replace the litter that has been removed with some more fresh litter up to the necessary level.

However, it is still advisable occasionally to remove all the contents, wash the tray and then refill it. Always wash your hands thoroughly after this cleaning process to promote good hygiene.

■ **Left:** *Indoor cats will sometimes replace prowling on fences by walking on worktops in your kitchen.*

Sleepy cats

Cats can spend sixty per cent of a day sleeping. They will seek out the most comfortable and warm places, which often do not include the lovely bed you have purchased for your pet. Instead, because cats often seek height for security and warmth for comfort, they may 'disappear' to sleep in your airing cupboard or laundry basket, on shelves above radiators and on the top of cupboards. Don't be alarmed by this behaviour as it is perfectly normal for cats.

■ Left: *Happy cats spend much of their day napping in the most warm and comfortable places.*

Play

Whatever toys you offer your cat he will find his own targets for fun. Play has its roots in 'hunting, stalking and pouncing'. Therefore many cats will play happily with an empty box or carrier bag, a discarded packet or dead spiders!

It is good for you to interact with your cat through play. Try to set aside a few moments to play with him at least once a day. It is possible to make your own 'toys' – for example, some feathers tied together and drawn or dangled on a string will always lure a healthy cat into play. The variation of 'prey on a string' can even include an enticing fresh food treat.

Games can be played without you. These can include toy mice, ping pong balls, wool and catnip soft toys. A cat may play in short bursts or intense sessions. A visit to your local pet store will quickly show you the vast range of toys that are available and you will soon be relieved of your money.

The range of toys for cats is almost endless. Track toys, where the cat sends a ball around a circular track, are popular, as are feather toys, 'fishing rod' types and roll-along toys.

■ Left: *Encouraging play with your kitten can create a positive interaction. Make time for play every day.*

■ Left: *Kittens will play with any object that captures their imagination. It may be a special cat toy or a piece of string or some newspaper or foil screwed up into a ball.*

Dangers in the home

A kitten is far more likely to explore and taste new substances than an adult cat. Youngsters are often more active and are usually brimming full of the desire to explore their surroundings.

The kitchen probably represents the most dangerous area for any cat, no matter what its age. Not only is this the room where food is made available but it will also include cookers that have burning hot circles of heat which can hold boiling foods. It is home to sharp knives, plastic bags, rubbish bins (which often contain a frightening array of dangerous items, such as sharp cans and glass), household detergents and a washing machine. Any of these everyday items and appliances can become a potential trap for an exploring cat.

To prevent your kitten from accessing the kitchen and to have 'peace of mind', it may be wise to install a child gate, completely covered with a fine-mesh barrier. Although an adult cat could probably launch itself on to most human heights it is unlikely that a kitten would attempt such a leap.

Although an adult cat would rarely attempt to eat a poisonous house plant, a kitten might be tempted to lick or even nibble on a leaf. It is always best to exclude or remove such plants. Detergents or medicines should always be kept safety put away inside closed cupboards.

Once you and your family have developed the habit of taking these potentially lethal aspects into consideration, your cat will be as safe as is humanly possible.

IDENTIFICATION

It is vital that your cat has some means of identification on its collar or through a recognised, widely used electronic method. You may lose your pet and, without some identification, the finder would be unable to locate and reunite you with your cat.

Microchips

If your cat is to have access to the outside world, beyond your home and garden, then it is vital to provide your pet with some means by which it can be identified to your home address. One of the most effective methods that is available today is called microchipping. This involves implanting a microchip, with the aid of a special hand-held unit, into the neck of your cat. The tiny microchip has your own unique identification code programmed into it. This registration number is then added to a computer data base which can be accessed by veterinarians, relevant animal rescue groups and authorities.

In an emergency, should your cat become lost or injured, a hand-held scanner can be used to identify your code. With this information, accessed through the Pet Log data base, an enquirer would be able to obtain your name, address and contact telephone number. Unlike cat collars, which can become detached from your pet, the microchip implant is always secure, and it will provide a permanent identification method.

Cat collars

Collars are the most economical method to locate an identification disc, tag or fob onto your cat. The best ones are made from leather or a man-made durable material and should be fitted lightly rather than tightly onto the neck. A contact number or abbreviated address can be engraved onto a disc or placed inside a barrel holder. There are many collar types available, although quick release or safety variations that have an elasticated section are the safest products, and either type is certainly worth the investment.

A young kitten, restricted to the home could be given a soft material collar (not a 'flea' collar) to get it used to wearing one. Once established as 'everyday wear', collars can be upgraded in size as the cat grows into an adult. The 'soft flea' collar is designed for semi-adult to adult cats and is not suitable for kittens. There is always be the danger of a soft collar becoming hooked onto a pointed object which could create a restriction and even lead to strangulation.

■ **Left:** *Microchipping your cat will ensure its identity can be quickly established in an emergency.*

Car travel

To make sure your kitten or cat becomes used to car journeys and travelling in a carrier, it is wise to offer it short trips, perhaps to the supermarket or a local town, from about three months onwards.

One of the first journeys will be to your local veterinary clinic for the standard vaccinations. Prior to these two separate immunization vaccinations, your kitten would not normally be allowed outside.

It is always wise to desensitize your cat from the carry box by allowing it to enter and exit freely over a few weeks. Put one of your old items of clothes inside. This could be 'scented' by adding it to your laundry basket of clothes to be washed. Your cat will associate with your scents and feel secure.

Practice makes purrfect

It is advisable never to make the first car journey the one to the veterinary clinic, as this may give your kitten a nasty association with car journeys (the only other car experience probably being when you removed your kitten from its mother and littermates). If a cat only travels in the car to receive a jab from a hypodermic needle, then it is likely to make the wrong association with car trips and you will have problems.

Do not feed your kitten or cat prior to a car journey as there is always a chance that he will regurgitate food if he becomes distressed. Larger carry boxes or travel crates will usually take a drip-feed water bottle; otherwise, make sure there is a dish of water in case your cat becomes thirsty.

Ideally, place your kitten in his carrier and transfer this to the back seat or hatchback space. Use a secure harness or a seat belt. Otherwise, place some solid item against the carrier to prevent any sudden shift should you have to brake sharply to stop the car.

Short but sweet

Make the first few journeys with a very short trip. On your return home, allow your kitten to exit the carrier at his own pace. Make sure there are some special treats in a saucer and access to water outside the box. This can make the experience of travelling in a car and being placed in a carrier

less of a trauma. These short trips should be undertaken three or four times per week. If your kitten shows little sign of distress, build up the journeys into significant trips that you may make on a regular basis. Always make sure your car is well ventilated and that there is no chance of extreme temperatures. On hot summer days, your adult cat could quickly succumb to heat exhaustion in a car. In the winter, extreme cold could cause hyperthermia.

Preparing your cat for journeys will pave the way for successful trips should you wish to use a cattery, move home or need to go to the veterinary clinic.

■ **Above:** *A carry box is essential for transporting your cat safely. Make the unit cosy and allow your cat to explore it outside of visits to the veterinary clinic in order to prevent a 'negative' association being formed.*

Moving with your cat

House moves can be traumatic enough for humans who know the reasons for relocating, whether for work or to upgrade for a growing family. However, cats have no idea why a move from one house to another is necessary and, as they are 'territorial by nature', the process can be doubly traumatic.

It is possible to make a house move for your cat as smooth as possible by taking a few basic precautions. Don't wait until the last moment to place your cat in a carrier or travel crate. If you are chasing your cat around the home when keys are about to be handed in, then everyone will be stressed.

Indoor cats

The process of relocating is made much easier if you have a house-bound cat. Confine the cat in one room for about twenty-four hours prior to the day of moving. Keep any food given down to a bare minimum and leave the carrying box or travel crate available for the cat to enter and exit at free will. It is best to end up with a hungry cat which is ready to eat once the move has been made because this will help prevent any potential travel sickness and make eating in the new home a priority. There is nothing like a hearty meal to make a cat feel at home!

Place an old sweater, which has been worn for a day or has been kept in the 'to be washed' laundry basket, inside the carrier or crate on moving day. Your cat can curl up on it and will be reassured by the familiar scent.

Outdoor cats

If your cat is a wanderer, do not risk trying to locate your pet on the day of the house move. The absence of a cat at the moment of the actual relocation can lead to accidental abandonment and also needless worry. Just keep the wanderer inside for about twenty-four hours prior to the move. Remember to close up the cat flap if you provide one for your cat. It is best to confine him to one room together with all his usual needs: litter tray, food, water and bedding. Harden your heart and ignore any cries to be released. The restriction in one room will help condition your cat to living in a confined space in your new home. This is necessary in the adapting period where the cat has to adjust to a new home as well as to new territory.

When you are ready to move (all the furniture is in the van), enter the room and be sure to close the door behind you. Place your cat in the carrier or travel crate and then gather up your accessories to take with you.

Small is beautiful

When you arrive at your new home, whether your pet is a house or an outdoor cat, select a small room where the cat (with the carrier or travel crate) can be placed, together with his used litter tray, food and water dishes. Cats are more 'secure' in a reduced territory as there is less to defend, and a bolt hole is always sought when the world around them is perceived as threatening or unfamiliar.

Always wait for a short time before offering your cat the option to leave the carrier or crate. Open the door of the carrier or crate and allow him to exit when he is ready to do so. Allow him to explore the room without any fuss or bother. You may wish to pop in from time to time to offer a stroke and a special food treat, but

 **Right:** *Cats are territorial by nature and they find house moves disturbing. Follow the guidelines to ensure that your cat is secure before and after removal to your new home.*

beware of the cat making a mad dash for the nearest exit – many cats get lost in house moves. It is always wise to take precautions by confining your cat when there is likely to be much coming and going of family and removal men.

Over a few days, gradually open up the house to your cat, allowing him to explore from room to room. Always prevent initial access to the garden or street because your cat will quickly become disorientated in unfamiliar territory and could easily end up in real difficulties. There will be unknown roads, potentially aggressive rivals for the territory and many other unforeseen dangers. The next week or two should consist of a gradual exploration of home, garden, yard, street or lane, all under your guidance and tuition. Tinkle a bell with a name call to announce meals or treat times on a random basis and then you can call your cat anytime, using this signal.

■ **Left:** *Start from the carry box and allow your cat to explore its new home, taking each room one at a time.*

New beginnings

Never trust an outdoor cat to make its own 'mental map' of your new home and surroundings. This is a gradual process and the new territory needs to be 'written' over the old territory if your cat is not to become lost in the first days of exploration. Some cats will attempt to return to their familiar territory and they can become completely disorientated. Stories of cats travelling for many miles and finding their way home do not apply to most cases. A cat that is lost and hungry can find itself in all kinds of trouble.

The process of new territory 'orientation' needs to be systematic – first the home, then the garden and then the surrounding roads and houses. Try to imagine what it would be like if you were a young infant exploring the world for the first time.

It is best to spend several weeks 'orientating' your cat rather than rush the process in the first week and lose your pet. Some cats who will walk on a harness can be guided around the block, if they have been used to lead-walking from an early age.

GOING TO THE CATTERY

There are a number of obvious reasons why cats need to be housed temporarily in a boarding cattery. These times include family holidays, when a house move is not straightforward or when there is no one to take care of your cat in the event of hospitalization. Sometimes your cat may board for just a few days whereas at other times it may be a few weeks.

The best option for your cat is to remain at home with a relative, friend or a neighbour feeding him every day. If this is not possible, then using boarding catteries may be the only option. Your vet may be able to recommend a suitable cattery or you can look through the local directories to find one nearby. Always be sure to inspect the establishment before placing your cat in it. Although some boarding kennels also board cats, it is wise to look for a specialized cattery unless your cat is familiar with dogs and barking.

Holiday jabs

It will be necessary to make sure that your cat has been immunized or given booster jabs to prevent any health problems. A travel crate or carrier is essential for boarding because it offers your cat a part of its territory when it stays at the cattery. Never hold a cat whilst travelling or during the transfer from car to cattery because of the potential for panic and escape. The cattery is unlikely to be near your home and, as such, represents a new territory that is unknown to your cat. It is best not to fuss your cat before or on his return because this can highlight the separation experience.

Chapter Seven

HEALTHCARE

The arts of medicine and surgery relating to the cat, be it a blue-blooded show specimen or an alley cat, are now highly sophisticated veterinary specialities. The health problems that can afflict the species are being increasingly researched, and much is known about both how similar and how different cats are compared to dogs or humans when unwell or in trouble.

My main aim in this section of the book will be to explain a range of different symptoms, what you should do about them, and some simple, useful first-aid with an emphasis on the 'first'. You must always seek veterinary help as soon as possible for all but the mildest and briefest of medical conditions.

I will also outline the basic principles behind some of the most common diseases of cats, together with the various ways in which the veterinary surgeon can counter-attack these afflictions.

Prevention being better than cure, regular inspection of your pet is important and simple and will not take you too much time. **Look:** to see that its behaviour, movements and posture are all normal; that eating and drinking are as usual; that the mouth, ears, eyes and anus are clear and clean. **Feel:** run your hands over the cat's body to check for any lumps, skin disease or painful places. **Listen:** for tell-tale coughs, sneezes or wheezes.

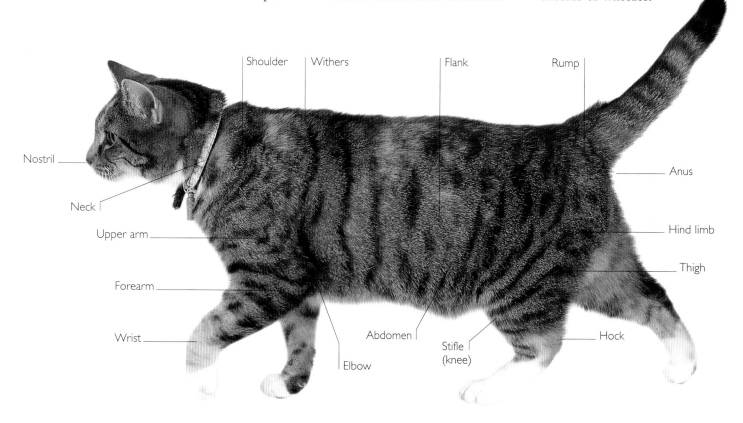

Shoulder | Withers | Flank | Rump

Nostril

Anus

Neck

Hind limb

Upper arm

Thigh

Forearm

Wrist

Abdomen

Hock

Elbow

Stifle (knee)

NURSING A SICK CAT

In all your pet's ailments, no matter whether they are mild or serious, you will normally have to be prepared to do something, usually acting as a nurse. There are some essential techniques to be learned when it comes to handling a sick cat, administering medication, taking its temperature and all the other aspects of nursing. Here is some basic information to help you.

Handling a cat for examination

There are four main methods of handling a cat. Remember that a sick cat may struggle and try to escape or even react aggressively to the person handling it, so some cats may need a greater degree of physical restraint than other ones.

Wrapping the cat

To keep the cat immobile and calm, wrap it firmly in a large strong cloth, towel, sack or blanket.

■ **Right:** *Wrapping a cat in a blanket is the most common way of restraining it if it is distressed or acting aggressively.*

Restraint holding legs

If your cat is an escape artist and struggles, you may have to restrain him by holding all four legs.

Holding by the 'scruff'

You can hold your cat by the scruff and press down firmly onto a flat surface to restrict the scratching ability of the paws.

■ **Above:** *When 'scruffing' your cat, press down firmly but gently on the rear end and talk reassuringly to him.*

Cradling in the arms

If the animal is quiet and is not in any pain, then cradling it in your arms is an effective and gentle way of handling a pet cat. Make sure that you hold your cat firmly and close to your body in order to prevent him escaping.

■ **Above:** *Cradling your cat in your arms, holding him close to your body, is an effective way of restraining him.*

Administering medicine

This is not easy, ever. Although the vet will try to select drug preparations that are as attractive as possible to cats, liquids and crushed tablets mixed with their food are usually detected quickly. Puss then marches off in high dudgeon, going without a meal rather than take his medicine.

The key technique to master is to hold the cat's head, bending it back on the neck until the mouth automatically opens a fraction.

Then keep the mouth open by pushing the lips on each side between the teeth with your index finger and your thumb.

Giving a tablet

If giving your cat a tablet, drop it accurately onto the groove at the back of the tongue. Give a quick poke with the index finger of the other hand (or carefully with a pencil if you feel timid about your finger), pushing the tablet over the back of the tongue.

Close the mouth immediately. Some drugs can be prescribed by the vet in the form of palatable tablets which, with luck, the cat will voluntarily scoff.

Giving liquids

With the same grip on the cat's head, liquids can be dropped slowly into the patient's mouth. However, do not be impatient and flood your pet's mouth with fluid. The cat will only choke, panic and splutter furiously.

■ **Left and below:** *Give your cat a tablet by holding the head back, then pushing the lips each side to ease the tablet in. To aid swallowing, gently rub the cat's throat until it swallows.*

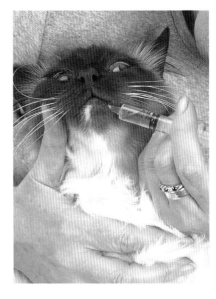

■ **Left:** *You can inject liquid into the mouth via a syringe. This method may be easier for cats who won't cooperate.*

Pre-tranquilizing

If your pet cat is as wild as a mountain lion but has to be taken to the vet's surgery for some reason, it is often possible to make things easier for all concerned by giving him some valium or some other sedative under the vet's instructions before leaving home.

■ **Left:** *Give liquids by holding back the head and dropping or spooning them into the cat's mouth.*

THE UNWELL CAT

I shall begin, like Alice, at the beginning and look at the mouth of the cat. After the mouth we shall travel together from head to tail through the various systems of the feline body. If you look after your cat properly, groom him regularly and feed him a high-quality, nutritious diet, then you will help to prevent many of the common diseases and health problems that may affect cats. It is also a good idea to check him regularly for the warning signs of potential illness or poor health. By recognising them in the early stages, you can prevent many occurring or, at least, treat them at an early stage before they become serious. You should also ensure that your cat is vaccinated against the principal infectious diseases. Ask your veterinary surgeon for advice on this.

The mouth

This sharp end of the animal should be inspected from time to time to see if all is in order. Once- or twice-weekly cleaning of the teeth with some cotton wool or a very soft toothbrush dipped in salt water or, best of all, one of the tartar-inhibiting toothpastes which is specially designed for pets will stop the build-up of troublesome plaque and tartar. I can hear you saying that no-one cleans their cat's teeth that often, but it would save untold problems for the older cat in years to come if you spend just a few moments every two or three days on this very easy job.

Tartar

Common symptoms

■ Salivating (slavering)
■ Pawing at the mouth
■ Exaggerated chewing motions
■ Tentative chewing as if dealing with a hot potato

If tartar, a yellow to brown, cement-like substance, accumulates to any extent, it does not produce holes in the teeth that might need filling. Instead, it damages the gum edge, lets bacteria in to infect the tooth socket and thereby loosens teeth. Chronic infections in the tooth surroundings can lead to serious disease in distant parts of the body, such as the kidneys or heart. There is always some degree of gum inflammation (gingivitis) with tartar and usually an unpleasant smell.

What you can do

Open the cat's mouth and look for a foreign body stuck between the teeth. A piece of bone often wedges between the teeth and against the roof of the mouth. Fish-bone pieces sometimes lodge between two adjacent molars at the back of the mouth. You can probably flick a foreign body out with a teaspoon handle or a similar instrument. If there is no foreign body, look for smooth, red, ulcerated areas on the tongue. These can be caused by licking an irritant substance but are more commonly caused by the viruses associated with feline influenza and sometimes those causing feline infectious enteritis, feline infectious anaemia and possibly feline leukaemia or feline immuno deficiency virus (FIV). (See pages 113–117 for more information on these important diseases.)

Tooth decay due to tartar

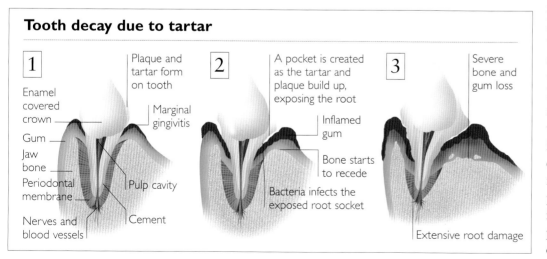

1
Enamel covered crown
Gum
Jaw bone
Periodontal membrane
Nerves and blood vessels
Plaque and tartar form on tooth
Marginal gingivitis
Pulp cavity
Cement

2
A pocket is created as the tartar and plaque build up, exposing the root
Inflamed gum
Bone starts to recede
Bacteria infects the exposed root socket

3
Severe bone and gum loss
Extensive root damage

The skull and teeth

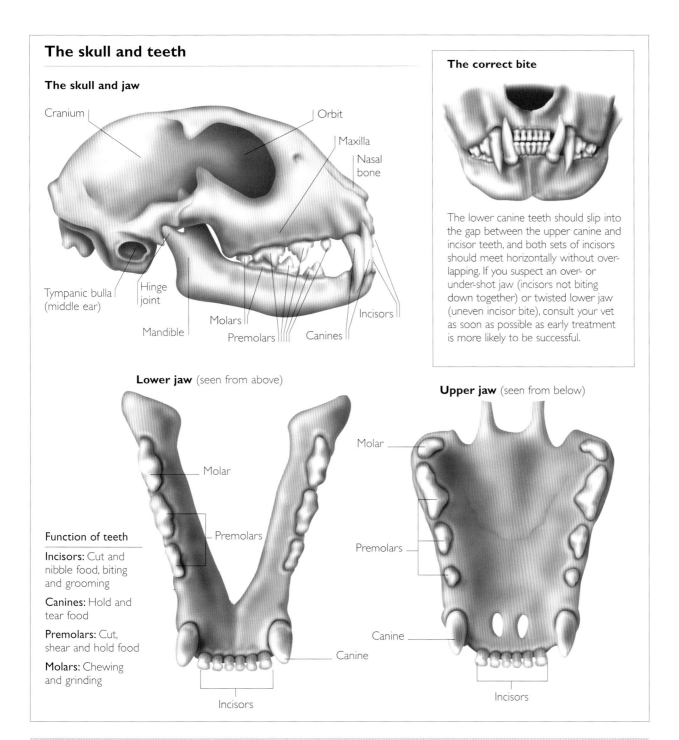

The skull and jaw

Cranium

Orbit

Maxilla

Nasal bone

Tympanic bulla (middle ear)

Hinge joint

Mandible

Molars

Premolars

Canines

Incisors

The correct bite

The lower canine teeth should slip into the gap between the upper canine and incisor teeth, and both sets of incisors should meet horizontally without overlapping. If you suspect an over- or under-shot jaw (incisors not biting down together) or twisted lower jaw (uneven incisor bite), consult your vet as soon as possible as early treatment is more likely to be successful.

Lower jaw (seen from above)

Molar

Premolars

Canine

Incisors

Upper jaw (seen from below)

Molar

Premolars

Canine

Incisors

Function of teeth

Incisors: Cut and nibble food, biting and grooming

Canines: Hold and tear food

Premolars: Cut, shear and hold food

Molars: Chewing and grinding

FELINE DENTISTRY

This is easily tackled by the vet who has the anaesthetics, instruments (de-scalers, etc.) and drugs to attend to mouth matters. If many teeth have to be removed from an elderly cat, do not worry. Food such as minced, cooked liver, poached fish, cereals with milk and the 'in-gravy' sort of canned cat food are easily ingested, even by totally toothless veterans. No teeth at all is better than having septic gums and rotten teeth that create misery and can poison the whole system.

Tooth anatomy

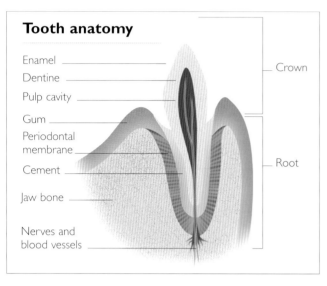

Enamel

Dentine

Pulp cavity

Gum

Periodontal membrane

Cement

Jaw bone

Nerves and blood vessels

Crown

Root

Mouth ulcers

Common symptoms

■ Profuse slavering
■ Unwillingness to eat
■ Dullness

If your cat has mouth ulcers, you should get veterinary help, since a course of antibiotic injections may be needed to prevent secondary infection. Ulcers can often result from a Vitamin B deficiency, and nicotinic acid tablets may be prescribed where this is suspected.

Toothache

Common symptoms

■ Pawing at the mouth
■ Chewing

Diseased teeth may be a cause of toothache. To check whether your cat has loose, diseased teeth, touch each tooth gently with your finger or a pencil. Look for wobbling of the tooth or some sign of pain from the cat. Do not give aspirin to relieve suspected toothache; aspirin is poisonous to cats.

Tongue or lip swellings

Common symptoms

■ A translucent 'cyst-like' swelling under one or both sides of the tongue
■ Difficulty in eating
■ A swelling, sore or an ulcer on a lip

A swelling that appears quite rapidly under one or both sides of the tongue is called a ranula. It is not a tumour or cyst, nor is it serious. Ranulas arise because of the blockage of a salivary duct. The vet can successfully treat the condition, either under sedation or light anaesthetic.

A chronic swelling, which is often topped by an open sore or an ulcer on a cat's lip, may be an eosinophilic granuloma, which is commonly called a 'rodent ulcer'. True rodent ulcers in human beings are cancerous tumours. Occasionally this is also the case in the cat, but most of them are not tumours.

The cause of eosinophilic granulomas is still not fully understood. Whereas some may be due to bacterial, particularly staphylococcal, infection, in other cases, abrasion by a rough tongue or fang tooth, virus disease or autoimmune disease has been implicated. Applying creams or ointments to 'rodent ulcers' is always problematical. The medication is usually quickly licked off and a dressing is impossible. Systemic treatment by means of oral preparation or injections or other forms of physical treatment are indicated.

The eyes

Common symptoms

■ Sore, runny or mattery eyes
■ A blue or white film over the cat's eye
■ The protrusion of a white skin (the haw, third eyelid or nictitating membrane) over some or most of one or both eyes from the inner corner

What you can do
If the eye is obviously sore and inflamed, if the eyeball has a blue or white area on it, or if the lids are swollen, then infection, wounding or foreign bodies, such as grass awns, may be involved. If the cat is not very concerned, you can drop Golden Eye liquid (available from the chemist) into the affected eye – one drop, three times daily. For

GENETIC EYE DISORDERS

A gene present in some Siamese cats produces faulty 'circuitry' in the optic nerve that connects the eye to the brain. The effect of this is to reduce the animal's binocular vision and give rise to some degree of double vision making the cat squint as it tries to merge the duplicate images.

The eye

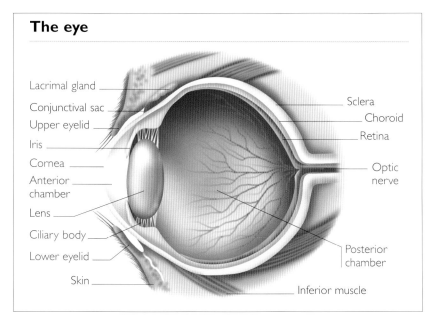

Lacrimal gland

Conjunctival sac

Upper eyelid

Iris

Cornea

Anterior chamber

Lens

Ciliary body

Lower eyelid

Skin

Sclera

Choroid

Retina

Optic nerve

Posterior chamber

Inferior muscle

more troublesome or persistent cases, consult your vet.

An alternative is to apply Golden Eye or similar ointment. This is usually a job requiring two people. One holds the cat, the other gently steadies the cat's head and, with the nozzle of the eye ointment tube parallel to the eyeball, not pointing at it, squeezes out about 1 cm (1/2 in) of the ointment so that it falls between the eyelids onto the cornea. The eyelids should then be held closed for a few seconds to let the ointment melt.

The nose

Common symptoms

■ Running, mattery nostrils
■ Snuffling
■ Sneezing

The appearance of symptoms like those of the common cold in humans generally means an outbreak of feline influenza. After recovery from the latter

Third eyelid

The partial covering of the eye by the third eyelid is a common and curious phenomenon. It often happens in otherwise apparently healthy cats. It can be as a result of weight loss, when the eye sinks back as the fat padding within the eye socket is reduced, or it may be an early symptom of feline influenza. Don't worry; the cat isn't going blind, but you must keep a careful watch on the creature.

disease, many cats remain snuffly and catarrhal for many months or even years.

What you can do

Bathe the delicate nose tip with warm water. Soften and remove any caked mucus. Anoint a little petroleum jelly into the nose. Feline influenza needs veterinary attention so never delay in seeking professional health.

What you can do

Should other symptoms develop, see the vet. If it persists for long without other signs, try boosting the food intake and give fifty micrograms of vitamin B12 daily in the food or as a tablet.

Veterinary treatment

The vet has a number of ways of dealing with the varieties of eye disease: using local anaesthetic drops to numb the eye for the removal of irritant objects; or applying drugs, not just by using ointment and drops but also by an injection under the conjunctiva, the pink membrane round the eye. He can also examine deep into the eye with his ophthalmoscope and can identify infecting bacteria by taking swabs of the cat's tears. Nowadays the vet can deal with a squint, blocked tear ducts, cataractous lenses and many other eye conditions by surgery.

The nose and palate

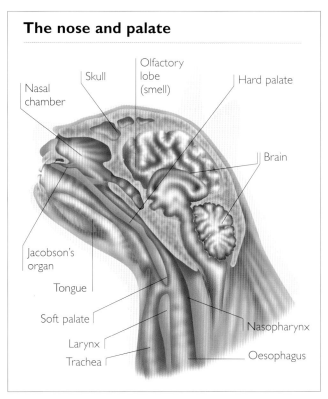

Nasal chamber

Skull

Olfactory lobe (smell)

Hard palate

Brain

Jacobson's organ

Tongue

Soft palate

Larynx

Trachea

Nasopharynx

Oesophagus

The ears

Common symptoms

- Shaking the head
- Scratching the ear
- Tilting of the head to one side, sometimes associated with loss of balance and a staggering gait
- Sudden 'ballooning' of an ear flap
- Tiny white 'insects' moving slowly around inside the ear
- A bad-smelling, chocolate-coloured or purulent discharge from the ear

What you can do

If ear trouble flares up suddenly, you can pour in liberal quantities of paraffin oil (liquid paraffin), warmed to body heat. Do it in the garage – puss will flick any excess oil all over your chintz curtains if you do it in the lounge.

If the cat is simply an ear-flicker and the ears seem dry but contain the 'insects' referred to above (actually otodectic mange mites), get some ear mange drops from the pet shop.

Veterinary treatment

Any discharge constitutes canker and may need antibiotic treatment by the vet. Head-tilting and loss of balance may indicate Otitis Media (middle ear disease). This is inflammation behind the ear-drum in the middle ear. Infection usually enters this area via a channel (the Eustachian tube) that runs from the throat, so it often follows throat and respiratory infections. It needs immediate veterinary treatment, since the modern drugs used by the vet can reach the inflammation in the middle ear and in almost all cases prevent permanent damage to the balancing organs and the spread of the infection to the brain.

Haematoma

The sudden ballooning of the ear flap of a cat is due to bleeding within the flap. It is a haematoma (really just a big blood blister), usually as a result of the cat scratching its own ear vigorously but sometimes caused by a blow or a bite from another animal.

Anatomy of the ear

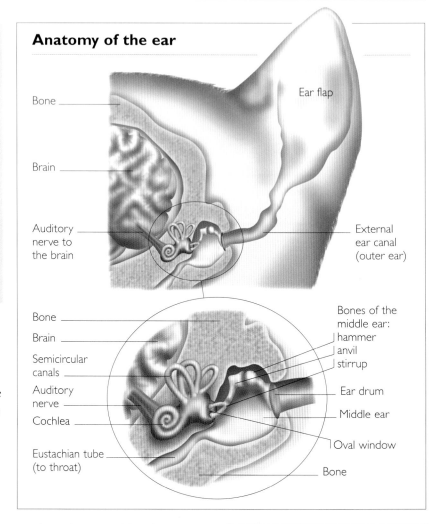

Bone
Brain
Auditory nerve to the brain
Ear flap
External ear canal (outer ear)

Bone
Brain
Semicircular canals
Auditory nerve
Cochlea
Eustachian tube (to throat)
Bones of the middle ear: hammer, anvil, stirrup
Ear drum
Middle ear
Oval window
Bone

Aural haematoma

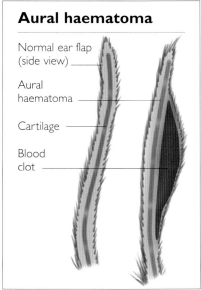

Normal ear flap (side view)
Aural haematoma
Cartilage
Blood clot

It annoys the cat because it feels strangely heavy but is not painful like an abscess unless secondarily infected, which is uncommon. The cat shakes its head, trying to dislodge the weight. The condition is identical to that seen in human boxers who are repeatedly cuffed round the ears. Left untreated, the blood inside the haematoma clots and shrinks into a gnarled scar, thereby crumpling the ear into a 'cauliflower' shape.

Veterinary treatment

The vet can avoid puss taking on the appearance of a punchy prize-fighter by giving him a general anaesthetic, draining off the blood, usually through an incision, and then stitching the ear in a special way which may involve attaching steel buttons for a week or so. (This may look odd but it serves a most

useful purpose.) A haematoma is not a serious condition and the success rate following surgery is very high. Nevertheless, the cause of the original scratching (mites, canker or whatever) must be treated simultaneously to avoid a recurrence of the condition.

■ **Left:** *You can use some ear-cleaning fluid to gently clean the ears.*

Deafness

In the cat, deafness can be either temporary, due to infection in the outer or the middle ear, or the accumulation of wax or discharge, or the build-up of large numbers of parasites, or it may be permanent, brought on by disease of the inner ear, or degeneration of the ear structures as old age creeps on, or a hereditary factor. There is a gene, frequently found in white cats, particularly ones with blue eyes, that induces withering of the tissues of the inner ear and, thus, deafness.

Veterinary treatment

The vet will determine the type of deafness a cat has and what, if any, treatment there may be.

The chest

Common symptoms

- Coughing
- Gasping
- Sneezing
- Laboured breathing

Cats can suffer from bronchitis, pneumonia, fluid build-up in the chest cavity, including pleurisy, and other chest conditions. Coughing and sneezing, all the miserable signs of a head cold, perhaps including eye or nasal discharge, may be signs of feline influenza (cat 'flu). Laboured breathing without any 'cold' symptoms may even be a sign of pleurisy or of heart disease in older cats.

Feline influenza

This disease is usually caused by a mixture of viruses and secondary germs. The most important of the 'flu viruses are those of feline rhinotracheitis and feline calicivirus. Feline influenza may be mild or severe and sometimes ends fatally. In such cases, the damage may be done by secondary bacterial infections of the lung. It is not a cold, wet-weather disease, particularly; many major outbreaks occur in summer, and it is often found in epidemic form in catteries during the hot holiday months.

What you can do

Protect your pet against feline influenza by ensuring that your cat is vaccinated and boosted regularly. Incidentally, there is no connection between human and cat forms of 'flu. Keep a cat with chest trouble warm and dry. Do not let him exert himself. Give him nutritious food, finely minced or liquid, if he will accept it.

There is no harm in the odd drop of brandy or whisky spooned in. Keep the nostrils unblocked as far as possible by sponging the nose and greasing it with a little petroleum jelly. In simple cases where the cat does continue to eat and his breathing is not too distressed, a quarter of a teaspoonful of Benylin syrup (obtainable from your chemist) may be given every two or three hours as a cough mixture.

The respiratory system

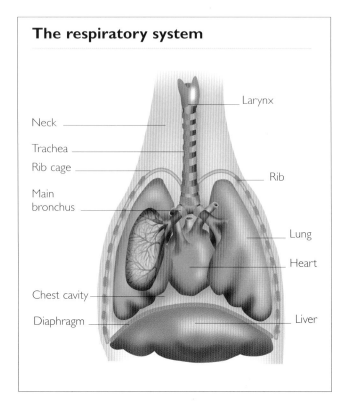

Neck

Larynx

Trachea

Rib cage

Rib

Main bronchus

Lung

Heart

Chest cavity

Diaphragm

Liver

Veterinary treatment

More serious cases will be treated by the vet using antibiotics, drugs to loosen mucus in the lungs and, where the heart is involved, special cardiac medicines. Where fluid accumulates in the chest in pleurisy cases, the vet may tap this off under sedation.

Very many cats with dicky hearts can live happy, long lives once their problem has been diagnosed and a maintenance treatment prescribed.

A primary course of vaccination against feline influenza begins at eight to nine weeks of age with one injection followed by a second three to four weeks later. Some vaccines also protect against other cat diseases. Booster doses of the vaccine are best given annually.

Feline chlamydial infection

This is an ailment whose signs can resemble those of feline influenza. Eye inflammation and discharge are often pronounced. The cause is a germ, which is not a virus, called *Chlamydia psittaci*, which is closely related to the one that is found in parrots (psittacosis) and another that has killed a large number of koala bears.

Veterinary treatment

The germ can be treated by your vet who may use antibiotics, such as tetracyclines and erythromycin. A vaccine is also available and this, too, can be given from nine weeks of age, either alone or in combination with the vaccines for feline influenza and feline enteritis.

The stomach and intestines

Common symptoms

■ Vomiting
■ Diarrhoea
■ Constipation
■ Blood in droppings
■ Bad breath
■ Excessive thirst
■ Overeating
■ Lack of appetite
■ Flatulence

There are numerous causes for any of these symptoms and sometimes more than one symptom will be observed at the same time.

Vomiting

This may be simple and transient, due to a mild inflammation (gastritis) of the stomach or the presence, particularly in the longhaired breeds, of a fur ball. If severe, persistent or accompanied by other major signs, however, it can indicate the presence of serious conditions, such as feline infectious enteritis, tumours or an obstruction of the intestine.

Gastritis

Pure gastritis is not common and it is generally caused by the ingestion by the cat of poisons or irritant chemicals.

Fur balls

These are very common. As the cat grooms itself, it swallows hairs which gradually build up into a soggy mass which, when regurgitated, is frequently sausage shaped and can be mistaken for a dead mouse. If the fur ball is not vomited out, its presence in the stomach, growing ever larger, produces erratic appetite and eventually weight loss and poor condition in the affected cat.

Diarrhoea

This may be simple, the result of too much liver or too many yeast tablets or a mild bowel infection. However, it may be more serious and profuse, as in cases of feline infectious enteritis, feline infectious peritonitis or bacterial infections, including Salmonellosis.

Constipation

This may be a result of old age, accumulation of fur balls in the intestine or faulty diet, or it may be an indicator of obstruction.

Blood in the stools

This may be merely from the scratching of the intestinal lining by gobbled bone splinters, or it can be the effect of an acute food-poisoning attack.

Bad breath

Bad breath can result from mouth infections (gum ulcers and tooth decay, etc.), digestive upsets or Vitamin B deficiency.

Excessive thirst

This is an important symptom that may indicate the presence of a significant disease, such as diabetes, kidney or liver problems, hormonal upsets, uterine disease (such as pyometra) or certain toxic conditions.

Overeating

Overeating may be quite normal when recovering from an illness or after giving birth, but it can also indicate the presence of parasites, diabetes, pancreatitis or hormonal disease.

Lack of appetite

Poor appetite can be the result of a bewildering variety of disorders, ranging from the very mild to the serious. Flatulence may be of dietary origin or may indicate an intestinal problem, such as the faulty absorption of nutriments (malabsorption).

What you can do
Use your common sense. If any of these symptoms persists for more than a few hours or if they are

accompanied by profound malaise and weakness on the part of the cat, you need skilled help. In simple cases or until you see the vet, just remember that water and salt loss through vomiting or diarrhoea is the killing factor, and you can do something to combat this. Spoon frequent small quantities of glucose and water, seasoned to your taste with table salt, into the cat.
◆ Where vomiting is the prime symptom, give no solid food but concentrate on liquid replacement. Persevere if vomiting continues. Don't use milk or brandy. Half a teaspoonful of Maalox or baby gripe water can be given.
◆ Where diarrhoea is the main sign, concentrate on administering fluid. Gently introducing a third of a capful of strong, sweetened coffee at body temperature via the rectum through a human enema syringe is safe and sensible; do it slowly. A teaspoon of Kaopectate mixture can be given by mouth. Do not try human kaoline and

morphine diarrhoea mixtures.
◆ During the early stages of constipation, try spooning two or three teaspoonfuls of mineral oil (liquid paraffin) into the cat. The tiny, ready-to-use, disposable enemas, available at the chemist, are very effective. Use a half to one tube, as directed for humans on the instructions. If constipation is a chronic problem, add bulk to the cat's diet in the form of bran flakes or isogel granules.

Veterinary treatment
Severe or persistent cases always need veterinary attention. The vet can examine the alimentary tract of the affected animal in various ways: with his fingers, by X-ray, sometimes with barium meal, by stethoscope, gastroscope, ultrasound and, occasionally, by an exploratory operation.

Careful diagnosis by a skilled, qualified practitioner is essential before formulating treatment for the cat's abdominal problems.

The digestive system

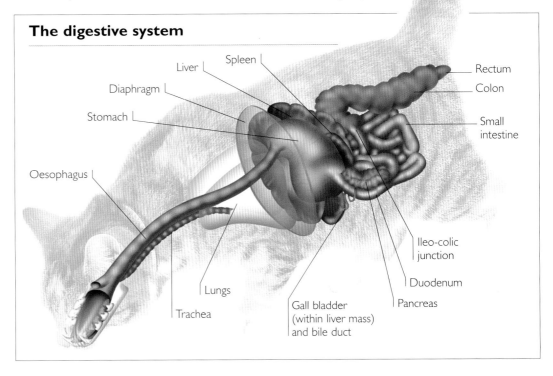

Liver
Spleen
Rectum
Colon
Diaphragm
Stomach
Small intestine
Oesophagus
Ileo-colic junction
Duodenum
Lungs
Pancreas
Trachea
Gall bladder (within liver mass) and bile duct

Feline infectious enteritis

Common symptoms

- Depression
- Vomiting
- Diarrhoea (not always present)
- Rapid dehydration
- Sitting in a 'hunched-up' posture
- Evidence of a painful abdomen when handled

One of the major virus diseases of cats, feline infectious enteritis is highly contagious, and the virus is resistant to many antiseptics. It is not purely a complaint affecting the intestines; it attacks the liver and white cells of the blood also. It can run a very short and fatal course within a matter of hours after an incubation period of two to nine days, and the symptoms are variable (see box above).

What you can do

The cure for feline infectious enteritis, a terrible scourge, is prevention. Therefore have your cat vaccinated from eight weeks of age onwards, and make sure that it is boosted regularly. Special dead vaccines can be given to queens to boost their immunity and thereby provide plenty of antibodies in the colostrum for new-born kittens.

Veterinary treatment

The vet cannot kill the virus but may use antibiotics to control secondary bacterial attack. He will certainly be concerned to protect the affected animal from dehydrating through fluid loss, and this may mean saline transfusions, under the skin or intravenously. You can help by keeping the patient warm and giving frequent, small spoonfuls of warm glucose and water.

Peritonitis

Common symptoms

- Abdominal pain
- Fever
- Diarrhoea or constipation
- Vomiting
- Lack of appetite
- Sitting in a miserable 'hunched-up' posture

This is a disease of inflammation of the lining of the abdominal cavity. It can be caused by the perforation of the abdominal wall, stomach or intestines, by the presence of tumours or by germs arriving through the blood or lymphatic systems. Urgent veterinary attention is always required for such cases.

Feline infectious peritonitis

Feline infectious peritonitis is a special type of peritonitis. It is due to a virus which usually strikes young cats under three years of age. As well as the peritoneum, the virus invades the liver, kidneys and brain, and the disease most frequently has a fatal outcome after a few weeks. The symptoms are those that are mentioned above, often with swelling of the abdomen due to fluid accumulation, and possibly jaundice and breathing problems.

Treatment

Unfortunately, no vaccine is yet available to protect against this dangerous disease. Veterinary treatment is aimed at countering dehydration and secondary bacterial infection, draining off dropsical liquid and supporting the body's organs with vitamins and certain hormones.

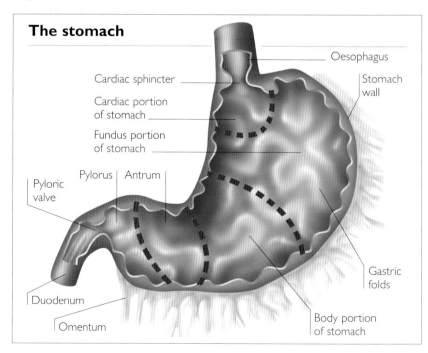

The stomach

- Oesophagus
- Stomach wall
- Cardiac sphincter
- Cardiac portion of stomach
- Fundus portion of stomach
- Pyloric valve
- Pylorus
- Antrum
- Duodenum
- Omentum
- Gastric folds
- Body portion of stomach

Feline immuno deficiency

Another virus disease that can produce similar symptoms to the above ones is feline immuno deficiency, often called feline Aids or 'faids'. There is absolutely no evidence that people can be infected by cats, although the virus is in the same family as the one that causes human Aids.

This ailment is becoming very common, and infected cats can carry the virus, without showing any signs of it, for years. It is probably transmitted by bites although close, long-term contact is also thought to be necessary. Diagnosis can be confirmed by a simple blood test.

Milk-sensitivity diarrhoea

Although saucers of milk or cream are traditionally associated with felines, cow's milk is not a natural drink for cats and some individuals cannot tolerate it even though they like it. Chronic diarrhoea in such cases is due either to allergy or to the cat being deficient in the milk-sugar-digesting enzyme called lactose.

Most mild cases usually respond to the simple remedy of diluting the cat's milk with water. However, more severe intolerance necessitates excluding milk, all milk products and most cereal products (which are found in some proprietary cat foods) from the affected animal's diet.

NUTRITIONAL PROBLEMS OF THE CAT

Nowadays, with a multitude of balanced, complete cat foods available widely in canned, semi-moist and dry pelleted forms, nutritional disease is far less common than it used to be.

Obesity

Fat cats of the non-human variety are still to be found in abundance. Lack of exercise, over-indulgence by owners and puss's sheer greed can lead to excess pounds that put strain on the heart, liver and joints. No cat should weigh more than 8 kg (17½ lb). The heaviest cat I know of was 'Spice', a nine-year-old ginger and white tom with thyroid trouble. He lived in Ridgefield, Connecticut, USA, and weighed 19.5 kg (43 lb). Too much fat in the diet, as fatty fish of the salmon or herring type, or over-generosity with oils from canned fish, can damage the heart and induce fat tissue disease. Signs are dullness, tenderness when handled, circulatory problems and sometimes fever. While you correct the diet, the vet may prescribe large doses of Vitamin E.

Vitamin deficiency

A purely lean meat diet can result in Vitamin A and/or Vitamin D deficiency in the cat.

◆ Signs of **Vitamin A** deficiency include poor condition, bone, skin and eye disease, infertility and abortion. Treatment is by giving cod liver oil and feeding liver.

◆ **Vitamin D** deficiency causes bone disease and is corrected by Vitamin D injections, cod liver oil supplements and a more balanced feeding regime.

◆ **Vitamin B** is actually a complex of several different vitamins. Commercial cat foods contain added Vitamin B to replace any vitamins lost during processing. Excess feeding of raw fish can produce a deficiency of Vitamin B, with resultant damage to the nervous system, which may be manifested in convulsions or strokes. Too much over-processed food may lead to Vitamin B6 deficiency with anaemia, weight loss and, again, convulsions. Treatment is by injections of Vitamin B, oral supplements or yeast or B-complex tablets and correcting the diet.

Mineral deficiency

◆ **Calcium:** This is essential, and in substantial quantities, for growing kittens, and pregnant and lactating queens. If a cat's diet is deficient, rickets may occur in the young, and brittle bones in adults. Lactating queens may develop hypocalcaemic lactation tetany. The commonest reason for insufficient calcium in the feline diet is too much lean meat. Milk, fish (including the bones) and balanced commercial foods will correct the faults. Treatment will require calcium supplements or sterilized bone flour in the food and perhaps, if the vet advises it, Vitamin D.

◆ **Iodine:** Because they live on high-protein diets, relatively large amounts of iodine are required. Iodine is, however, toxic if over-dosed so it must be given carefully and then only where the diet consists of home-made food. To supply a sufficient quantity, lightly season such food with iodized tablet salt or give the multi-vitamin trace element tablets which are specially formulated for small animals.

Note: Although cats also require many other minerals to maintain good health, deficiencies are very rare as meat, fish and proprietary foods contain adequate amounts.

Disease of the liver and pancreas

Right: *Cats will drink from many sources but if you think that your cat is drinking excessively, this may be a symptom of liver or kidney related disease or diabetes.*

Two major abdominal organs that are involved in food digesting and metabolism are the liver and the pancreas. Both can suffer damage or can become diseased.

Liver

Common symptoms

These can be very variable, mild or severe, sudden in onset or long-lasting and can include:
■ Jaundice
■ Vomiting
■ Diarrhoea
■ Constipation
■ Excessive thirst
■ Enlarged abdomen
■ Dullness
■ Depression
■ Collapse
■ Coma

The liver can be physically damaged by road accidents and other trauma or affected by tumours, malnutrition, poisons, parasites (particularly migrating young larval forms), infections or after malfunction of other organs.

Veterinary treatment

Liver disease always needs urgent attention from the vet who will be aided by special blood, urine and stool tests. Treatment depends on the exact nature of the condition and is likely to include Vitamin B complex injections, transfusions of fluid, corticosteroids and glucose to raise blood sugar levels and protect liver cells. Recently I have found silymarin, a chemical found in the plant milk thistle, to be invaluable in supporting the liver in acute crises.

What you can do

Keep the cat warm. Administer small amounts of fluid, preferably glucose or honey and water, frequently. If the animal is eating, the diet should be one of low-fat, high-protein content.

Pancreatic disease

Acute pancreatitis

Common symptoms

■ Vomiting
■ Abdominal pain
■ Fever
■ Shock
■ Collapse

Sudden inflammation of the pancreas is not common in the cat and the causes are still largely undetermined, although too much fat in the diet may play a part. Veterinary treatment, which may involve giving fluid transfusions, analgesics and anti-inflammatory drops, must be administered very quickly, but the chances of recovery are generally low.

Chronic pancreatitis

Common symptoms

■ Pale, putty-coloured stools, often visibly fatty
■ Excessive appetite
■ Loss of weight and condition

Milder, long-lasting damage to, and inflammation of, the pancreas interfere with its production of food-digesting enzymes and thus reduce the absorption of fat by the body. Your veterinary surgeon can confirm the diagnosis by testing the cat's stools.

Treatment of this condition is by provision of a low-fat diet and the addition of pancreatic enzymes in powder form to the affected animal's food.

Diabetes

Common symptoms

▨ Increased appetite and thirst
▨ Loss of weight
▨ Development of cataracts in the lenses of the eyes (in some cases)

Diabetes mellitus ('sugar diabetes') is caused by a fall in production of the vital hormone, insulin, by certain cells which lie within the pancreas. The disease is more common in older, fat cats, and some breeding lines have an increased tendency to suffer from it. Diagnosis is confirmed by blood and urine tests.

What you can do

Treatment for diabetes is by the regular administration of insulin injections and adjustment of diet. Don't worry. You'll find it easy. Insulin is cheap and can easily be given by the owner without upsetting the cat.

The vet will demonstrate how to inject the insulin, usually into the scruff of the neck. Most cats don't feel a thing! Frequency of injections and the dosage will vary from time to time, according to illness, stress or changes in your pet's diet. Everything will be explained and you must be guided by your vet who will also show you how to assess progress by using testing strips, which are dipped into a puddle of the cat's urine.

The oral anti-diabetic tablets used in humans don't usually work in cats and, anyway, they are more difficult to administer than an injection.

The patient's diet will be changed to one that is completely free of carbohydrates (including sugar-containing treats) and cereals. For more detailed advice on what to feed, ask your vet.

The urinary system

Acute nephritis

This inflammation of the kidney, which is caused by infection or poison, is less common in the cat than in the dog. The usual signs of it can include vomiting, thirst, inflammation of the mouth, depression, convulsions and coma. Urgent veterinary attention is indicated, and treatment will involve fluid therapy and, in cases of poisoning, the administration, if possible, of antidotes.

Chronic kidney disease

This is commoner, particularly in old animals, and can give rise to thirst, frequent urination, loss of condition and weight and, ultimately, uraemia (the retention of waste products in the blood) with vomiting, inflamed mouth, bad breath, dehydration and anaemia. Veterinary treatment may consist of fluid transfusions, vitamin supplements, anabolic hormones and other suitable drugs.

What you can do

Unlike the liver, destroyed areas of kidney tissue cannot be replaced by healing processes. So surviving, functioning kidney tissue must be helped and supported. The diet should be low in good-quality protein and rich in carbohydrates. Special proprietary 'kidney' diets for cats are available in veterinary prescription.

The urinary system of the male cat

Renal vein
Renal artery
Ureters
Colon
Bulbo-urethral gland
Prostate gland
Urethra
Prepuce
Kidney
Bladder
Penis

The kidney

Renal artery
Renal vein
Renal capsule
Ureter
Medulla
Cortex

Other urinary problems

Common symptoms

- Difficulty passing urine
- Blood in urine
- Loss of weight
- Thirst

Difficulty passing urine

The lower parts of the urinary tract, the bladder and urethra, are the most frequent ones to cause trouble, particularly in males. Cats on mainly dry-food diets, cats taking insufficient water and tom cats castrated very early are more prone to develop 'gravel' in the urine. This deposit of salt crystals in the bladder can eventually block up the urethra (water pipe) of male animals. The cat strains to pass urine and its owner may mistake the position adopted for one of constipation. When the bladder is over-full and tight as a drum, the cat is in considerable pain, will resent being handled and may actually turn to look at its hind quarters and spit angrily. Do not try to squeeze the cat's swollen bladder yourself. It is very easily ruptured. Seek veterinary help at once.

Blood in the urine

This generally indicates bladder infection (cystitis). This complaint is commoner in females. It, too, requires veterinary treatment.

Loss of weight and thirst

Loss of weight and thirst, particularly in old cats, can be due to kidney disease although other diseases, including diabetes, can exhibit these signs.

What you can do

As a preventative measure, make sure your cat always has plenty of fresh water available and a good proportion of moist food. Do not have a tom castrated too early. Wait until he is at least nine months old. Don't give too much dried food. Add a little salt to the cat's food to encourage it to drink.

Veterinary treatment

The vet can deal with urinary problems using special urine-active antiseptics and antibiotics. He can catheterize a cat's bladder painlessly to free blockages, and take urine samples for analysis. The kidneys can be X-rayed by contrast radiography and, if necessary, the bladder and urethra can be operated upon quite safely.

The reproductive system

As the male cat's reproductive system is rarely afflicted by any medical problems, I shall concentrate in this section on the problems of the female's genitalia.

Infertility

As with other species, failure to breed can be caused by a variety of factors. The ovaries may be inactive with resultant absence of sexual cycling, or they may be overactive through the presence of cysts. Parts of the genital system may be in an abnormal state, as in the case of blocked fallopian tubes. Disease, such as an infection of the uterus or vagina or pyometra (see page 122), may be grumbling away and showing, for the moment, few symptoms. Only professional veterinary diagnosis can sort out these problems. Anti-infective, hormonal or surgical treatment will be used as indicated.

The female reproductive system

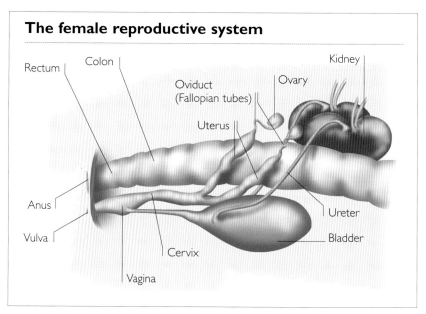

Rectum
Colon
Kidney
Oviduct (Fallopian tubes)
Ovary
Uterus
Anus
Vulva
Ureter
Bladder
Cervix
Vagina

Miscarriage

Premature onset of labour is not common in the cat but it does sometimes occur. A pregnant queen may begin to strain and bear down even though birth is still a long way off. There may be a bloody or other-coloured discharge from the vulva and the animal may appear to be dull, lacking in appetite, and will sometimes vomit.

What you can do

If you are sure that these events are premature or have any doubts about the timing, then seek urgent veterinary assistance. If you think that the queen may well be around sixty days pregnant, you can wait three hours and then contact the vet if no kitten has been born.

Metritis

Common symptoms

Signs are those of infection and septicaemia:
■ Loss of appetite
■ Depression
■ Fever
■ Vomiting
■ Thirst
■ Discharge of bad-smelling, bloody, purulent or a chocolate-coloured material from the vulva

Infection of the uterus can follow a birth, particularly in older queens or ones that are debilitated or out of condition for some reason, perhaps after the birth of a dead kitten, particularly one that has been delivered by forceps or by Caesarean section, or where all or

The pregnant female

Rectum | Amnotic fluid surrounds the foetus | Ureter | Kidney | Cervix | Bladder | Foetus | Placenta | Umbilical cord

some of the placenta has been retained after an otherwise normal birth. Urgent veterinary attention is indicated in such cases. Treatment will involve antibiotics, fluid replacement and, often, drugs to shrink down the uterus.

What you can do

Keep the cat warm and give it warm, nourishing liquids, such as beef tea, protein hydrolysate and glucose or honey and water.

Prolapse of the uterus

Occasionally, following a difficult birth, part or all of the uterus will balloon out of the vulva as a swollen red mass. What you see is the lining of the uterus and it can easily become damaged and infected as the cat moves about.

What you can do

You must seek urgent veterinary help. Meanwhile, you can keep the prolapsed uterus clean and moist by sponging it very gently with some cotton wool and warm

water before smearing on a little petroleum jelly and then covering it with either a piece of clean gauze or some cloth.

If the prolapse has not been 'out' long, the vet may be able to replace it under sedation or anaesthetic. However, if much time has elapsed and the prolapse has swollen markedly or become infected, an abdominal operation may well by necessary.

The male reproductive system

Colon | Prostate gland | Bulbo-urethral gland | Rectum | Scrotum | Vas deferens | Testis | Urethra | Penis | Prepuce | Bladder

Pyometra

Common symptoms

- Purulent discharge of some colour (white, pink, yellow, chocolate) from the vagina
- Dullness
- Lack of appetite
- Thirst
- Vomiting

Although this term strictly means 'pus in the womb', it is not primarily a uterine infection in the cat, but is rather a condition of hormonal origin. Over a period of time, under the influence of an abnormally functioning ovary, changes occur in the uterine wall with the formation of microscopic cysts. These lead to inflammation of the walls and the filling of the interior of the uterus with pus-like fluid. It is this fluid degenerating that eventually poisons the cat through its blood stream.

This disease is commonest in queens that have never had kittens or maybe just one litter. It looks like a septic infection and can make the animal very ill through absorption of the nasty fluid that distends the womb, although in many cases the pus is sterile. It is not an infectious disease although secondary bacterial invasions are a danger.

What you can do

If you are not planning on breeding, have a female spayed when young. If discharges are seen, clean the vulval area with warm water and weak antiseptic and take the little lady along to the vet.

Veterinary treatment

The veterinary surgeon may use hormone treatment together with drugs to reduce the amount of fluid in the womb, and antibiotics to tackle any opportunist bugs. The main veterinary weapon is normally surgical: hysterectomy, or the removal of the diseased womb through a side or mid-line incision under general anaesthetic. However, if puss is in a weak and toxic state because of the diseased womb, then the vet may delay operating for some time in order to try to strengthen her with vitamins, anti-toxic drugs and a course of antibiotics.

STOPPING UNWANTED PREGNANCIES

It is responsible, caring and humane pet ownership to take steps to avoid unwanted pregnancies in the cat. Most commonly, toms are castrated ('doctored', 'neutered') and queens are ovaro-hysterectomized ('spayed'). Apart from making the sad euthanasia of newborn kittens unnecessary, these operations have other important advantages.

Toms stray less, don't get into macho fights on rooftops by moonlight and desist from spraying their territory with pungent urine markers. Queens aren't pestered by neighbourhood lotharios several times a year, and their owners are spared the love-lorn howling of a female in heat.

Oestrus suppression

If you do want to allow your queen to have kittens, but in a controlled and orderly fashion, there are other methods of oestrus ('heat') suppression available. Injections or tablets of certain sex hormone preparations, such as testosterone, progesterones or megestrol, can be prescribed by the vet either to temporarily postpone (useful at holiday times), permanently postpone or suppress (if already begun) an oestrus period. These techniques enable a return to normal sexual cycling when desired. However, I am against using them repeatedly as a replacement for spaying, particularly in queens that have never had a litter of kittens. Over-use of these hormonal preparations can lead to ovarian or uterine disease, such as cysts or pyometra, at a later date.

If you do use chemical birth-control methods on your cat, discuss with your vet which is the most appropriate regime in your case. The contraceptive pills used in cats can have side-effects, such as increased appetite, unwanted weight gain and sluggishness. They cannot normally be given to diabetic animals.

Spaying

Spaying is best performed when your cat is between four and nine months of age. It can be done from three months onwards to almost any age. Kittens under three months of age and queens in oestrus ('heat') or more than four weeks pregnant must NOT be spayed.

Castration

Toms can be castrated from six months or age but it is best to wait until they are nine months old in order to avoid urinary blockages in the penis in later life.

Blood and circulatory problems

The heart

Common symptoms

■ Laboured or faster-than-normal breathing

■ Cat tires quickly and easily 'runs out of puff'

■ Coughing, wheezing or gasping

■ A lilac-blue tinge to the gums

Important: Where any one or more of the above signs persists for more than a day or two, seek veterinary advice.

Cat hearts can be afflicted by a number of different conditions. Kittens may be born with congenital defects in the heart walls ('holes in the heart'). Virus and bacterial disease, such as feline influenza, can cause long-lasting damage to heart tissue. Occasionally the heart can be the site of tumours and, in elderly cats as in old people, the passing years may bring weakness or a blockage of the heart valves.

In some countries, worm parasites which live within the circulatory system ('heart worm') can induce serious heart failure.

Over-active thyroid glands or diets that are deficient in the amino-acid taurine may also affect the heart significantly.

Veterinary treatment

The vet will examine the cat's heart by means of a stethoscope and may also employ X-rays, ultra-sound, electrocardiography or blood analysis to establish a diagnosis. Treatment will depend on the nature of the disease. Weak hearts may be strengthened and their action markedly improved by using modern drugs, such as enalapril, benazepril or propento phylline, under strict veterinary supervision. Whatever the specific treatment, old, tiring hearts often benefit from daily administration of 50 milligrams of Vitamin E or wheatgerm oil in the food.

Heart worms

These afflict cats (and some other mammals) living in the Far East, Australia, the USA and Southern Europe. The condition is only seen in the United Kingdom in cats imported from one of the above regions. The parasites are transmitted in larval form by either mosquitos or fleas.

Treatment is difficult and quite problematical because dead worms in the circulatory system can cause more trouble than living ones. Their corpses still act as foreign bodies in the blood, which may cause thrombosis. Protein chemicals released by dead worms may cause reactive shock in the cat.

Prevention in high-risk areas involves controlling fleas and mosquitos and also keeping pets indoors at night in mosquito-proof quarters. If you live in a 'heart worm' area, you should seek veterinary advice on any further precautions you can take.

How the heart works

The cat's heart consists of two pairs of chambers: the atria and ventricles. Deoxygenated blood enters the right atrium and is then pumped out through the right ventricle to the lungs where it is oxygenated. This blood flows into the left atrium and from there through the left ventricle to the body's organs.

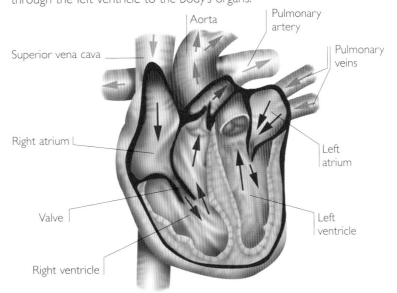

The circulatory system

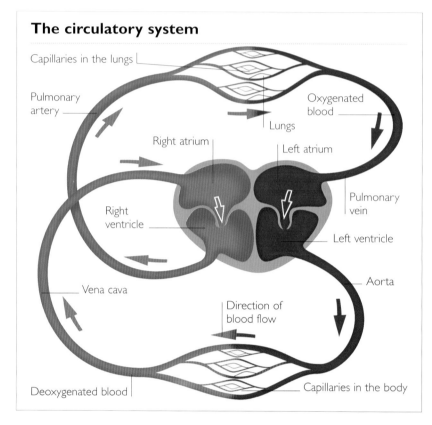

Capillaries in the lungs

Pulmonary artery

Oxygenated blood

Lungs

Right atrium

Left atrium

Right ventricle

Pulmonary vein

Left ventricle

Vena cava

Aorta

Direction of blood flow

Deoxygenated blood

Capillaries in the body

Anaemia

Common symptoms

- Pale mouths and eye membranes (the conjunctiva lining the eyelids)
- In severe cases, as the animal becomes 'oxygen hungry', breathlessness, fatigue, weakness and restlessness will occur

Anaemia is the reduction in the number of red cells circulating in the blood and/or a diminution in the amount of oxygen-carrying haemoglobin in the red cells. If you suspect it, see your vet as treatment must depend on cause.

Causes of anaemia
1 Destruction of red cells by parasites (as in feline infectious anaemia – see right), poisons, bacterial toxins or an immune reaction which may follow an incompatible blood transfusion.
2 Loss of blood by wounds, chronic bleeding, internal tumours, ulcers or other lesions, by blood-sucking parasite or by ingestion of a chemical, such as warfarin, the common rodent poison that inhibits normal blood clotting and results in internal bleeding from organs or tissues.
3 The absence, reduction in the numbers or abnormal production of new red cells in the cat's bone marrow caused by certain acute or chronic infections, tumours, poisons, chronic kidney disease, tuberculosis or a diet lacking in certain essential elements.

Veterinary treatment
The vet will examine the cat clinically and will also take a blood sample for analysis. The treatment that is given will depend on the type and cause of the anaemia and may include iron supplements, a course of vitamins and even a blood transfusion from a compatible donor cat as well as specific therapy of the underlying condition.

Feline infectious anaemia

This debilitating disease is caused by a minute protozoan parasite (*Haemobartonella felis*), which, like the malarial parasite in humans, lives inside the cat's red blood cells. It may be there in small numbers and cause few or no apparent ill-effects.

However, when it is present in much larger numbers and it becomes more virulent (when a cat's resistance is lowered for some reason), it can wreak havoc by destroying the cells. The infested cat is soon dull, weak and very out-of-condition. It loses weight progressively and the eye membranes and mouth lining become pallid.

Veterinary treatment
The veterinary surgeon will analyse a blood sample to determine the severity of the anaemia and also to confirm the presence of the parasites. Sometimes feline infectious anaemia affects cats that are also afflicted with feline leukaemia (see opposite) – in such cases, the outlook is not good. Where, however, the feline infectious anaemia is present alone, treatment, which will consist of certain antibiotics, anti-anaemic therapy and, in advanced cases, blood transfusion, normally assures a very favourable prognosis.

Feline leukaemia

Common symptoms

■ Fever
■ Lethargy
■ Weakness
■ Loss of weight
■ Anaemia

Note: Other signs are exhibited where the virus has particularly targeted certain organs. Vomiting and/or diarrhoea, together with enlargement of the liver and spleen, may occur in the abdominal form of the disease. Where the kidneys or thymus are involved, urinary problems or laboured breathing and coughing respectively may be seen. Sometimes the eyes are invaded, thereby producing severe inflammation and blindness.

Leukaemia is uncontrolled production of white blood cells. White cells, of which there are several types, ordinarily serve vital functions within the body of participating in immunity defences against infections and other undesirable intrusions by outside trouble-makers. Too many circulating white cells can clog up blood and lymphatic vessels and invade and damage organs.

There are many forms of leukaemia that can afflict man or other animals, and one form in the cat, and not transmissible to humans, is caused by a virus. Feline leukaemia is contagious and spreads from cat to cat by direct contact. The virus is unable to live for long outside the body and can easily be killed by ordinary disinfectants. While some cats are naturally immune to the disease, others can carry and transmit the virus without showing any signs of illness. These latter are dangerous individuals wherever groups of cats are maintained as in breeding catteries, etc. Once detected (this can be done by blood testing), they should either be isolated from other cats or euthanased.

What you can do

Diagnosis of feline leukaemia is in the hands of the vet. Treatment can be attempted, but there is no cure at present and it is usually wisest to euthanase an affected cat to prevent transmission to others. If one cat in a house is positive on blood testing, all the other cats should be screened also in order to detect any carriers. The good news is that the disease can be prevented by a vaccine given by the vet when a kitten is nine weeks old, with a second dose at twelve to thirteen weeks. 'All-in-one' vaccines combining protection against feline leukaemia, feline influenza and feline infectious enteritis are also available.

Thrombosis

Common symptoms

■ Sudden collapse and shock
■ Pain
■ Paralysis (total or partial) of the hind legs, which usually feel very cold to the touch
■ Disappearance of the pulse in the femoral arteries of both hind legs – normally, this can be felt easily on the inside of the hind leg between knee and groin

The blocking of an artery or vein by a clot floating in the blood stream is thrombosis. It can have sudden and grave effects, much depending on the site of the blockage. Cats occasionally suffer from sudden thrombosis of the aorta, the main artery running down the length of the body. Termed iliac thrombosis, this is usually due to a piece of inflamed tissue breaking away from a diseased heart valve and floating away to jam at some point in the aorta.

What you can do

Seek the most urgent veterinary attention. Surgical intervention and the administration of clot-dissolving drugs may succeed but the recovery rate is low and recurrences are likely to occur.

■ **Below:** *Make sure you complete the course of injections and avoid tragedy striking a kitten like this Persian charmer. Adverse reactions to vaccinations are rare.*

Skin ailments and parasites

Common symptoms

■ Thin or bald patches
  in the fur
■ Scratching
■ Wet or dry sores
■ Fine black 'coal dust' flea
  droppings

External parasites

(Not to scale)

Flea

Louse

Sarcoptic mange mite

Tick

There are many kinds of skin disease in cats, and their precise diagnosis will usually require an examination and, often, sample-analysis by the vet. Some kinds are parasitic, others non-parasitic; both are quite common and you should look out for them at your regular grooming sessions.

The presence of just one single flea on a cat – which is terribly hard to track down – may set up widespread itchy skin irritation as an allergic reaction to the flea's saliva injected when the little devil sucks. In late summer, orange

GENETIC SKIN DISORDERS

Some cats carrying Rex genes can be more or less hairless. Other genetic abnormalities include 'splitfoot' (a cleft in the fore feet), polydactyly (extra toes), badly positioned ear flaps, undescended testicles, death of kittens in the womb where both parents carry the Manx gene, cataracts in Himalayans, and spasticity of muscles in Devon Rex.

Cutaneous asthenia ('rubber kitten syndrome' or 'torn skin syndrome') occurs occasionally in Siamese and Himalayans. The condition is characterized by thin, fragile skin that tears easily.

Anatomy of the skin

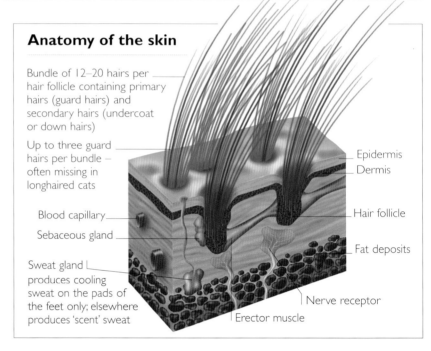

Bundle of 12–20 hairs per hair follicle containing primary hairs (guard hairs) and secondary hairs (undercoat or down hairs)

Up to three guard hairs per bundle – often missing in longhaired cats

Blood capillary

Sebaceous gland

Sweat gland produces cooling sweat on the pads of the feet only; elsewhere produces 'scent' sweat

Epidermis

Dermis

Hair follicle

Fat deposits

Nerve receptor

Erector muscle

specks in the fur of the head and ears or between the toes reveal the presence of harvest mites.

Points to consider, which will be useful to the vet in forming a diagnosis, are as follows:
◆ Is the cat a very fussy eater who may not be taking in a broad, balanced diet? If so, it may have a vitamin deficiency
◆ Does the condition occur at regular intervals or at certain times of year? This may indicate an allergy
◆ Is the cat neutered? Hormonal upsets can cause skin disease.

What you can do

If you see or suspect the presence of any of the skin parasites, such as fleas, lice, ticks, mites, obtain one of the anti-parasitic aerosols or powders for cats from the pet shop or chemist. Other modern, highly effective anti-parasite treatments available from the vet include injections, drops that are absorbed harmlessly into the cat's

body after being applied to the skin, and preparations for mixing with the animal's food.

Flea infestation

Fleas and, less commonly, lice and ticks can cause damage to the cat's coat. Look out for 'insects' or fine black 'coal dust' – actually the droppings of fleas among the hairs. Remember that parasites are most numerous in hot weather. Cats can become infected with feline, dog or, rarely, human fleas. Apart from damaging the skin and causing itching that may be intense, fleas can carry tapeworm larvae and certain virus diseases.

What you can do

As the flea's eggs are dry and not, like those of the louse, cemented to hairs, they drop off the cat's body. Carpets, bedding, furniture, etc. can thus become flea-ridden. It is therefore very important to use one of the special veterinary aerosols containing methoprene and permethrin for use about the house. Simply applied to carpets and furniture once every seven months, this product prevents re-infestation of your cat by flea eggs hatching in its environment. I have found that this procedure protects my five cats so well that any preventative treatment of the cats themselves is hardly necessary.

Lice infestation

Two kinds of louse, biting lice and sucking lice, can infest cats. They can be found anywhere on the body but they seem to be particularly fond of the head. Heavy lice infestation can result in poor condition and anaemia.

Tick infestation

Cats living in the country may pick up ticks when exploring fields or woodland. These blood-sucking parasites swell up as they feed until they resemble, and are the size of, blackcurrants. Don't pull ticks off as this tends to leave their mouth parts buried in the cat's skin with consequent abscess formation. Apply one of the anti-parasitic preparations mentioned earlier or, if you have it, apply a small drop of chloroform to the tick's body and then wait for it to loosen its attachment.

Mange mite infestation

Irritating mange, caused by an invisible mite, can cause dry, motheaten-looking areas round the head and ears. These parasites, barely visible to the naked eye, burrow into the skin. Several

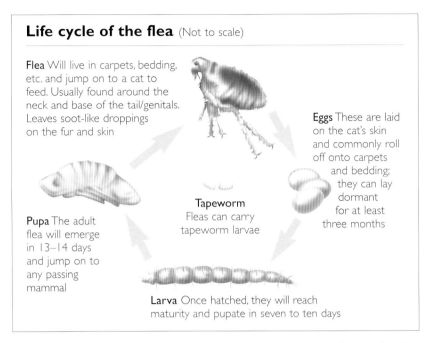

Life cycle of the flea (Not to scale)

Flea Will live in carpets, bedding, etc. and jump on to a cat to feed. Usually found around the neck and base of the tail/genitals. Leaves soot-like droppings on the fur and skin

Eggs These are laid on the cat's skin and commonly roll off onto carpets and bedding; they can lay dormant for at least three months

Pupa The adult flea will emerge in 13–14 days and jump on to any passing mammal

Tapeworm Fleas can carry tapeworm larvae

Larva Once hatched, they will reach maturity and pupate in seven to ten days

species of lice can infest the cat but the commonest is Notoedres. It generally lives in the head area and produces dermatitis with scaliness, scurf and loss of hair.

Other mites

Harvest mites or chiggers may be the cause of itching and areas of dermatitis on a cat's skin in the autumn, and fur mites are sometimes behind the excessive production of dandruff by a pet.

Ringworm

A 'ringworm' fungus, Microsporum or Trichophytes, can cause skin disease. Signs may be insignificant (areas of scaly, powdery skin) or more obvious – small, circular bald areas with wet or crusty edges. Ringworm, a very subtle thing in cats compared to the form it takes in man or cattle, may need ultra-violet light examination or fungus culture from a hair specimen for diagnosis, but it can now be treated by drugs given orally.

Note: Ringworm and some kinds of mites afflicting cats, such as the fur mite, can be transferred to humans, so take care that bedding and litter are burnt and boxes and utensils are sterilized in a hot, cat-safe disinfectant, where a pet is known to have an infestation.

Although cat fleas and lice may occasionally bite you, they cannot take up residence upon you, so any preventative precautions are unnecessary. Treating the pet is all that is necessary.

■ **Below:** *The traditional and reasonably effective way of removing fleas is with a flea comb, but, unlike modern anti-flea medications, it is time-consuming and not fool-proof.*

Non-parasitic skin disease

Eczema, dermatitis, weeping sores – any or all of these can be due to bacterial infection, food allergy, sunburn (in white cats), vitamin deficiencies or other nutritional faults, hormonal problems or contact with irritant chemicals. Itchy thinning of the hair over the trunk with points of oozing, red scabs is one of the commonest skin diseases. Often named 'Fish Eczema', this complaint has nothing to do with eating fish but is glandular in origin.

What you can do

It is best to seek veterinary advice for, as I have said so many times before, satisfactory treatment depends on accurate diagnosis. Where cats have wet sores, clip away the hair around the lesions with scissors – air always helps healing while matting of the fur always makes matters worse. Do not apply creams and ointments without veterinary advice – the animal will lick them off and may suffer ill effects. The same applies to powders.

Certainly you can gently bathe an inflamed area with some warm water and weak antiseptic and then dab it gently dry. However, if your cat incessantly licks or bites a diseased area, discuss fitting an Elizabethan collar made of plastic with your vet.

Veterinary treatment

The veterinary treatment of non-parasitic skin disease is usually very effective.
- ◆ **Bacterial infections** can be combated by antibiotics.
- ◆ **Food allergies** will require identification of the precise cause (the allergen), which is then withdrawn while immediate relief is obtained from anti-histamine or corticosteroid drugs.
- ◆ **Nutritional deficiencies** are corrected by the administration of nutritional supplements to a properly balanced diet.
- ◆ **Hormonal problems** are treated by the administration of hormones, orally, by injection or by subcutaneous implant.

Internal parasites

Although parasites can make their home in almost any of the cat's organs, including the heart, lungs, and eyes, the most important and commonest ones are found in the gastro-intestinal tract. They are worms and there are three main types of worm – roundworms, tapeworms and flukes.

Roundworms

Two kinds of roundworm, Toxocara and Toxascaris, most commonly infest cats. They live in the intestinal canal and 'share' the food passing through. They do not suck blood. Their eggs are passed out in the cat's stools and pass to other cats either directly or after being ingested by insects, mice or rats, which are then, in turn, eaten by a cat. Immature, larval worms of microscopic size can penetrate the placenta to invade kittens in the womb and sometimes can also be found in a mother cat's milk. Once in a kitten's body, the larvae migrate, causing damage to major organs, such as the liver, heart and lungs, as they make their way to the intestines where they become adult. Consequently kittens can be much more seriously affected by these parasites than adult cats.

Other roundworms

Less commonly, cats may suffer from whipworms or threadworms. Although much smaller than

Internal parasites (Not to scale)

Whipworm: up to 5 cm (2 in)

Hookworm: up to 3 cm (1 in)

Dipylidium: (30–40 cm) Usually single sections are seen stuck around the cat's bottom

roundworms, they have a similar life cycle. The eggs and larvae require no intermediate host (see tapeworms, below) and can pass directly from cat to cat.

Threadworms live in the small intestine and cause inflammation and haemorrhage by burrowing into the bowel wall, whereas whipworms prefer life in the large intestine. The symptoms again are of weight and condition loss, diarrhoea and anaemia.

Hookworms

Common symptoms

- Anaemia
- Weakness
- Diarrhoea (frequently streaked with blood)

More commonly encountered in the USA than in Great Britain, these dangerous blood-sucking worms enter a cat either via the mouth or by burrowing through the skin. Once inside, they migrate to the small intestine. Like roundworms, they can cross the placental barrier to infect the unborn foetus.

Tapeworms

Common symptoms

- 'Rice grain' segments seen stuck to the cat's rear end

These parasites, with segmented bodies, visible to the naked eye and more dramatic looking, are not as dangerous as roundworms or flukes. They live in the cat's intestines and, again, 'share' the digesting food but do not suck the

PREVENTING AND TREATING PARASITE INFESTATIONS

◆ Regular worming against roundworms, tapeworms and hookworms, beginning with kittens at six weeks of age and continuing every two to three months for young cats and every three to four months for adults. Queens can safely be wormed before and during pregnancy.

◆ There is a wide variety of 'all-in-one' preparations which will eliminate most parasites (including, in some cases, ecto-parasites) available from your vet, pet shop or chemist. Some are in tablet form; others as injections or drops applied to the skin. Modern worming drugs are safe and effective and utterly free of the unpleasant side-effects that were once so common. Always seek professional advice before beginning your worming programme and follow instructions carefully.

◆ Other things you should do are: regular grooming and use of anti-parasitic powders, aerosols or drops to keep the cat free of larva-carrying fleas, disposal of litter by burning or placing in the dustbin, regular changing of bedding to discourage skin-burrowing worms, and stopping (if possible) your cat eating wild animals.

■ **Left:** *Guard the cat's eyes and nose with your hand when using an aerosol. Do not spray too close to the skin (it can cause mild frostbite if you do!).*

blood. When the segments pass through the cat's anus they appear like white grains of rice sticking to the hairs beneath the tail. These segments contain eggs which must be ingested by an intermediate host, such as a flea or a mouse. Inside the intermediate host's body, the eggs turn into larval form or crysticercus. Only when the intermediate host has been eaten by another cat will the larvae be able to change into another adult tapeworm. One tapeworm that is commonly found in the United States requires two intermediate hosts for its

successful passage to another cat: a tiny crustacean and then a fish.

Flukes

Common symptoms

- Digestive upsets
- Diarrhoea
- Jaundice
- Anaemia

These tiny, flat, leaf-like parasites are rare in Great Britain but are fairly common in Asia, mainland Europe and Canada. They lodge in the intestine, pancreas and the bile ducts of the liver and, as with tapeworms, require intermediate hosts (a small and a freshwater fish) for their life-cycle.

Other internal parasites

Occasionally protozoan parasites (Amoeba, Trichomonas, Coccidia, Giardia) will cause diarrhoea and other gastro-intestinal upsets in cats. The vet will identify their presence by laboratory tests on stool samples, and drug treatment is usually very effective.

Toxoplasmosis

One commoner and much more important parasite, which can affect humans and other animals as well as cats, is *Toxoplasma gondii*. Contracted usually by eating raw meat, this microscopic organism can attack the intestine and organs of the body. Signs are varied and can be subtle. It can be mistaken for Feline panleucopoenia.

Diarrhoea is the commonest symptom of both the acute and chronic forms of toxoplasmosis. The parasite spreads via the stools and sometimes can be picked up by humans. Although rare, this disease is a particular risk to pregnant women as it can be passed on to their unborn babies.

What you can do

Pregnant women should avoid close contact with cats. All cat food should be either a proprietary brand or, if prepared at home, well cooked. Change the cat litter daily (using rubber gloves if you are pregnant) and disinfect litter trays and their surrounds thoroughly. When gardening, use gloves to avoid contact with contaminated soil where cats have defaecated. Keep children's sand pits covered when not in use to prevent any contamination by cat faeces.

Veterinary treatment

Diagnosis and treatment of toxoplasmosis in cats can be undertaken by the vet. Diagnosis involves blood tests. Treatment may involve the prescription of sulphonamides, the antibiotic clindamycin or other drugs.

Problems of the nervous system

This section deals with disorders that may affect the brain or spinal cord of the cat, or the nerves leading from them.

Encephalitis

Common symptoms

■ Dullness
■ Fever
■ Weakness and staggering
■ Paralysis
■ Epilepsy ('fits')
■ Dilated pupils
■ Coma

Inflammation of the brain can be caused by viruses, bacteria or protozoan parasites via the blood or from nearby tissues, e.g. an infected middle or inner ear. Poisons can also be responsible.

What you can do

Consult your vet immediately. Keep the cat in quiet, stimulus-free surroundings. Diagnosis of the cause of encephalitis is not always easy. The vet may suggest X-rays and/or blood tests to aid the clinical examination of your pet. The treatment depends on cause and normally involves the administration of drugs, such as antibiotics and corticosteroids.

Meningitis

This inflammation of the membranes enclosing the brain and spinal cord can have causes similar to those of encephalitis. The vet may drain off a sample of cerebro-spinal fluid from the spine by means of a hypodermic syringe in order to confirm the diagnosis. Treatment is as for encephalitis.

'Mad cow disease' of cats

Common symptoms

■ Wobbliness
■ Circling
■ Loss of orientation

Note: Similar signs can be caused by far commoner ailments of the cat, such as middle ear disease, and, if caught early, can usually be treated successfully by the vet.

Scientifically given the rather unwieldy title of Feline Spongiform Encephalopathy (FSE), this 'new' and rather strange disease first appeared in Great Britain shortly after the first cases of BSE were recorded in cattle in 1986. Still rare in domestic cats, it has also been seen in exotic felines, such as pumas and ocelots. I personally saw my first case in a cheetah at the late Windsor Safari Park.

The cause of the invariably fatal disease is a bizarre speck of maverick protein called a prion. Although we still have much to learn about prions, BSE and the probably closely related Creuzfeldt Jacob Disease (CJD) of humans and FSE, it seems likely that somehow the malady has skipped from one species to another.

Epilepsy ('fits')

These attacks usually begin quite abruptly. The cat will fall over, frothing at the mouth, its body shuddering, legs paddling and apparently unconscious. Frequently, urine and faeces are voided. After a few minutes the 'fit' stops, again suddenly, the animal becomes calm and shortly regains its feet, looking as if nothing had happened. The whole phenomenon looks painful, but in fact the cat does not suffer any pain during an attack.

Resembling an 'electrical storm' in the circuitry of the brain tissue, epilepsy can be due to a variety of causes, some very obscure and almost impossible to pinpoint. Tumours, head injuries or parasites may be responsible.

What you can do
When a 'fit' occurs, immediately reduce all environmental stimuli. Darken the room, cut down any noise from radios, etc., and put a guard around any open fire. Do not touch or stroke the cat – you may only extend the length of time that the 'fit' lasts. Do not try, under any circumstances, to

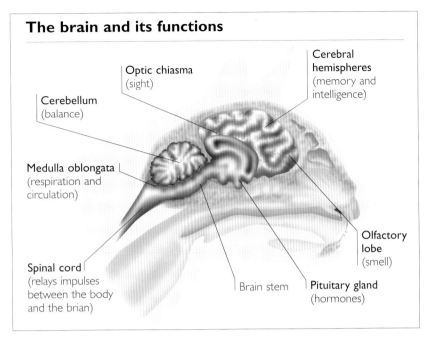

The brain and its functions

Optic chiasma (sight)

Cerebral hemispheres (memory and intelligence)

Cerebellum (balance)

Medulla oblongata (respiration and circulation)

Olfactory lobe (smell)

Spinal cord (relays impulses between the body and the brian)

Brain stem

Pituitary gland (hormones)

administer a 'reviver' of brandy or anything similar.

Seek veterinary attention if the epileptic attacks occur more than once a month, or if there are other signs in between the 'fits'. Epilepsy can be successfully controlled in most cases by the administration of a cheap drug by mouth.

Myelitis

Common symptoms

■ Total or partial paralysis of a limb or limbs
■ Pain and acute tenderness in the back

Inflammation of the spinal cord, myelitis is caused most frequently by bacterial infection spreading from nearby tissues. Most of my cases originated in deep cat bites to the back (a common site during fights between rival toms). Other possible causes are viruses (such as that of Rabies), parasites (such as Toxoplasma) and certain

poisons. Damage to the spinal cord can also be commonly found after accidents and produces signs similar to those of myelitis.

What you can do
Seek urgent veterinary attention. Handle the cat very gently and avoid flexing of the spine when taking it to the surgery or clinic.

Veterinary treatment
The vet may use X-rays, spinal tapping and blood tests in making a diagnosis. The treatment may involve drainage of the spinal canal, the use of antibacterial drugs to control secondary infections and analgesic and anti-inflammatory preparations.

Where paralysis is present, the outlook is very gloomy if distinct improvement of some degree is not made within one month. If such definite improvement does occur, full recovery may take several weeks or months longer.

Physiotherapy, as instructed by the vet, may aid recovery and will depend on you. Good nursing and

The nervous system

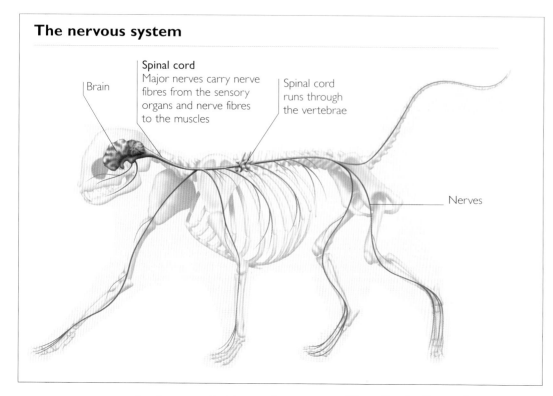

Brain

Spinal cord
Major nerves carry nerve fibres from the sensory organs and nerve fibres to the muscles

Spinal cord runs through the vertebrae

Nerves

hygiene are vital in paralytic cases where control is lost, temporarily, of the bowel or bladder.

Local nerve paralysis

Sometimes a nerve supplying one particular part of the body ceases to function and the area becomes paralysed. A limb or the tail is most commonly involved as a result of an accident. Unable to feel or control the appendage, the animal drags it about. Soon, friction with the ground results in abrasions and then ulceration.

If veterinary treatment, which is frequently difficult in such cases, does not result in distinct improvement beginning within one month of the actual injury, amputation should be considered. This operation, carried out under general anaesthetic, is not cruel. The animal is not crippled. Cats can get about just as well with only three legs or minus a tail.

Key-Gaskell syndrome (Feline dysautonomia)

Common symptoms

- Dilated pupils
- Protrusion of third eyelid
- Dullness
- Loss of appetite
- Dry mouth
- Vomiting and regurgitation
- Constipation
- Loss of bladder or bowel control

This puzzling disease, which has its origins in the nervous system, has only been recognised in recent years. The cause is unknown but may be perhaps due to toxic or infectious (virus) factors. It tends to involve only one cat out of a group and is no more likely to appear in vagrant alley-cats than in cosseted house-bound pedigrees. The prognosis in cases of the disease is poor with around seventy per cent of affected cats dying.

What you can do

Seek urgent veterinary attention. Good nursing is vital if a cat is to recover from this syndrome. Because swallowing is difficult due to paralytic dilation of the gullet (oesophagus), nutritional support must be provided by giving either dry food or little balls of moistened food which are easier for the cat to swallow. Liquid diets are risky and not advisable – regurgitation can lead to fluid getting into the lungs. A good idea is to feed the cat on the stairs, placing the food on a higher step than the animal. This helps passage of the food bolus down the gullet.

Veterinary treatment

The vet may investigate the animal by X-ray after administering barium in order to detect the dilated gullet. The treatment will be aimed at suppressing symptoms and usually includes drugs to strengthen the nervous system and the prescription of mineral oil as a laxative. Fluids to combat any dehydration may be administered by drip.

CONCUSSION

Accidental blows to the head may lead to concussion. Usually this is manifested by initial loss of consciousness followed by signs that may include paralysis, staggering or blindness. Luckily, in most cases, such signs are temporary, rarely lasting longer than five days. Treatment by the vet may include corticosteroid and/or diuretic drugs and vitamin injections.

Musculo-skeletal problems

Common symptoms

- Limping
- Swollen legs or feet

Cats develop diseases of the bones, joints and muscles far less frequently than their owners or pet dogs. Injuries are the main type of musculo-skeletal disorder and can range from minor sprains to broken bones and infections resulting from fighting wounds. The causes of limping or swollen limbs include accidental injury, wounds, fracture, bone infection, tumour (not very common) and arthritis, which is rare.

What you can do

Seek veterinary attention without delay. Do NOT give aspirin or human or dog-type analgesics before obtaining professional advice. Aspirin is toxic to cats.

Arthritis

This is treated by suitable anti-inflammatory drugs, including members of the cortisone family of chemicals. If you suspect that your cat may be affected, see your veterinary surgeon.

Fractures

See First Aid (page 138).

Infected bites

Apart from traumatic damage caused by accidents, a common reason for lameness or a painful, puffy, swollen foot or leg is an infected bite. During a fight, the needle-like teeth of an opponent can penetrate the skin and reach the bone which generally lies closer to the surface of the body than in dogs. Soft tissue infection and/or deeper involvement of the bone (periostitis or osteo-myelitis) quickly develop, but antibiotics control the situation. You may be asked to bathe the area several times a day with warm water containing a little table salt or Epsom salts.

The skeleton

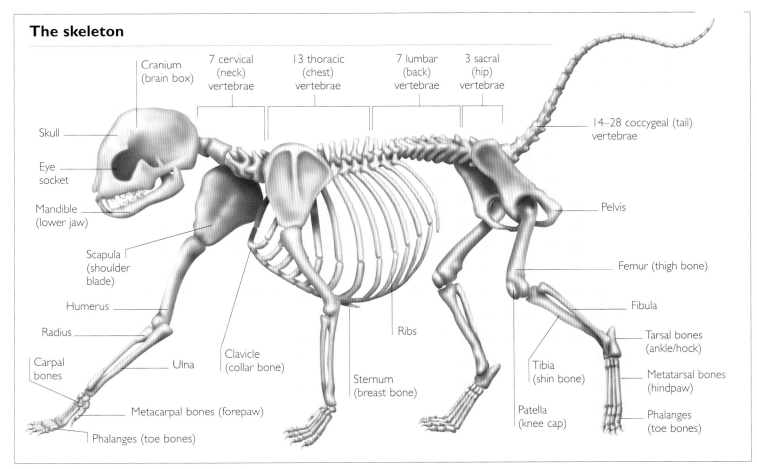

Cranium (brain box)

7 cervical (neck) vertebrae

13 thoracic (chest) vertebrae

7 lumbar (back) vertebrae

3 sacral (hip) vertebrae

14–28 coccygeal (tail) vertebrae

Skull

Eye socket

Mandible (lower jaw)

Scapula (shoulder blade)

Humerus

Radius

Carpal bones

Ulna

Clavicle (collar bone)

Metacarpal bones (forepaw)

Phalanges (toe bones)

Ribs

Sternum (breast bone)

Pelvis

Femur (thigh bone)

Fibula

Tarsal bones (ankle/hock)

Metatarsal bones (hindpaw)

Phalanges (toe bones)

Tibia (shin bone)

Patella (knee cap)

THE OLD CAT

Inevitably, time catches up with cats. Should your pet survive beyond seventeen years, he is doing very well indeed. Very few reach one score, although the longevity record at present stands at thirty-four years as achieved by a tabby queen from Devon. Certainly, cats tend to last longer than dogs, where the majority do not pass sixteen and the record is twenty-seven years.

Old cats need special attention and understanding. After years of faithful companionship, it would be a churlish owner who did not give a thought to coping with their feline geriatrics.

Physical changes

Venerable cats change physically. They frequently become rather thin. This may be accompanied by a change in appetite with an increased or decreased demand for food. They may become more thirsty. Certainly some of these are the results of a failing liver and kidneys – conditions that, in the absence of other symptoms, are difficult for the vet to treat.

The right diet

If your cat's appetite increases and he drinks more, give extra food at each meal or, better still, more meals daily. High-quality protein food (fish, meat and poultry) and a variety of vegetables and fruit are good for the pussy pensioner.

A teaspoonful of lard mixed with the usual food will provide valuable extra calories for an old, lean cat whose intestines no longer absorb nutriments very efficiently and who no longer carries an insulating layer of subcutaneous fat.

Give your elderly cat more water or milk to drink if he wants it; denying the increased thirst would be dangerous.

Fibre is important

Age may bring fussiness, and a concentration on high-quality protein may produce bowel sluggishness and constipation, as happens in some old people. Although oily fish, such as canned pilchards, help the free movement of the bowel, the basic fault generally is that in providing rich and tasty morsels to the old-timer, owners do not give enough bulky roughage, the stuff that gives healthy exercise to the intestines.

A little paraffin oil (liquid paraffin) mixed with the food can be used occasionally as a laxative (say, two teaspoonfuls once or twice weekly), but the regular daily use of paraffin oil is a bad practice, as it cuts down the absorption by the cat of the vitamins A, D and E in his diet.

If your cat will not take fibre in his food in the form of bran or some crumbled, toasted wholemeal bread, then the daily use of a bulk-acting granular laxative is the answer. An ideal one is made from certain plant seed husks. Laxatives of this type are usually well accepted by cats, especially when they are mixed with meals. Once swallowed, they absorb liquid, swell and make bulk that stimulates contraction of the lazy intestine-wall muscles.

Mouth and teeth

In old age, a special watch should be kept on the mouth. Regular servicing by the vet throughout a cat's life should have stopped the

■ **Right:** *The senior citizen cat requires a modified diet and a thoughtful owner.*

■ **Above:** *Old cats who have infirmities should be discouraged from any risky situations. This one-eyed veteran on a bird table in a tree lacks the stereoscopic vision useful for accurate jumping down.*

build-up of tartar. A fondness for soft snacks in a cat's dotage may encourage rapid tartar formation with secondary gum damage, inflammation in the tooth sockets and loosening teeth. Catch these things early. Septic areas in the mouth and bad teeth can only contribute to kidney and liver run-down. General anaesthesia for major mouth surgery (multiple extractions, etc.) can be risky in old age, so do not neglect cat mouth hygiene in youth and middle age. Deal with tartar when you first see it. Clean the old cat's teeth once or twice weekly with a soft toothbrush or some cotton-wool dipped in salt and water.

Regular grooming

There is a tendency for cats to lose personal pride when past their prime. They either forget or cannot be bothered to groom themselves. In longhaired cats, watch out for knots which may build up in the coat. Groom your cat daily with a comb and brush.

Leaking and bowel control

Some old warriors lose control of their bowels or water-works on the odd occasion. This may be forgetfulness, but it may be that nerve control of the various valves involved is weakening. If it becomes troublesome, let your vet check over the animal. Cystitis can be a cause of involuntary 'leaking' and should be treated. Lazy bowels may simply need more bulk content (see opposite).

Diseases of old age

Deafness or failing eyesight usually arise gradually, if at all, and the owner should be able to compensate intelligently for them. For example, remember that a deaf cat cannot hear if you are moving furniture, vacuuming the carpet or bringing a strange dog into the room – all potential dangers from the immediate

vicinity of which a cat with good hearing will quickly remove itself. With a blind cat, keep its food dishes in the same place and protect it from open fires and similar dangers; try to avoid rearranging familiar furniture.

Making life easier

Although there is no elixir of life available yet for man or his pets, there are some drugs that the veterinarian may prescribe that can counteract some of the symptoms of old age. One is sulphadiazine, which is claimed to combat senility, lack of lustre, greying of hair and general lack of interest and vitality where such signs are due solely to old age. Others are the range of anabolic hormones that encourage tissue building, oppose wastage of bodily protein, speed up the healing processes, and generally increase appetite, alertness and activity. The vet must decide whether your cat is suitable for treatment with any of these compounds. All elderly cats should be checked over by the vet two or three times a year.

WHEN THE TIME COMES...

In ancient Egypt, folk would shave off their eyebrows as a token of deepest grief if a cat died naturally. If you are fortunate, your cat will die in his sleep when his time comes. Alternatively you, as a humane, responsible owner, may have to make the tough decision for him. If a cat is in pain that is not likely to be quickly relieved, if the condition is a hopeless one where the animal is literally diseased and obviously unhappy, or if it is an embarrassment to itself (paralysed, continually fouling itself, etc.), then it is not only false sentimentality but also irresponsible ownership to deny the creature a dignified, peaceful end.

FIRST AID AND EMERGENCIES

Nine lives or not, when cats, as they frequently do, get into scrapes, prompt action by their owner can make all the difference between tragedy and a quick return to normal. When an accident occurs, get someone to phone the vet at once while you give practical first aid. Remember also that it is usually quicker for you to take the animal to the veterinary surgery or clinic than to wait for a veterinary surgeon to come to the house – speed of treatment is often a crucial factor in deciding the outcome.

Emergency action

1 The first thing to do is to get the cat out of danger. Move it gently by either slipping a sheet under it to form a hammock that you can carry. Anything that is warm and strong enough to take the cat's weight can be used as a hammock – a warm coat is ideal. Or, second best, pick the cat up by its scruff. Generally, it is wisest not to raise the head, other than very briefly, to avoid blood, saliva or vomit running down the throat and blocking the windpipe.

2 Do not give anything by mouth. Keep the cat warm in a quiet place until your vehicle is ready or the vet has arrived.

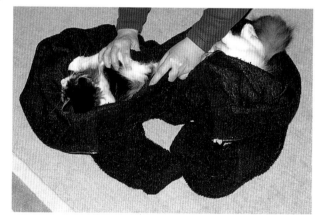

3 Place a hot water bottle, covered with a cloth to prevent scalding, next to the cat.

4 Now check the cat's pulse by feeling on the inside of the thigh before also checking the animal's breathing.

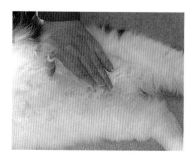

SCRUFFING

Only scruff an injured cat if it is aggressive and you are sure there is no damage to the head or neck. Take a firm hold of the loose skin around the back of the neck and lift the cat while supporting its rear with your other hand.

5 If the breathing is irregular or not apparent, open the mouth, pull the tongue forwards, wipe away any accumulation of blood or froth, loosen the collar if the cat is wearing one and, if you still can't see it breathing, give artificial respiration. There are several ways of doing this (see box on right).

6 If you cannot detect the pulse on the inner surface of the thigh, feel for the heartbeat by placing your fingertips on the chest wall just behind the front leg.

7 Should the heartbeat be non-apparent, very weak or very slow, then give heart massage by rubbing the area over the heart with both hands. Do not be heavy-handed; the cat's ribs can be crushed by the application of too much force.

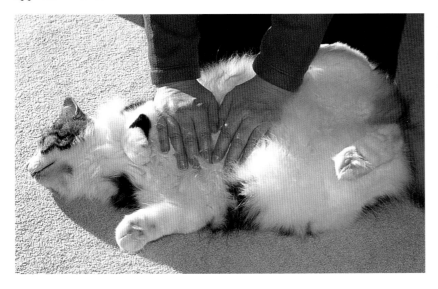

ARTIFICIAL RESPIRATION

1 Unless there is a possibility that the back or hind legs are injured, you can swing the cat, head down, by its hind legs like a pendulum. This will clear away any fluids, which may be blocking the cat's airway, by centrifugal force. Make sure that you grip the cat's feet firmly before starting.

2 If the chest is not damaged, in your opinion, you can place the palm of your hand on the cat's uppermost ribcage as it lies on its side. Press down at 5-second intervals, releasing the pressure straight away so that the chest expands, filling the lungs with air. Do not press too firmly – cats are far more delicately built than dogs or humans. Rough or too heavy artificial respiration can damage the lungs and heart.

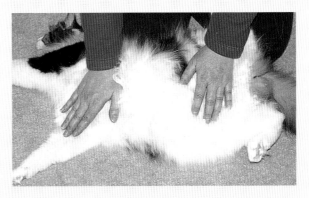

3 Another method, again with the cat lying horizontally, is 'mouth to nostrils'. Check first that the airway is not blocked by any fluid, mucus or blood, and then apply your lips to the cat's nostrils. Blow in some air steadily for three seconds, pause for two seconds and then repeat the procedure.

Burns

These can be caused by extreme cold or electric current, but the commonest ones result from hot liquids spilled on the cat. The cat's fur does afford a little protection, but nevertheless skin damage, the evidence of which may take some days to develop, is frequent.

1 Apply cold water or ice to the affected area immediately.

2 Then anoint the burn with a greasy ointment, such as petroleum jelly. Seek veterinary attention even though you may not be able to see any damage to the skin at that time.

Fractures

If, when first examining the cat, you detect a possible fracture of a limb, pad the site with gauze and then splint with two 1.5-cm (¹/2-in) wide pieces of thin wood either side and bind with a bandage. But don't waste too much time if you find this difficult – get the cat to the vet.

Heavy bleeding

If bleeding is heavy and persistent, this must be staunched.

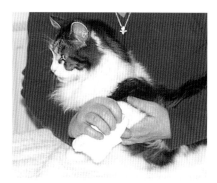

■ **Right:** *Steady, firm pressure on the bleeding point with anything you have to hand is the crucial thing in cases of haemorrhage.*

1 Apply firm pressure with the fingers, preferably over a pad of cotton wool, gauze or a screwed-up paper tissue. Maintain the pressure until veterinary attention has been obtained. There are pressure points that can be used to stem severe bleeding (see below).

2 Dressing a wound will apply pressure and keep the area clean but never wrap a bandage too tightly on a limb or tail. It is easy inadvertently to form a 'tourniquet', cutting off the blood supply to the extremities with sometimes disastrous consequences. Do not waste time applying antiseptics, creams or powders to any wound.

Shock

A shocked animal will feel colder than normal and have pallid gums and eye membranes. Don't give alcohol or other stimulants, but keep it warm and seek veterinary assistance without delay.

■ **Right:** *There are pressure points that can be used to stem severe bleeding.*

Head and neck
Press on the artery (in a groove in the lower part of the neck where it meets the shoulder)

Fore limb
Press firmly on the artery where it crosses the bone 2–5 cm (1–2 in) above the inside of the elbow joint

Tail
Press firmly on the artery where it runs along the underside of the tail

Hind limb
Press on the artery where it crosses over the bone on the inner thigh

Other emergencies

'Fits' or convulsions
(See page 131.)

Foreign body in the mouth
Hold the cat firmly to prevent him wriggling and then open the mouth, pushing down the lower jaw with a pencil. If necessary, use a torch to locate the object which can then be dislodged with fingers, a teaspoon handle or tweezers.

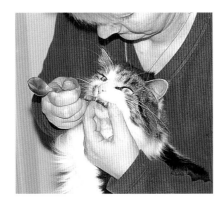

Foreign body in the nose
Leave it alone. Control any bleeding by application of cold compresses, and seek veterinary help.

Foreign body in the eye
You can try to wash it out by gently pouring warm (body-heat) water or human-type eye wash into the eye. If the object is not swept out, seek veterinary help.

POISONS

Internal contaminating
Cats sometimes ingest toxic substances, whether when out hunting they eat some rodent poison or by licking their coat after it has been contaminated with some noxious chemical. Licking puddles of anti-freeze tainted water in the garage is another not infrequent cause of poisoning.
Note: Various poisonous chemicals produce similar signs and symptoms – don't try to diagnose which one unless you have hard evidence and can take a sample of the causant chemical to the vet.

External contaminating
Where the cat's fur has been contaminated, wash the animal using human hair or baby shampoo, then rinse and dry thoroughly before contacting the vet for immediate examination.

Note: In all cases, there is no time to lose – professional help and advice are essential.

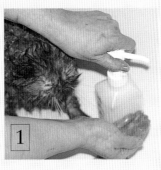

1 *Use plenty of human hair shampoo (baby shampoo for around the eyes and face).* 2 *Shampoo the affected area thoroughly.*
3 *Rinse all traces of shampoo off, then, if necessary, repeat the whole process again. Seek professional advice as soon as possible as your cat may have licked the affected areas.*

COMMON POISONS

Chemical	Source	Symptoms
Aspirin	Tablets	Vomiting, liver damage
Lead	Paints (particularly old flaking woodwork)	Nervous signs, paralysis
Ethylene glycol (anti-freeze)	Car radiator drips	Convulsions, wobbliness, depression, coma
Phenols, Cresols, Turpentine, Tar products	Disinfectants (usually ones that turn white when added to water), tar, wood preservatives	Burnt mouth, characteristic smell, vomiting, convulsions, coma
Warfarin	Rodent poisons	Stiffness, haemorrhages, diarrhoea
Arsenic	Horticultural sprays, rodent poisons	Vomiting, diarrhoea, paralysis
Phosphorus, Thallium	Rodent poisons	Vomiting, diarrhoea
Metaldehyde	Slug killer	Incoordination, salivation, rapid breathing, convulsions, coma

Advanced cat care

Many devoted cat lovers proceed to more advanced aspects of cat care, including showing and breeding. Showing your cat brings its own rewards, and devotees claim that there is nothing more exciting than the thrill of exhibiting their cats and joining the ever-growing ranks of the Cat Fancy. Whether you have an elegant pedigree cat or a much-loved non-pedigree, you can still show him and compete for rosettes and trophies. You may even think about breeding from your cat, but breeding brings its own responsibilities and must only be undertaken in a considered manner. There are so many stray and unwanted cats in the world that you must breed responsibly and find good homes for all the kittens.

Chapter Eight

SHOWING YOUR CAT

All over the country, almost every weekend of the year, people from all walks of life rise with the lark and often travel great distances to indulge in their passion for cat showing. For many cat lovers (known as 'cat fanciers'), there is nothing to beat the excitement of exhibiting their beautiful cats and meeting and socializing with like-minded people. Elegant Orientals, luxurious longhairs and even pampered non-pedigrees, all have a place in today's modern cat show. They all compete for rosettes, trophies, occasionally prize money and, of course, the ultimate accolade – Best in Show!

If you think that you would like to join the ever increasing ranks of the Cat Fancy, then you would be well advised to visit one or two shows, if possible with a friend who is exhibiting, as this will give you a good insight into show life. The day of the cat show can be very long and tiring, with exhibitors arriving as early as 7.30 a.m. and not leaving until 5.00 p.m. With travelling time added to this, you can appreciate that cat fanciers are a dedicated bunch of people.

What makes a show cat?

When you buy a pedigree kitten, it does not automatically mean that he or she will be destined for great things on the show bench. Each breed has its own Standard of Points – the ideal description of a perfect specimen of its breed.

The breeder will have assessed the litter of kittens and decided whether they are pet, breeding or show quality, and will not want kittens sold as pets to be shown. Pet kittens will undoubtedly make superb family companions, but

■ **Left:** *Pet cats have their own classes at cat shows where they can compete for just as many prizes as their pedigree cousins.*

they will have one or more faults that will preclude them from showing or breeding. Breeding-quality kittens will probably be good examples of the breed, but they may have a minor fault, such as slightly irregular markings, which will not necessarily pass on to their offspring but will most certainly stop them gaining top show awards.

Your chosen breed of cat is, of course, very much a matter of personal taste, but it may be advisable to take into account your lifestyle, and that of your family, before making your final decision. Longhaired cats, such as Persians and Chinchillas, will require daily grooming and might trigger allergies in someone who, for example, is asthmatic. Semi-longhaired cats, such as Birmans and Maine Coons, also require regular grooming, although their coats do not tend to matt quite so easily as their longhaired cousins. Some of the Oriental breeds, such as the Siamese, can demand a lot of attention and therefore may not suit families who spend much of the day away from home.

So you can see that it is essential to research your chosen breed of cat well, for whatever show cat you buy, he or she could be part of your family for fifteen years or more

ENTERING A SHOW

Above: *The UK Supreme Cat Show where once a year Champions/Grand Champions, Premiers/ Grand Premiers and Open Class winners from the GCCF Championship shows gather to compete for the title, Supreme Cat of the Year. It is the only show where cats are housed in lavishly decorated pens – a wonderful sight to behold.*

All shows throughout the UK are organised by individual cat clubs, which all come under the control of a central body called The Governing Council of the Cat Fancy (GCCF). Area cat clubs will accept entries from all breeds of cats, even if they reside in a different part of the country; there are other clubs that are specific breed clubs, and these will only accept entries from the breed of cat their club represents. There are also clubs that represent particular sections of the Cat Fancy, such as the Long Haired and Semi Long Haired Cat Club and the Short Haired Cat Society. These clubs will accept entries from any breed of cat that comes within the section that they represent. At most shows you will also find a Household Pet section where many beautiful non-pedigree cats of all colours, ages, sizes and coat types, compete for rosettes and trophies and, of course, the prestigious title – Best in Show Household Pet.

For a small fee, the GCCF will supply you with a list of all the UK shows that will take place throughout the current show year. The list details the date and venue of each show together with, most importantly, the name and address of the Show Manager.

Once you have selected the show that you wish to enter, you will need to write to the Show Manager, enclosing a stamped addressed envelope, to request a schedule and entry form. Requests for schedules need to be made approximately three months in advance of the show date, and it is always a good idea to apply to a number of shows at the same time and tick these off on your list. Plan your show diary well; the GCCF rules say that you may not enter your cats in shows more frequently than once a fortnight!

The show schedule

When your first show schedule comes through the letter box, find a quiet moment in the day and make yourself a cup of coffee. Put your feet up and read through it thoroughly before filling in the entry form. The numerous pages of rules and instructions can seem quite daunting to the first-time exhibitor, but by following the show rules and regulations carefully and checking anything you are not sure of with either the Show Manager or the GCCF, entering your first show should be relatively trouble free.

At all the shows there are three types of classes for all cats, whether they are pedigree or non-pedigree, and each cat, or kitten, must enter a minimum of four classes. All exhibits must enter the 'open' class appropriate to their breed; for example, a three-year-old neutered Ragdoll female will only compete against others of her like. Adults, kittens and neuters will all have their own classes, and these will be split into separate male and female classes. 'Miscellaneous', or Side, Classes allow cats to compete against other breeds in their section in a variety of different ways. If you have a Somali kitten that has never been shown before, it may enter the Debutante Kitten class where it could be competing against Birmans, Turkish Vans,

Norwegian Forest Cats and indeed any other breeds that fall into the Semi Longhair Section.

All the cat clubs will offer their own 'Club' classes at their shows, which are only open to fully paid up members of the club. At some shows there will be 'Club' classes which are sponsored by individual clubs, and you may enter these if you happen to be a member of that particular club.

Completing the entry form

Once you have selected the classes in which you wish to enter your cat, then fill out the entry form carefully and clearly. You will need to fill in the full pedigree name of your cat and its mother (dam) and father (sire), and it is important that this information should be copied precisely from the GCCF pedigree registration certificate. It is essential that this information is completed correctly as any mistakes could lead to your cat's disqualification.

Many exhibitors will include a stamped addressed postcard with their entry form, detailing the classes that they have entered; the Show Manager will sign this and return it to you in due course as a confirmation of your cat's entry into the show.

Show equipment

Cats that are shown at shows held under the rules of the GCCF are judged in complete anonymity, and all judges are instructed to pass any pen that may bear any distinguishing features. Therefore it is important to purchase the correct show equipment.

SHOW CHECKLIST

◆ White litter tray
◆ White blanket
◆ White water bowl
◆ White food bowl
◆ Bottle of drinking water
◆ Pet-safe disinfectant and cloths
◆ Cat litter
◆ Litter scoop and plastic bag
◆ Cat food – dry biscuits or wet food is acceptable, but don't forget the can opener!
◆ Grooming tools
◆ Narrow white ribbon or thin white elastic
◆ Vaccination certificate
◆ Show schedule and confirmation of entry card
◆ A secure cat carrier, complete with some cosy bedding – NEVER carry your cat into a show or take it in on a harness or lead!

Each cat is housed within an identical pen to its neighbour, and it should be provided with a plain white blanket, white litter tray, white food dish and a white water bowl. If you have any problems obtaining any of these items from your local pet shop, you will be able to buy them from one of the many trade stands at the show.

In addition, you will need to take a variety of things that are essential for your cat's comfort. Many cat fanciers choose to have a show bag and checklist for this purpose. The items listed (below left) are the essential things that all cats, longhaired or shorthaired, pedigrees or non-pedigrees, need. Experience and the individual cat's requirements, may increase the size of your basic kit as time goes by. Once you are sure that you have all the right equipment, you can sit back and relax until a week or so before the show when your cat's show preparation will begin in earnest.

■ **Left:** *A judge and her steward move along the row of exhibits. They judge each cat or kitten in its pen.*

SHOW PREPARATION

You do not have any control over your cat's physical appearance; that is down to genes and Mother Nature. To turn your pet into a real 'show stopper' he must undergo some form of show preparation. Regardless of whether your cat is a pedigree or not, don't let him down by skimping on this preparation. Take the time and effort to groom him to perfection and watch him turn heads on the show bench.

General health

It is unkind to subject a sick cat to the stress of travelling and showing, and equally unfair to the exhibits penned nearby, who would almost certainly be at risk of infection. It is essential that your cat is in the peak of good health when he is shown. Every cat, pedigree or non-pedigree, must be vaccinated against cat 'flu and enteritis, and the final dose or booster should be given by your vet not less than seven days before the show. It is a wise owner who administers flea and worm preventatives on a regular basis, as all cats must have coats that are free from parasites, such as fleas and ticks.

Grooming a shorthaired cat

Shorthaired cats seldom, if ever, need bathing, and, indeed, over-grooming may strip out some of their delicate coat. Use a fine-toothed metal comb to remove any dust and loose hair, followed by gentle grooming with a soft natural bristle brush following the lie of the coat. To bring out the natural shine, it is best to polish it with a chamois leather or a piece of silk. Some exhibitors swear by 'hand grooming' – with a clean hand, gently stroke the cat along the lie of the coat.

Seek advice from a seasoned exhibitor, as each breed will have special coat requirements. For example, the Russian Blue should have a plush, upstanding coat and a bran 'bath' will help this. Warm the bran in the oven on a baking sheet, or in a saucepan over a low heat, and then gently rub it into the coat, avoiding the ears and eyes. Brush the coat the wrong way to remove every last trace of bran.

Claws, eyes and ears

Thoughtful owners will clip the ends off their cats' claws the night before the show to avoid the cat accidentally scratching the judge or steward. Do not use scissors or human nail clippers as these will flatten the claw, making it split and crack – use specially shaped claw clippers. Remove any staining from the eyes and gently clean just the visible parts of the ears – never poke anything into them.

SHOW TIPS

Once you have prepared your cat for a show, do not let it go outside – a roll on your driveway in a large patch of oil, or a dip in your neighbour's fish pond will be sure to ruin all your hard work. Similarly, do not feed your cat 'messy' food – a dish of sardines could quite easily stain the beautiful pale coat of a Turkish Van or Chinchilla. If you are unsure of how well your cat travels, it is perhaps wise not to feed it on the morning of the show – a cat who has been travel sick will not make a good exhibit!

Grooming a longhaired or semi-longhaired cat

The coat on these cats should look full and impressive, with every hair separate and standing away from the body, particularly around the head and neck – this fur is referred to as the 'ruff'. To achieve this, an adult cat should be bathed approximately five to seven days prior to the show, whilst kittens can be left until one or two days before the big day.

Bathing your cat

Bathing is not a natural procedure for any cat, so make the experience as stress-free as possible – for both of you! Ensure that the room where you bathe him is warm and draught-free and that you have all the equipment on hand to dry the coat quickly (see the panel).

Stand your cat in a wash-hand basin or bath, which contains about 5 cm (2 in) of lukewarm water. If your cat seems rather nervous, put a towel or a rubber mat under his feet, to help him grip and feel a little more secure. Thoroughly wet the entire coat, taking great care to avoid the head and ears.

Gently massage shampoo all over the body, legs and tail. Avoid the head, and don't forget the feet and the area under the tail. Rinse thoroughly with plenty of warm water until it runs clear from the coat. Wrap the cat in a large, preferably warm, towel. You will need another towel almost immediately as the first one will quickly become sodden. Blow-dry the coat with an ordinary hair dryer on a cool setting. Brush in the opposite direction to the lie of the coat to ensure that every hair is separate, thereby giving the coat a wonderfully full look.

WHAT YOU WILL NEED

◆ Two or three large bath towels
◆ Cat or kitten shampoo
◆ Hand-held hairdryer
◆ Brush and comb.

1 *Use a shower rose with lukewarm water to wet the coat thoroughly.*

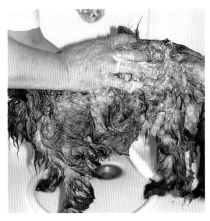

2 *Avoiding the ears and eyes, massage the shampoo into the body.*

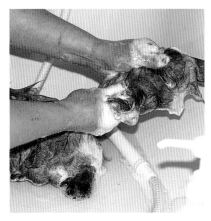

3 *Wet the tail and the area below it, and gently massage in the shampoo.*

4 *Rinse thoroughly with lukewarm water to remove all the shampoo.*

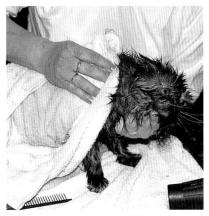

5 *Wrap in a large, warm towel and gently towel-dry the cat.*

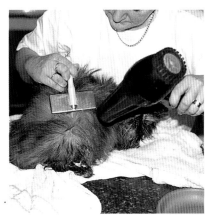

6 *Blow dry, brushing in the opposite direction to the 'lie' for a full look.*

GROOMING

Some exhibitors use grooming powder to get rid of any final traces of grease and help lift the coat. However, no traces of powder should remain or the cat may face disqualification!

THE SHOW DAY

When you arrive at the show venue, you will be greeted by a member of the Show Management Team, who will hand you an envelope containing your cat's prize card, a catalogue voucher, an exhibitor's pass and a tally with your exhibit number marked. You will need all of them throughout the day. Next, you will join the queue of people waiting to take their cats through the vetting-in process.

Vetting-in

All cats entering the show must be examined by a veterinary surgeon for any signs of ill health, and you should be prepared at this point to show your cat's vaccination certificate. The vet will check the eyes, ears, mouth and coat of each cat, and if for some reason your cat shows any signs of illness or parasites, such as fleas, you will not be allowed to take part in the show. Your cat will either be placed in an isolation pen for the day, well away from the main show area, or you may go straight home but, unfortunately, your entry fee will be forfeit, so make sure your cat is in optimum health.

Penning your cat

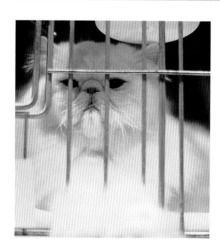

Right: *Groomed, penned, ready and waiting, this lovely Persian is waiting for the first rosette to appear.*

Once inside the show hall, you will need to find your cat's pen; this will bear the number that is on your show envelope and tally. Before you place your cat in the pen, you will need to thoroughly clean it, using pet-safe disinfectant. Arrange the white blanket, litter tray and water dish in the pen before you put your cat in. Give him a final grooming, but do not use any spray or powder in the show hall, as this is strictly against the rules. Place the tally around your cat's neck, using narrow white ribbon or thin white elastic, and check that it is not too tight. You may feed your cat at this point if you wish, but the food dish must be removed before the judging starts. Finally, place your show bag and cat carrier under the pen, and check that you have left nothing that could be considered a distinguishing feature inside or on top of the pen.

Judging

This usually begins at 10 a.m. and the exhibitors are not allowed to remain in the show hall whilst the main Open Class judging takes place. The judge and his or her steward will move around the hall, judging each exhibit by its pen. The judge will write an assessment of each cat in the judging book and then fill in an award slip for each class. The award slip is then displayed on the award board so that exhibitors may mark the class results in their show catalogue.

Definition of awards

The adult male and adult female class winners may have been given a 'CC', which means that they will have been awarded a 'Challenge Certificate'. A cat that has gained three 'CCs', at three shows, awarded by three different judges, will gain the title of 'Champion'. At some shows, judges will award a 'Best of Breed' certificate by choosing the best cat from their male and female 'CC' winners.

Cats that have been neutered do

not compete with entire adults, but the winner of the male and the female neuter class are awarded a 'PC' or 'Premier Certificate'. Three 'PCs' will earn the cat the title of 'Premier'. Kittens do not gain titles, but they will compete for first placing with others of their own sex. As with the neuter and adult class winners, the male and female kitten class winners will then compete against each other for 'Best of Breed'.

Cats that have gained the title of 'Champion' or 'Premier' can then compete for the title of 'Grand Champion' or 'Grand Premier' by winning three 'Grand' certificates at three shows, and which are awarded by three different judges.

If your cat is entered in the Non-Pedigree Section, there will not be a standard of points for the judge to apply to each Open class. Each exhibit will be assessed on its own merits, and the judge will be looking at the general condition of the cat as well as its grooming and general show preparation. He or she will

be looking for any particularly attractive features that will make it stand out from other cats, and, most importantly, assessing it on its temperament whilst it is being handled by the judge.

At around 1 p.m., exhibitors and the general public will be allowed into the show hall, and you may return to your pen and feed your cat. Afterwards, during the afternoon, Miscellaneous Class judging takes place, and, hopefully, as more awards cards are placed on your cat's pen, you will need to claim your rosettes, and possibly even trophies, from the awards table.

Show etiquette

Even though you are back in the show hall, judging will still be taking place. It is most important that you do not make yourself known to the judge as this action can result in your cat being disqualified. If you see a judge and steward making their way towards your cat, you should move well

■ Left: *A judge and steward carefully examine a kitten to see how closely it conforms to the breed standard.*

away and not make any attempt to speak to the judge while he or she is still working. Most judges are quite happy to speak with the exhibitors once they have finished their work and will be pleased to give their assessment on your cat. Always remember to congratulate the winner of your cat's class – next time it could be you. Most of all, remember – win or lose, you take the best cat home!

■ Left: *The National Cat Show at Olympia is the oldest and largest cat club show in Britain. Visitors and judges from all over the world attend this popular annual event.*

Chapter Nine

BREEDING

A charming litter of kittens is enough to melt the heart of any cat lover, and it may even tempt you to enter the world of cat breeding yourself. But beware; in spite of the very high cost of buying one of these pedigree cats, you can be certain that the breeder has not made a fortune, and certainly not a living, from cat breeding alone.

You may have a very pretty non-pedigree female who, in all probability, will make an excellent mother, but it is quite simply untrue to say that all females should have a litter of kittens before being spayed (neutered). Sadly, too many rescue centres and foster homes throughout the country are full of cats and kittens

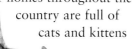
Above: *Every year, far too many unwanted kittens are abandoned or left at rescue centres.*

from people who let their cat have 'just one litter'. It is irresponsible to do this, and unless you can breed responsibly and can find good homes for all the kittens, you should have your cat spayed.

Cat breeding is a very costly and time-consuming hobby, and it is fraught with many responsibilities and duties. If you feel that breeding is the next step in your hobby of cat

Above: *Charming and inquisitive, these Persian kittens are a responsibility.*

ownership, then do some research first. Join a relevant breed club, visit a few cat shows and meet up with some breeders. Finally, have a chat with your vet about some of the problems that can occur during pregnancy and kittening, and also the possible costs involved!

Buying a cat for breeding

If you are a novice cat breeder, do not fall into the trap of buying a male to keep one female company. Because of their natural instinct to mark out their territory by urine 'spraying', adult males, known as 'stud' cats, have to live in outdoor runs. They will need a lot of your attention and affection, as well as a steady stream of visiting female cats, called 'queens', so that they do not become frustrated, nervous

or even spiteful. Some breeds of cat can be particularly vocal, so a frustrated, noisy stud cat at the end of your garden could even cause you to fall out with your next-door neighbours.

Once you have decided which breed of cat you would like to own, you can then embark on the search for a breeding queen. Many breed clubs organise their own Kitten Register where prospective

new owners will be given details of breeders in their area who have kittens for sale. Details of all the breed clubs can be obtained from the Governing Council of the Cat Fancy (GCCF), or from specialist cat journals and magazines which can be purchased from most large newsagents and retail outlets.

You should not attempt to buy a pet-quality kitten, usually at a cheaper price, from which to breed. These kittens will make wonderful pets, but they will probably have at least one fault that will make them unsuitable for breeding. Most breeders will safeguard their kittens, and their

reputation, by placing them on the 'non-active register' when they register their pedigree with the GCCF. Reputable stud owners will refuse to accept a 'non-active' cat, and the GCCF will not register her kittens so you will not be able to sell them as 'pedigree' cats!

The calling queen

A female cat's season or heat is known as a 'call', and once your cat reaches sexual maturity you will understand why! The age at which a queen will first come into call can vary greatly, with some foreign breeds, such as the Siamese, calling as early as six months of age, whereas some of their longhaired cousins do not call until they are ten or twelve months old. It is usually best to allow your female to have one or two full calls before sending her to stud for the first time.

■ **Right:** *Excessive friendliness is one of the first signs of your queen coming into 'call'.*

The early signs

The first signs of calling will be excessive friendliness: rubbing around anyone and anything at every available opportunity and then rolling furiously on her back – even the family dog is likely to come in for some of this show of

affection! The observant cat owner will also notice that their pet is paying far more attention to her grooming routine than is usual and perhaps less attention to her food bowl. Over the next day or two, your queen will crouch down very low on her front legs when she is touched or stroked; she will flick her tail to one side and will paddle furiously with her back legs. Then you will hear that unmistakable sound that only a queen in season can make, and you will know why it is called a 'call'.

Preparations for mating

It is wise to ring the stud owner at the beginning of your cat's call to make the arrangements for taking her to be mated. Do not forget to make sure that all her vaccinations are up to date – she

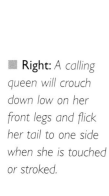

■ **Right:** *A calling queen will crouch down low on her front legs and flick her tail to one side when she is touched or stroked.*

will need to be vaccinated against feline infectious enteritis and cat 'flu, and she should also be free from feline leukaemia. Worming and flea treatments should also be carried out prior to mating; you must not give your cat these treatments during her pregnancy without first seeking veterinary advice. You will probably be asked to bring your cat on the second or third day of her call, and she will usually stay for two or three days. Please remember to clip her claws before you go; no one appreciates having the ear of their prize stud cat torn during the throes of passion!

Returning from stud

When your queen returns from stud, it is quite likely that she will still be in call. Do not worry, this is quite normal and does not mean that she has not conceived. In fact, you should keep a very close watch on her during this early period and make sure that she does not escape and then rendezvous with the local feline Romeo; cats can give birth to a

Left: *A stud will sniff to see if the queen is ready to mate and whether his advances will be welcomed.*

litter of kittens which has been sired by more than one male!

At around twenty-one days from the first day of mating, you should be able to tell if she is in kitten. Experienced breeders will ask you if she has 'pinked up. This simply means that her nipples appear to be swollen and will have a deep pink glow. Often the surrounding hair will recede slightly.

The average pregnancy lasts for sixty-five days, but it is important not to panic if your female goes into labour before or after this date, as anything from sixty-three to seventy days is often quoted as being 'normal'.

Pregnancy

A normal, healthy queen does not need any special treatment – she is quite capable of racing around the house and playing with all her favourite toys – and she should be allowed to carry on a normal life. However, it is a good idea to keep stress to a minimum. Bringing a new puppy or a kitten into your home or hosting a noisy party had better be left until after the kittens are born and leave for their new homes. You should ensure that

your queen receives a high-quality diet, and make sure that she always has access to fresh, clean drinking water. As her pregnancy progresses, you should offer her smaller, more frequent meals.

◆ **Early pregnancy:** Four to five weeks into her pregnancy, your queen will begin to look like an expectant mother; her abdomen will start to become swollen and her appetite will increase.

◆ **Middle pregnancy:** By week

seven of the queen's pregnancy, you may be able to see the kittens moving and, by placing your hand gently on her tummy, you should be able to feel their movement – never poke or prod!

◆ **Late pregnancy:** Eight weeks into her pregnancy, the queen's shape will have changed quite considerably: her abdomen will appear very pear-shaped and she will have quite a swagger when she walks. Because of her size and

Right: *With her swollen abdomen, it should be obvious, even to the novice, that this queen is pregnant. Although she is enjoying a stroll in the sunshine, she should not be allowed to wander too far.*

Above: *This home-made wooden kittening box is lined with a fleece-type sheet to keep the kittens warm.*

shape, she may have trouble with her grooming routine. You can help by gently washing her anal area with cotton wool moistened with warm water, and gently brushing her coat to keep it free from any dirt and tangles.

The maternity ward

About a week before your queen is due to give birth, she will begin to search for a suitable place to deliver her kittens. Wardrobes, piles of old newspapers under a desk or even the airing cupboard will seem very inviting to your mother-to-be, but they are hardly suitable places to raise a family. Providing her with a clean box in a quiet secluded part of the house is the answer. Choose a place that is warm – about 22°C (72°F) is ideal – and draught-free. It must be well out of the way of busy household activities.

The kittening box

The ideal kittening box should have an entry hole at the front, which should not be too close to the ground, as very young kittens may fall out. It should have a removable lid for access to your queen should she get into difficulties during her delivery. If you decide to use an ordinary cardboard box, this should be scrupulously clean and

also very strong – the birth process can be a very wet, messy business.

Line the box with layers of warm, clean, absorbent material, such as flannelette sheeting or towels which can be removed as they become soiled. You may even wish to add several layers of newspapers, as many queens seem to enjoy ripping and shredding these to make a real 'nest'. However, this can become very messy as the kittens are born, so you will need to remove the pieces as soon as they start to get soggy.

KITTENING EQUIPMENT

There are a few essential items that you should have on hand just in case your queen needs some assistance. They are as follows:
◆ Electric heater pad – approximately half the size of your kittening box
◆ Towelling squares – clean face flannels are ideal
◆ Blunt-ended scissors – surgical scissors are available from most chemists
◆ Dilute disinfectant – pet-safe products only, obtainable from your vet or pet shop
◆ Absorbent kitchen paper
◆ Waste bag – for disposal of soiled equipment.

The birth

The vast majority of cats give birth to their kittens without any problem or human assistance. The owner who fusses or interferes at every stage can cause the mother to become stressed, and she may move her kittens to somewhere quite unsuitable or, worse still, she may abandon them altogether. Be on hand to watch for problems and reassure your new mother, but at all times remain calm.

First stage of labour

This begins when small uterine contractions move the first kitten towards the cervix. The queen's breathing will quicken and small contractions may be seen as slight ripples along her side. Some females appear to enjoy this first stage and will purr loudly, whilst others will appear restless and may pace and even growl. She may go repeatedly in and out of her litter tray and she may lose all interest in food, although many females will eat just moments before giving birth. This first stage may take an hour, or it may last for up to twenty-four hours; do not panic – like humans, no two births are the same.

Second stage of labour

This begins when the kittens' journey towards the birth canal stimulates the mother to start 'bearing down' or pushing. The first contractions may be up to an hour apart, but they will increase gradually in their frequency until just before the birth when they may be only a few seconds apart.

You will soon see a fluid-filled 'bubble'; this is the sac containing your first kitten!

As the kitten is born, the queen will break the sac, which will allow the kitten to take its first breath. Her licking and nibbling can appear quite rough, but this will help to stimulate the kitten's breathing and will remove all traces of the birth fluids and sac.

Kittens are usually born head first, but occasionally the tail and hind legs appear first, and more rarely there may be a breech birth. A breech kitten is born tail first, with one or both of its hind legs tucked up under its body. Breech birth kittens usually take slightly longer to be born and the process will require more effort from the queen, but they are usually managed without any human assistance.

Third stage of labour

This third stage is the delivery of the placenta. Each kitten has its own placenta and when this is delivered, the queen will bite through the cord approximately 3 cm (1 inch) away from the kitten's body. She will usually proceed to eat the placenta, although if she has a large litter she may not eat every one.

Human assistance
Very occasionally it may be necessary for you to act as a 'midwife'. Your queen may be unsure of what to do, or she may have two kittens born in quick succession – so speed is of the essence. With clean, disinfected hands, carefully break the sac and then, with a clean cloth, clear away any fluids from around the

■ **Left:** *Newborn kittens will root instinctively for a nipple, and the queen will settle down to feed and care for her family.*

kitten's mouth and nose. You will then need to cut or tear the cord, first pinching it firmly between your thumb and forefinger. The kitten must then be rubbed dry with a towelling cloth, which will help to stimulate its breathing. If the kitten does not appear to be breathing, hold it in the palm of your hand with your first two fingers supporting its head and neck, and then gently swing it in a downward arc. This should serve to release any fluid that may be trapped in its lungs.

Important: If your queen appears to have been pushing for quite some time without any effect, or a kitten seems to be stuck, do not delay – you must call your veterinary surgeon immediately.

After the birth

Once all the kittens have been born and the queen has washed them thoroughly, they should all

begin instinctively to root for a nipple and feed for the first time. You should remove any heavily soiled items and place a heater pad under the bedding at one end of the box, without disturbing the new family too much. When the queen leaves the nest, the kittens will move towards the heat. Scent

■ **Above:** *This kitten is only a few days old, and without stimulation from its mother, it cannot urinate or defecate.*

seems to play an important part in the mother/kitten bonding process, so it is very important to leave some of the birthing sheets in place.

The growing kittens

■ Right: *With its eyes still firmly shut, this kitten uses its heightened sense of smell and touch to locate its mother's nipples.*

One to three weeks

During the first three weeks of life, the kittens are still totally dependent on their mother. She will feed them and wash them, and keep them warm and safe. However, by handling them on a daily basis, you will be able to check their progress and, most importantly, the kittens will become accustomed to humans. Healthy kittens should gain weight rapidly, usually doubling their birth weight by the end of the first week; during this time their cords will have dried up and

Above: *Handling the kittens every day will help them to get used to humans. Do this inside the nest box so as not to distress the mother.*

Left: *Totally dependent on its mother, this tiny kitten cuddles up to her for warmth as well as food.*

dropped off. Most kittens will begin to open their eyes at around five to ten days, and they should be fully open a few days later.

Three to six weeks

At three weeks of age, kittens will begin to realise that there is life outside their box, and they will take their first few wobbly steps away from the nest. They are still very small and vulnerable, so it is advisable to confine them to the safety of one room by erecting a barrier across the doorway; their mum will appreciate this, too. She will know they are safe while she takes a well-earned break!

Weaning normally takes place at around three to four weeks when the kittens are coming out of their box with confidence. You should take care not to overload a kitten's delicate digestive system; offer only one small meal a day to begin with, building up gradually to four meals daily by the age of six weeks. There are as many different ideas on 'first foods' as there are breeds of cat – canned baby food, milky baby rice or cereal food, or sardines are some of the more popular choices.

Six to nine weeks

At about six to seven weeks, the barrier across the doorway will have been conquered and the kittens will be ready to explore the rest of the house. You must keep a very close watch from now on as many dangers await them – guard open fires, keep electric wires and cables well hidden, and never ever leave washing machine or tumble dryer doors open. The kittens' diet should now include a proprietary brand of kitten food to replace some of their milky or baby food meals, but they will still be feeding from

LITTER TRAYS AND TOYS

Once the kittens are eating, your mother cat will be most reluctant to clean up after her brood and who can blame her! The kittens should now be provided with a small, shallow litter tray. If you place this close to their mother's large tray, you will usually find that curiosity and natural instinct will soon have all the kittens using their tray. Any kittens who have not got the message can be popped onto the tray if they look as though they are about to squat somewhere unsuitable.

With the kittens growing in confidence and ability, you should now provide a variety of safe toys. Avoid toys with glued-on eyes or lengths of wool, which could break off and might be swallowed. Probably the best fun to be had is with a table tennis ball or a cotton reel.

Left: *Providing good-quality, safe toys will ensure your kittens get plenty of exercise and hours of amusement.*

■ **Right:** *Through play, kittens learn the skills that will equip them for adult life.*

their mother from time to time – if she lets them. Your kittens should be wormed at around six to eight weeks of age, and it is wise to talk with your veterinary surgeon about the best regime to follow.

It should be possible to assess the potential of pedigree kittens at around six to eight weeks, although this may vary according to the breed, and it will be necessary to register them with the GCCF. If you are a novice breeder, you would be well advised to seek the opinion of the stud owner or another experienced breeder.

Nine to twelve weeks

■ **Below:** *At about nine weeks and at twelve weeks of age, kittens should be vaccinated to help protect them against 'flu and enteritis.*

At nine weeks, your kittens should be taken for their first injection against feline infectious enteritis and cat 'flu – it is vital that they are vaccinated against these two diseases as the immunity they received in their mother's first milk (colostrum) will have gone. Several other vaccines are available which

will safeguard your kittens against a variety of diseases – talk to your veterinary surgeon about the best ones to use.

Very occasionally the kittens will have a slight reaction to the vaccine, which may make them go off their food and appear rather quiet for about twenty-four hours. However, more serious symptoms should always be brought to the attention of your veterinary surgeon immediately. The second part of this vaccination will be given at the age of twelve weeks,

and it will become fully effective seven days later, and then your kittens will be ready to leave and go to their new homes.

SOCIALIZATION

Socializing with the rest of the human family and any other pets is a very important part of the kittens' development, and visitors should be encouraged to handle and play with them wherever possible. However, your kittens are still much too young to be allowed to venture outside, and without vaccine protection they would be susceptible to some potentially fatal diseases.

Choosing the new owner

Your final duty to your kittens can be the most difficult. Having cared for your queen throughout her nine-week pregnancy, sat with her while she gave birth, and then nurtured and cared for her fast growing family, only the very best of homes will do.

If your litter is a pedigree one, you can advertise your kittens with the relevant breed club, or in the pages of one of the numerous specialist cat magazines. Non-pedigree kittens can be advertised in your local newspapers or on the notice boards at veterinary surgeries. Wherever you advertise and whatever your kittens, pedigree or non-pedigree, your goal should always be the same – matching the right kitten to the right home.

Every kitten is a unique individual, with a character all its own – the lively extrovert of the litter may not suit a quiet, retired couple, whilst the gentle, shy kitten might not be at all happy living with a large family and several dogs. Chat with prospective new owners over the telephone and find out a little about them, their home environment and their family. If you are happy with the conversation, then invite them round to see your kittens. Ask to meet everyone, not just Mum or Dad; that way, you can see which kitten responds best to the whole family.

Do not exclude people who have not owned a cat before; remember you too were once a first-time cat owner. Look for someone with good common sense, who is willing to listen and learn from your experiences and who will seek veterinary advice when necessary.

Your kittens should leave your home in perfect health with a diet sheet and vaccination certificate and, if they are pedigree, their pedigree chart and their pedigree registration papers. Finally, do not let all the kittens leave on the same day, as your queen will probably find this too stressful. Stagger their departure and by the time the last kitten leaves, you might even see your queen breathe a big sigh of relief!

▧ **Left:** *If choosing a new kitten, it is very important to involve the whole family. Make your choice wisely; don't rush your decision. Your pet could be part of your family for the next fourteen years or even longer.*

The most popular cat breeds

Some of the world's most popular and best-loved breeds of cat are featured in the following pages with detailed information and expert advice on their history and origins, their temperament, family suitability and whether they are best suited to living indoors or outdoors. If you are considering acquiring a pedigree cat, you can check on how much grooming and individual attention each breed needs.

Chapter Ten

CAT BREED GUIDE

Right: *The gentle Bengal is actually a modern breed of cat. Its popularity stems from its resemblance to a small wild cat.*

There are numerous breeds of cats, and they come in an extraordinarily wide range of patterns and colours.

They include the flat-faced Persian with its long, glamourous, silky coat, the water-loving Turkish Van, the elegant oriental breeds from Burma and Thailand, and the traditional working cats of Northern Europe and the New World. In addition, there are the relatively new breeds, which include the floppy Ragdoll, the wild-looking Bengal and Ocicat, and the silky-coated Balinese. The modern descendants of some of the world's oldest cats can still be found – the distinctive, spotted Egyptian Mau, which dates back to the revered pharaonic cats of Ancient Egypt, the sinuous Abyssinian and the fine-haired Angora, which hails from the earliest cats of Ancient Turkey.

HOW TO USE THE BREED GUIDE

Temperament
Longer bars mean a good temperament and indicate a breed that is noted for its friendly nature, making it more suitable as an affectionate family pet.

Family suitability
Longer bars mean that a breed is friendly and adjusts well to family life, and will socialize well with people in a range of surroundings.

Grooming
Longer bars mean that you must be prepared to spend more time grooming your cat and tend to apply to longhaired and semi-longhaired breeds.

Outdoors/indoors
Longer bars mean a greater ability to adapt successfully to life indoors as a house cat or a need to have access to outdoors.

Summary
This sums up the specific breed's main attributes, temperament and suitability as a family pet.

Longhair

Persian

Temperament

Placid, quiet, gentle, affectionate

Family suitability

An undemanding family pet

Grooming

Regular daily grooming essential

Indoors

The perfect indoor cat

Summary

An aristocratic cat with a loving nature

Among the oldest and most popular breeds, the precise origins of the Persian are still obscured in mystery but it is probably descended from the Angora. Exotic-looking longhaired cats were prized in Turkey and Iran for hundreds of years before they appeared in Western Europe. Persians became popular in Italy in the eighteenth century after their introduction by Pietro della Valle. Their glamourous, silky coats were much admired and they later spread to France and Britain where their selective breeding began in 1871. In Britain and Europe, where they are called longhairs, each colour is considered to be a separate breed, whereas in the United States all the colours are Persians but they are shown in five categories: solid, shaded, smoke/tabby, parti-coloured and point-restricted colours.

■ **Below:** *This Red Shaded Cameo Persian is raising its plumed, bushy tail.*

Coat

The abundant, luxurious coat is resilient and fine-textured, and

■ **Right:** *These Red and Blue Persian kittens are only thirteen weeks of age.*

should have a healthy shine. The dense neck ruff should fall to a frill between the front legs, and the fur should stand out all over the body.

Appearance

The magnificent Persian has a large, powerful, cobby body set on muscular legs with large, round paws. The heavily plumed and bushy tail is carried low. The large, round head has a flattened face with full cheeks and widely positioned, small, round-tipped ears. The large, round eyes, which are set wide apart on the head, are very expressive, and their brilliant colour should always match that of the coat.

Temperament

The calm and docile Persian is affectionate, sweet-natured and easy-going. Its extremely placid, undemanding nature makes it the ideal family pet, and it is very sociable to other cats as well as people. This quiet cat likes nothing better than to stretch out and relax, although some Persians are good hunters. Cats with some Siamese blood – such as the Colourpoint, Chocolate and Lilac varieties – are more active and lively but generally they will all live happily indoors.

Daily care

A Persian will need intensive grooming for at least 15 minutes every day to keep the coat tangle-free. A soft, natural-bristle brush will remove dead hairs. As the coat moults heavily through the year (but especially in summer), regular grooming will prevent fur balls forming in the stomach.

■ **Above:** *This Blue Smoke Persian male has a luxurious, silky coat.*

Coat colours

An exceptionally wide range of colours and patterns are permissible, and for precise information you should consult the relevant governing body or breed club.

British Angora

Developed in the 1960s, this elegant cat is not the ancient longhaired breed which originated in Angora (Ankara), Turkey, but an attempt by modern breeders to recreate it. Today's Angora is a longhaired type of the Oriental and is not related to the Turkish Angoras. This breed is known in the United States as the Oriental Longhair.

Coat

The medium-length, glossy coat is renowned for its soft, silky texture. The fur is exceptionally fine but there is no woolly undercoat. Except for the chin, neck, tail and underside, which have a tendency to frill, the coat should lie flat and should not knot. A lot of hairs are shed during the summer.

Appearance

An oriental-looking, graceful cat with an elegant body, the Angora is long-legged with small, oval paws. Its plumed tail is long and tapering tail. It has a long, well-proportioned head with a straight nose, large, pricked ears and

Above: *This Lilac Angora stud cat has the distinctive long, silky coat.*

oriental, slanting eyes which are usually a vivid green. However, they may be blue or even odd-eyed (one blue and one green) in white cats.

Temperament

The Angora is the perfect indoor house cat. Although it loves to sleep, it has a lively temperament. Serene, gentle and affectionate, it has a tendency to attach itself to one person within the household and actively seeks affection, often vocally – this is probably due to its Oriental ancestry.

Daily care

If you own an Angora you must be prepared to groom it on a daily basis. However, grooming is easy and it requires less than a Persian as there is no undercoat. Angoras hate water and will resent being bathed so you may prefer to use a dry shampoo.

Coat colours

The permitted colours are those of the Oriental Shorthairs, including White, Black, Blue, Chocolate, Lilac, Cinnamon, Caramel, Fawn, Red, Cream and Apricot. Tortie colours, Smokes, Tabbies and Shaded are also allowed. For more information, consult the GCCF.

Temperament

Sweet, friendly, intelligent, vocal

Family suitability

Good pet but one-person oriented

Grooming

Daily grooming required

Indoors

Likes to live indoors

Summary
A devoted companion and house cat

Left: *This Angora male is a Black and Silver Tabby.*

Maine Coon

Temperament

Boisterous, alert, independent

Family suitability

Home-loving but one-person oriented

Grooming

Less then other longhairs

Outdoors

Prefers to be outside; not an indoor cat

Summary

A friendly, healthy companion and good hunter. An ideal family pet

Although its exact origins are obscure, this cat is the oldest feline breed in North America. It was probably developed by crossing working cats with longhaired Angoras in the north-eastern seaboard state of Maine. However, longhaired feline immigrants may have been brought to America by the Vikings centuries earlier and this may account for the longhaired gene. A commonly held belief that the Maine Coon is related to the racoon is, in fact, genetically impossible! This beautiful cat was officially recognised in the United States in 1967 and is now popular in Britain and Europe, too.

Coat

The medium-length double coat is dense and shaggy with lustrous, silky-textured, soft fur. The undercoat is covered with a waterproof topcoat which enables

the cat to survive in the cold New England winters. Although the coat is thick on the body and long on the withers, it is shorter on the cat's head. A thick ruff develops around the neck in winter.

Appearance

Among the largest domestic breeds of cat, the powerful Maine Coon is large and muscular with a medium-long flowing, plumed

■ **Left:** *Maine Coons come in a wide range of colours and patterns.*

tail. Male cats can weigh as much as 9 kg (20 lb). The rounded head has large, expressive, oval eyes, which may be green, yellow, gold, copper, or even blue in white cats. The ears are tall and tufted.

Temperament

Intelligent and home-loving, the Maine Coon will make an affectionate and friendly family pet. However, it does have a tendency to attach itself to one person. It is not well suited to indoor life, being a capable hunter and enjoying being outside in the garden. It is less likely to exhibit behaviour problems if it is allowed a degree of freedom and space. This quiet cat does not purr or miaow in the usual way but makes a chirruping noise.

Daily care

Unlike Persians and the other full-coated cats, the Maine Coon needs regular but not daily grooming. Healthy and robust, it will cope well with low temperatures and will happily sleep anywhere – sometimes in the oddest places.

Coat colours

A wide range of colours and patterns are permissible, including eight Tabby combinations, which most closely resemble a racoon's coat. However, Chocolate, Lilac and Siamese-type patterns are not acceptable.

■ **Right:** *Maine Coons can adapt successfully to indoor life but they love to have outdoor access.*

Turkish Van

This beautiful Angora cat is a native of the snowy Lake Van region in Turkey, where it has been domesticated for hundreds of years. Unlike other small cats, it likes water and loves swimming. In 1955, two photographers, Sonia Halliday and Laura Lushington, brought two Turkish Vans back to Britain and started breeding from them. The breed was recognised in 1969 and spread to America in 1982. The cat is well respected by the Turkish people who live around Lake Van, some of whom believe that the white patch on the cat's face is the thumbprint of Allah.

Coat

The semi-long, dense coat is spectacular with soft, fine, silky fur. In winter, the coat becomes immensely thick to protect the cat from the bitterly cold weather, but it moults profusely in spring and summer. The Turkish Van also has

a frontal ruff, well-feathered ears, tufted toes and a thick, plumy tail.

Appearance

This medium-sized cat is very similar in appearance to the Turkish Angora. The strong, muscular body is set on medium-length legs with small, tufted paws. The long tail is dense and feathery. The wedge-shaped head has a long nose with a pink tip. The tufted ears are large, pointed and pink inside. The large, oval eyes, which are rimmed with pink, are an amber yellow.

Temperament

This is an elegant cat which is nonetheless extremely hardy and long-lived. The Turkish Van is tranquil and highly intelligent and makes an affectionate family pet. It is not afraid of water and,

■ **Left:** *Gentle and friendly, the Turkish Van has a pink-tipped nose, tufted ears and oval eyes rimmed with pink.*

■ **Above:** *The Turkish Van is the only breed of cat that really loves the water and enjoys swimming and bathing.*

unlike other breeds, loves to swim, to play with water and to be bathed. In spite of its outdoor heritage, it will adjust to indoor life so long as there is access to a terrace, patio or outside run.

Daily care

Like other longhairs, it needs daily grooming to remove tangles and keep the coat looking healthy. In spring and summer, when it sheds its winter coat, more intensive grooming is required to remove dead hairs. It enjoys being bathed but must always be thoroughly dried afterwards.

Coat colours

The coat is always White with darker markings on the face and tail. Auburn is the most common colour but Cream, Tortoiseshell and Black are also permitted.

Temperament

Gentle, intelligent, lively

Family suitability

Good pet but one-person oriented

Grooming

Requires daily grooming

Indoors

Adapts well with access to patio

Summary

An affectionate cat which loves water

Longhair

Norwegian Forest Cat

Temperament

Intelligent, a skilful hunter, independent

Family suitability

Affectionate, a good family pet

Grooming

Only occasional grooming required

Outdoors

Needs to roam freely in open spaces

Summary
A low-maintenance pet but it would be very cruel to keep it indoors as a house cat

This cat's origins go back as far as ancient times when, according to Scandinavian myths, it pulled the chariot of the Norse goddess Freya. Known as the Norsk Skaukatt, it is native to Norway and a northern cousin of the European Wild Cat. It still lives wild in the dark Norwegian pine forests, but it has also been domesticated and makes a good companion pet. First shown in 1938, it has grown in popularity throughout Europe but is still not recognised in the United States.

Coat

The long, thick coat protects this cat in the harsh, cold Norwegian winters. Its dense undercoat keeps the body warm and is covered by long guard hairs. This outer coat is water-resistant and acts as a shield against heavy rain and snow. In

Below: *Whatever the colour, the coat is always very long.*

Coat colour

All coat colours and patterns are acceptable, apart from Chocolate, Siamese and Lilac.

Above: *This cat loves to climb and to have free access to a large garden.*
Right: *The large ears and prominent whiskers are both distinctive features.*

addition, in winter the cat grows a thick, full ruff, shirt-front and knickerbockers for extra warmth.

Appearance

This medium-sized cat has a strong, powerful body with long legs and a thickly furred long tail. Its claws are strong for climbing and gripping on rocks and trees, and the thick tufted fur between the toes helps to protect the feet and keep them warm. It has a triangular head with large, tufted ears and long whiskers. The eyes are almond-shaped.

Character

Although this cat is affectionate and enjoys human company, it is not suited to life as an indoor cat. Intelligent and independent, it needs the opportunity to roam

freely in open spaces, to climb and go hunting. Its agility, strength and skilful climbing ability make it a good hunter and working cat.

Daily care

You might think that the profuse, long coat requires daily grooming, but it needs only an occasional session. This cat sheds its coat, with the exception of its tail, once a year. Although it often catches and eats its own food if allowed to roam freely, it should eat a high-protein meat and fish diet.

Birman

Also known as the Sacred Cat of Burma, the Birman was originally kept by Buddhist monks, and it was even worshipped by them as a deity. The distinctive markings are said to have originated when a sacred cat leapt onto the body of a monk, who had been slaughtered by an invading Thai army, and its back turned golden, its paws white and its eyes sapphire blue. For many centuries, the Birman was a Burmese temple cat, but in the 1920s a breeding pair was sent to France and by the 1960s the breed became popular in Britain and the United States.

Coat

The Birman has a long, fine, silky coat with a thick, long ruff around the neck. The hair on the back is particularly silky, while underneath it is wavy and slightly curled. Although the fur is quite long and thick, it does not have a tendency to matt.

Appearance

This medium-sized cat has a long, low, stocky body with strong legs and large, round paws with their familiar white 'boots' or 'gloves'. The round-tipped ears are mounted on a round head which has large and slightly slanting sapphire blue eyes.

Temperament

The Birman's appeal lies not only in its very beautiful and mysterious appearance but also in its gentle, pacific nature. Affectionate and intelligent, it is a good pet for a relatively quiet family. A sociable cat who loves to play, it tolerates children, dogs and other household

Below: The paws have distinctive 'boots'.

pets. It is very faithful to its owner and may sometimes ignore other people in the owner's absence.

Daily care

This healthy cat can adapt well to an indoor or outdoor existence. Whereas some Birmans will make excellent house cats, others love to play and hunt outside in the garden. Regular grooming is essential to keep the cat's long, silky coat in optimum condition.

Above: The Birman is an ancient breed which originated in Burma.

Coat colours

The pale body colour is usually a milky white or creamy gold with Siamese points, including:
◆ **Blue point:** Creamy coat with greyish-blue mask, ears, legs and tail
◆ **Chocolate point:** As above but chestnut brown instead of Blue
◆ **Lilac point:** As above but pearly grey instead of Blue
◆ **Seal point:** As above but dark seal brown instead of Blue.
Also Cream, Red, Tortie and Tabby points.

Right: Mysterious and alluring, the Birman is a gentle, sociable cat.

Temperament
Intelligent, affectionate, sociable

Family suitability
Loves to play; ideal family pet

Grooming
Regular grooming required

Outdoors/indoors
A good indoor or outdoor cat

Summary
A handsome, faithful companion

Longhair

Ragdoll

Temperament

Gentle, undemanding, tranquil

Family suitability

A good family pet

Grooming

Regular grooming required

Indoors

Likes to live inside

Summary

A relaxed and gentle indoor cat

This relatively new breed of cat originated in the United States in the 1960s when a breeder, Ann Baker, mated a white longhaired female, Josephine, with a Birman male. Ragdolls were bred selectively to cultivate their docile, gentle nature, and their name comes from their unique characteristic of going limp and totally relaxed when they are handled. The first breed to have its own trademark, its early development was strictly controlled and it was not recognised in the UK until 1981. There is still a very popular

■ **Below:** *The limp and gentle Ragdoll has distinctive, amazingly blue eyes.*

■ **Right:** *A pretty cat, the Ragdoll will make an ideal pet for most families. It is very affectionate and loves to play and be handled by its owners.*

misconception that these cats cannot feel pain or sense impending danger as the original Josephine had fractured her pelvis in a road traffic accident. However, this is not true.

Coat

The medium-length coat is dense and silky with long guard hairs covering a minimal undercoat. Although the fur is short on the face, shoulders and front legs, it is medium in length on the body and longer around the neck with a luxurious ruff. The full coat only develops when the adult cat is mature.

Appearance

Ragdolls are large with a long, muscular body; males can weigh up to 9 kg (20 lb). The chest is broad and deep, and the short, sturdy legs have round, well-tufted paws. The long, tapering tail is well plumed, and the head is large and triangular in shape. The forward-tilting, rounded ears are well-furnished and wide set. The oval eyes are vividly blue and the cheeks are full.

Temperament

This cat is renowned for its gentle temperament which it probably inherited from its Persian and

Birman ancestors. It makes an undemanding pet and likes to live indoors. Relaxed and tranquil, it enjoys being handled and is the perfect pet for easy-going owners.

Daily care

Ragdolls need regular grooming even though their semi-long coat tends not to matt. You can use a brush and comb or just 'comb' through the fur with your fingers.

> **Coat** colour
>
> The coat is always pointed and patterned. It may be Seal, Blue, Chocolate or Lilac. Colourpoint, Mitted or Bi-Colour patterns are all acceptable but a good contrast is required. On mitted cats, the paw pads are white.

Balinese

This longhaired version of the Siamese is a natural mutation from Siamese parents with a longhaired mutant gene. It originated from a Siamese litter that was born in California during the 1940s. Two women, Marion Dorset and Helen Smith, were instrumental in developing the Balinese breed, and it was not officially recognised in the United States until the 1960s (later in Europe). It has no connection with the island of Bali but derives its name from its natural grace and agility which are reminiscent of traditional Balinese dancers.

Coat

The medium-length coat is shorter than that of most other longhaired breeds of cat. Soft, fine, silky and ermine-like, the Balinese does not have a downy undercoat. However, although its coat is naturally non-matting, it does have a tendency sometimes to curl.

Appearance

With the classic conformation of the Siamese, the Balinese has a long, well-muscled body set on long, slim, tapering legs with

Coat colours

The body should be evenly coloured with darker point colours restricted to the tail, feet and ears. In the USA, the solid points allowed are Seal, Chocolate, Blue and Lilac, but in the UK, Red, Cream, Tortie and Tabby points are also permissible.

■ **Above:** *This Red tabby point Balinese has the breed's characteristic long coat.*

small, oval feet. The hind legs are slightly longer than the forelegs, and the tail is long and tapering. Svelte, fine-boned and graceful, it is a very elegant cat. The wedge-shaped head is set on a long, slender neck. The large ears are pointed at the tips and wide at the base, and the bright blue eyes are almond-shaped.

Temperament

Although it is lively, spirited and intelligent, the Balinese is less boisterous than the Siamese. However, it retains its inquisitive characteristics and its tendency to be very vocal and demanding. Sociable and fun-loving, it hates to be left alone and will let you know in an imploring voice. It loves to play games with all the

family, especially children, and is extremely acrobatic. Although it will live indoors, it does need regular access to a small garden.

Daily care

Even though its coat is silky and non-matting, the Balinese does require a quick daily grooming session. Just a few minutes with a soft-bristled brush will keep the coat looking shiny and soft.

■ **Below:** *The ears of the Balinese are exceptionally large with pointed tips and a wide base.*

Longhair

Somali

Temperament

Lively, easy to train, playful, intelligent

Family suitability

Adapts well to a quiet family

Grooming

Will require daily grooming

Outdoors

Needs access to a garden or patio

Summary

An affectionate pet which loves to roam freely

This aristocratic-looking cat is a long-haired variety of the ancient Abyssinian (see page 182). Although naturally longhaired kittens do sometimes occur in Abyssinian litters, they are genetic mutations. The Somali was developed from mutant Abyssinian longhairs as a new breed in America in the 1960s. It was officially recognised in 1978 in the United States, and five years later in Great Britain. In latter years, Somalis have been crossed with Silver Persians to produce a silver-haired Snow Cat.

Coat

The medium-length, double coat is soft and silky and tangle-resistant. The best show cats have a really dense coat with ear tufts, a thick ruff and full breeches. There are at least three bands of colour on each shaft which produce a shimmering ticked effect. The Tortie, Silver and Tortie Silver varieties may have as many as ten bands of colour on an individual hair.

Appearance

A medium-sized cat with a long yet sturdy body and strong, slender legs with small, oval paws and tufts of hair between the toes, the Somali is fractionally larger than the Abyssinian. Its long, well-furnished tail, which tapers from base to tip, appears to float behind the body. It tends to stand with a slightly arched back as though it is about to leap into action. The round, tapering, wedge-shaped head has an elongated muzzle and large, pointed ears. The expressive, almond-shaped eyes may be amber, green or hazel with dark lids.

Temperament

Lively, intelligent and a good hunter, the Somali is an active outdoor cat which needs freedom and plenty of space. It loves to play games with its owner and can be even trained to perform tricks and walk on a lead. However, although it is sweet-

■ **Above:** *The Somali's almond-shaped eyes are expressive with dark lids, and the large ears are quite pointed.*

natured, it can be demanding, distrustful and very vocal.

Daily care

The Somali does not make a good indoor cat, and if it lives indoors it must have access to a garden, terrace, patio or an outside run. It will fret and will quickly become bored if it is confined for long periods to a relatively small space. Note that the longhaired coat will need daily grooming.

Coat colours

◆ **Usual:** Ruddy brown tipped with black
◆ **Sorrel:** Red tipped with brown
Also available in Blue, Chocolate, Cream, Fawn, Lilac and Red, although in the USA only the Usual (Ruddy) and Sorrel are recognised.

■ **Right:** *A skilful hunter, the Somali does not like to be confined indoors. Ideally, it should have access to a garden or at least an outdoor run.*

Siamese

Shorthair

Descended from the Asiatic wild cat, the elegant and regal Siamese was once confined to the temples and royal palaces of Siam. However, in 1884 the British Consul in Bangkok was given two Siamese cats by the King of Siam, and these were then exhibited in Britain. The breed soon became established in Europe and the United States.

Coat

The shorthaired coat of the Siamese is sleek and silky with thick, glossy, fine-textured fur.

Appearance

The aristocratic Siamese is very elegant, slender and fine-limbed. Medium-sized with a lithe, well-muscled, athletic body, it has long legs and a long, thin, tapering tail. The triangular-shaped head is set on an elongated neck and has a long, straight nose. The large, pricked ears are wide set on top of the head, and the slanting, almond-shaped eyes are a vivid blue. However, in the dark, they appear to shine red.

Coat colours

This beautiful cat has a pale coat (light Fawn, Beige, White or Ivory) with darker colour points on the face, ears, tail, legs and feet. The earliest and most common colour is Seal point, but the other acceptable colours are Blue, Chocolate, Lilac and Red points, and also Tabby and Tortie points.

Temperament

Hypersensitive, demanding and intelligent, the complex Siamese is a challenging pet to own and is not the right breed for busy people who work full-time. It craves human company and will insist on getting your full attention. It is incredibly vocal and will 'talk' to you by howling and miaowing. Boisterous, active and exuberant, it loves to play with adults and children. However, some Siamese can be nervous or unpredictable, or may become one-person oriented, pining and wailing insistently when that person is absent.

Daily care

Because the sociable Siamese hates being left alone, it is important that it gets lots of attention on a daily basis, so owners need to play with their cats regularly. It is an energetic cat which loves to run around and jump outside in

■ **Above:** *The inquisitive Siamese loves to have access to a large garden.*

the garden, so it may not adapt well to life indoors as a house cat. The Siamese should be fed a mixed diet of meat, fish, boiled rice and vegetables. Its short coat needs a quick daily brush to get rid of any dead hairs.

Temperament

Lively, sensitive, demanding, easy to train

Family suitability

Affectionate and lovable, a good family pet

Grooming

Minimal grooming required

Outdoors

A cat that loves to be outdoors

Summary

A cat that craves company and needs a lot of attention

■ **Below:** *This breed has a very distinctive, elegant appearance.*

Shorthair

Tonkinese

Temperament

Lively, people-oriented, demanding, playful

Family suitability

A fun-loving family pet

Grooming

Minimal grooming required

Outdoors

Prefers access to outdoors

Summary

A friendly, inquisitive cat which demands attention

■ **Below:** *This cat has extraordinarily vivid blue eyes.*

■ **Left:** *With its distinctive appearance, the Tonkinese is a very elegant cat.*

A cross between the Siamese and Burmese, this cat has its origins in the ancient copper cat of Southeast Asia. However, the modern breed was developed in North America during the 1960s and it later attained championship status there in 1984, although it was not recognised in Britain until 1991. Its name is derived from the Gulf of Tonkin which separates Burma and Thailand, the countries from which the Burmese and Siamese hail.

Coat

The Tonkinese has the dark colour of the Burmese marked with the darker points of the Siamese. The medium-short, close-lying coat is thick, dense and soft with a lustrous sheen like that of a mink.

Appearance

This medium-sized cat has a strong, muscular body and long, slim legs with dainty, oval paws. The hind legs are longer than the forelegs and the tail is long and tapering. The triangular head is set on a medium-long neck and has a square muzzle. The rounded ears are wide set and the almond-shaped eyes are blue-green (aquamarine).

Temperament

This fun-loving cat is extremely lively, energetic and inquisitive. It enjoys human company and loves to play with adults or children, insisting on their attention. It is quick to learn and will walk happily on a lead and harness. Although it will adapt to indoor life, it prefers a secure, spacious garden in which to exercise. A large outside, wired-in run,

Coat colours

In Britain, all the recognised Burmese colours are permitted including solids, Tortoiseshells and Tabbies. In the US, the colours correspond to the basic Siamese points: Natural Mink, Blue Mink, Honey Mink, Champagne Mink and Platinum Mink.

■ **Above:** *Tonkinese kittens love to play and enjoy lots of human attention.*

complete with climbing stations and scratching posts, is the perfect solution and this will keep the Tonkinese amused for hours. It is an extremely skilful hunter and always enjoys mousing.

Daily care

An easy cat to look after and groom, the Tonkinese requires only a quick combing session and a polish with a silk cloth to keep its coat really glossy and healthy. However, it is cruel to confine it inside the house and it will need plenty of outside access.

Burmese

This long-established oriental breed has lived in Burma for centuries. Brown cats were traditionally kept in Burmese temples where they were revered as divinities. The modern breed, which was recognised in the USA in 1936, and in Britain in 1952, is descended from Wong Mau, a brown Burmese female who was taken to America by Dr Joseph Thompson in 1930 and then cross-bred with a Siamese. However, as well as the original brown coat, a variety of colours is now permitted.

Coat

The shorthaired Burmese has a distinctive smooth, glossy coat with fine, close-lying fur. The texture is shiny, sleek and satiny.

Appearance

This is a medium-sized, muscular cat with an elegant body, straight

back and strong, rounded chest. In the USA, the Burmese is more stocky than the slimmer British breed. The tail is straight and the slender legs end in oval paws in the UK (round in the USA). The wedge-shaped head has wide-set rounded ears and distinctively high cheekbones. The enormous and expressive eyes, which are wide set, may be golden, yellow or amber.

Temperament

A confident, playful cat, the Burmese loves human company and will enjoy socializing with both your family and friends. Demanding, inquisitive and attention-seeking, it hates being left alone and is not a suitable pet for people who are out at work all day. When lonely or bored, it may engage in destructive behaviour. This intelligent cat can be trained, like a dog, to walk on a lead and retrieve objects. It loves to climb and observe family life from a great height, and it also enjoys car journeys. Although it has a loud voice, it is not as vocal as its Siamese cousin.

■ **Above:** *This appealing Brown Burmese kitten is only eight weeks old.*

■ **Above:** *The traditional colour for the playful, sociable Burmese is Brown.*

Coat colours

The usual colour is Brown, which darkens to a dark Sable as the cat matures. Although only Brown cats are allowed in the USA, other colours are permissible in Britain, including Blue, Chocolate, Cream, Lilac, Red, and Brown, Blue, Chocolate and Lilac Tortie.

Daily care

The Burmese loves to be outside in the garden but will adapt well to life as a house cat. Its needs only minimal grooming, but does require a lot of attention from its owner. You need to set aside time every day to play with your cat.

■ **Below:** *This intelligent cat is renowned for its huge, expressive eyes.*

Temperament

Intelligent, confident, sociable, playful

Family suitability

The perfect pet for a fun-loving family

Grooming

Minimal grooming required

Indoors/outdoors

A good indoor or outdoor cat

Summary

An affectionate cat who enjoys company

Shorthair

Singapura

Temperament

Quiet, affectionate, responsive

Family suitability

Adapts well to a quiet family

Grooming

Requires minimal grooming

Indoors

Adjusts well to indoor life

Summary

A quiet, loving cat with a lively nature

Right: *The diminutive Singapura has a very loving temperament and a gentle voice but it is naturally reserved and can be extremely shy.*

This relatively new breed was developed by an American couple, Tommy and Hal Meadow, in the 1970s from a natural breed of cat from Southeast Asia. They fell in love with the feral street cats of Singapore and brought some back to the United States. The name is derived from the Malaysian word for Singapore and this small,

■ **Left:** *The nose and almond-shaped eyes should be rimmed with black.*

slender cat has been adopted as Singapore's official symbol. It is still quite rare and the demand for kittens exceeds supply, making it an extremely valuable cat.

Coat

The short, sleek coat has silky, close-lying fur with bands of ticked guard hairs along the head, back, tail and legs. The base of each hair shaft is light while the tip is darker, usually dark seal brown.

Appearance

The Singapura is one of the smallest cat breeds: the males average only 2.7 kg (6 lb) and the females 1.8 kg (4 lb). Pretty and dainty, this cat has a muscular

body and medium-length legs with small, oval feet. Its slender tail is blunt-ended and medium long. The round head has a short nose outlined in black and large, deeply cupped and slightly pointed ears. The eyes, which are also black rimmed, are large and almond shaped. They may be green, hazel or yellowish gold.

Temperament

In its native environment on the streets and sewers of Singapore, this cat is naturally cautious and reserved. However, with a patient, loving owner, it reveals its lively, affectionate nature. Although it may be suspicious of strangers, it is very inquisitive and likes to observe everyday activities, often from a high vantage point. It is a quiet cat with a gentle voice.

Daily care

Responsive and adaptable, the Singapura usually adjusts well to an indoor life. Its short coat makes it easy to groom – all that's required is a quick brush and comb on a regular basis.

Coat colours

Although a wide range of colours and patterns are found on the native cats in Singapore, the only recognised colour in the US is Sepia agouti – a golden ivory tipped with dark seal brown – and cream or ivory in the UK. Every hair shaft should have at least two bands of dark sepia ticking. The underparts and legs are lighter in colour and untipped.

Exotic Shorthair

The ideal pet for people who want a docile, Persian-type cat without the bother and daily commitment of grooming a longhaired coat, the Exotic Shorthair was developed in the 1960s as a shorthaired version of the Persian/Longhair. The parents must be either a Persian and an American Shorthair, or two Exotic Shorthairs, or a Persian and an Exotic Shorthair. The result is a cat with the quiet and gentle temperament of the Persian, and the lively playfulness and shorter coat of the American Shorthair.

Coat

The Exotic's dense, soft coat is slightly longer than that of other shorthairs. Glossy, resilient and plush, it has a springy quality and should stand away slightly from the cat's body.

■ **Above:** *The flattish face of the Exotic is similar to that of the Persian.*

■ **Below:** *The soft, dense coat should be groomed every day in order to keep it healthy and in good condition.*

Appearance

This medium to large cat has a short, cobby body with strong, sturdy legs and large, round paws. The short, straight tail is carried low to the ground. The massive head with a round face and full cheeks is set on a thick, muscular neck. The nose and round-tipped ears are both small, and the large eyes are round and expressive. Wide set, their colour should match the cat's coat colour.

Temperament

The Exotic Shorthair combines the calm and affectionate nature of the Persian with the alertness of the American Shorthair. It is an ideal pet – eager to please, playful and friendly but not too boisterous. It is a skilful hunter and extremely adept at catching mice, enjoying access to outdoors, although it will happily adapt to indoor life.

Coat colours

Over fifty varieties are permissible, including most of the colours and patterns found in Persians and American Shorthairs. For more information, contact the governing body or relevant breed club.

Daily care

This popular cat is healthy and easy to look after. It likes to play with you and will enjoy a regular grooming session, preferably every day, to comb out dead hairs.

■ **Below:** *A glamorous cat, the Exotic is calm, playful and friendly.*

Temperament

Intelligent, gentle, affectionate, playful

Family suitability

The perfect family pet

Grooming

Regular grooming required

Indoors

Lives indoors but likes outdoor access

Summary

A hardy, robust breed which is calm and gentle

Shorthair

British Shorthair

Temperament

▭▭▭▭▭

Intelligent, calm, independent, easy-going

Family suitability

▭▭▭▭▭

A loyal member of the family

Grooming

▭

Minimal grooming required

Outdoors

▭▭▭▭▭

Needs outdoor access and freedom to roam

Summary

An affectionate pet and skilled hunter

Descended from the cats brought to Britain about 2,000 years ago by the invading Roman armies, the modern breed was developed by Harrison Weir at the end of the nineteenth century. For many years, the British Shorthair was the most popular cat at British cat shows but it was later overtaken by the more exotic Persian and Siamese although it has now regained its rightful place as one of the best-loved British cats. It is recognised in the United States as a distinct and separate breed from the American Shorthair, although available in fewer colours than in the UK.

Coat

The short, dense coat has plush, springy fur. It protects the cat from damp, cold British winters but has no woolly undercoat.

Appearance

A large, well-proportioned cat with a muscular body and deep,

▭ **Above:** *The kittens are naturally inquisitive and quickly learn to hunt.*

broad chest, the cobby British Shorthair has short, stocky legs. Powerful and strong, it is heavier than most domestic cats and has a thick, tapering tail with a rounded tip. The large, broad-cheeked head has small, rounded ears and a broad, straight nose. The large eyes are round and set wide apart. Usually gold, orange or copper coloured, they may be blue or even odd-eyed in white cats, or green or hazel in silver cats.

Temperament

A calm, easy-going cat, the British Shorthair is a good mouser and likes an independent, outdoor life. Some do adjust to indoor living but they prefer to have the run of a large and spacious garden. Intelligent and affectionate, they make good companions and will play happily with children.

▭ **Above:** *British Shorthair kittens are playful and grow up into calm cats.*

Daily care

The short coat rarely tangles and it just needs a regular brush to remove any dead hairs and to keep it looking glossy.

Coat colours

A wide range of colours and patterns is permissible, including White, Black, Blue, Cream, Tabby, Mackerel Tabby, Silver tabby, Red Tabby, Brown Tabby, Spotted, Tortoiseshell, Tortoiseshell and White, Blue-cream, Bi-colour, Smoke and British Tipped.

▭ **Right:** *This breed has a distinctive, cobby-shaped body and a broad chest.*

American Shorthair

This cat is descended from European domestic cats, which were taken to North America during the seventeenth century by the early settlers for rodent control on board ship and in the new settlements. Strong and hardy, they were valued for their companionship as well as their hunting skills. It was not until the nineteenth century that they were recognised as a breed in their own right, and until 1966 they were known as 'Domestic Shorthairs'.

Coat colours

Most colours are permitted, including White, Black, Blue, Red, Cream, Bi-colour, Shaded Silver, Chinchilla, Shell Cameo, Shaded Cameo, Cameo Smoke, Red Smoke, Black Smoke, Blue Smoke, Blue-cream, Tortoiseshell, Tortoiseshell Smoke, Van Pattern, Calico, Brown Tabby, Red Tabby, Silver Tabby, Blue Tabby, Cream Tabby, Cameo Tabby and Patched Tabby.

Coat

The short and resilient coat has coarse-textured, dense fur. It is not as plush as that of the British Shorthair. It is heavier and thicker in winter for protection against bitterly cold and damp weather.

Appearance

This medium to large, muscular cat is bigger than the British Shorthair with longer legs, a less rounded head and a longer nose. The powerful body has sturdy legs and strong feet with large paws. The large, full head has round cheeks, erect, rounded ears and distinctive whiskers. The jaws are well adapted to catching and killing rodents. The round eyes are brilliantly coloured, usually gold. However, some White cats have blue eyes, Silvers have green eyes, and Tabbies may have hazel eyes.

■ Left: *The American Shorthair loves to be outside hunting and stalking prey. A fearless hunter, it is extremely skilful at catching mice and rats.*

Temperament

Hardy, fearless, independent and active, this cat is an outstanding hunter and likes to roam freely outside. Although some individual cats do adapt well to indoor life, they prefer to have unlimited access to a spacious garden. They are excellent climbers and agile jumpers, and make good working cats. However, their friendly, affectionate nature predisposes them to be good companions, and they enjoy living within a family in a domestic environment.

Daily care

Easy to groom, the American Shorthair needs regular but not daily brushing to get rid of dead hairs and prevent furballs forming in the stomach. Naturally healthy and strong, they like to play and need some space in which to hunt.

■ Left: *Muscular and powerful, the American Shorthair has distinctive long whiskers and strong jaws. The round eyes are usually golden.*

Temperament

Intelligent, active, fearless, independent

Family suitability

Makes an affectionate family pet

Grooming

Minimal grooming required

Outdoors

Needs access to a garden and freedom to roam

Summary

A good hunter and gentle companion

Shorthair

Abyssinian

Temperament

Boisterous, demanding, gentle, intelligent

Family suitability

Likes to participate in family life

Grooming

Daily brush and rub with soft cloth

Outdoors

A cat that needs access to outside

Summary

An athletic, elegant cat which craves company and loves to play

One of the oldest breeds, the Abyssinian may be descended from the pharaonic cats of Ancient Egypt. It bears a striking resemblance to the cats depicted in ancient tomb paintings. In 1868, some British soldiers returning from the war in Abyssinia brought back a cat called Zula, the ancestor of the modern breed. However, a Breed Standard was not established until 1929. The gentle 'Aby' was severely affected in the 1960s and 1970s by the feline leukaemia virus but has made a comeback.

Coat

The thick, dense, glossy fur is similar in texture to that of a rabbit. Unlike the coats of many other breeds, it is resilient to the touch and not particularly soft. The overall ticking is the result of a minimum of four bands of colour on each hair shaft, which tends to be light at the root and darker at the tip.

■ *Above: This ancient breed closely resembles a small, wild cat.*

Appearance

The Abyssianian has a long, lithe, powerfully-muscled body with long, slender legs and small, oval feet with black pads. The thickly furred tail is long and tapering. The delicate, wedge-shaped head is set on a long, elegant neck, and the ears are large and pointed. The almond-shaped eyes may be amber, green or hazel, and are bordered with black or dark brown set in a paler outer oval. The dark nose is also rimmed with black.

Temperament

Gentle and intelligent, this cat is easy to train and gets involved in family activities. Lively and agile, it enjoys playing and learning new tricks. It craves attention from its owner; if not given, it may even develop anxiety and behaviour

problems. It may appear shy and unsociable to strangers. It has a distinctively sweet 'bell-like' voice, and, unlike most cats, it uses its paws rather than its nose to investigate unfamiliar objects.

Daily care

This cat is demanding and you must set aside some time each day to play with it. It gets bored and restless if kept indoors and should have access to a garden with trees to climb. Its coat will stay shiny if you brush and rub it with a soft cloth on a daily basis.

Coat colours
◆ **Usual:** Ruddy brown with black or dark brown ticking
◆ **Sorrel:** Copper red with chocolate ticking
◆ **Blue:** Blue-grey with steel blue ticking
◆ **Fawn:** Medium fawn with deep fawn ticking
Also available in Lilac, Silver, Silver Blue and Silver Sorrel.

■ *Right: This cat is extremely gentle but very demanding and you must make time to play with it.*

Egyptian Mau

This uniquely marked cat is descended from the revered domestic cats of Ancient Egypt, which were probably a spotted subspecies of the African Wild Cat. A first cousin of the Abyssinian, its name is derived from the Egyptian word for a cat. The modern breed was developed in 1953 when an imported female in Italy was mated with an Egyptian male. It was officially recognised in the United States in 1968, and ten years later in the UK. It is also known as the Spotted Oriental or Oriental Spotted Tabby.

Coat

The medium-length, dense coat tends to be silky with a high sheen. Its highly distinctive feature is the marking pattern, with randomly placed spots on the body, a striped head and banded tail. In the centre of its forehead is an M-shaped mark. There are two or more bands of ticking in each hair, and the texture varies according to the colour. Thus bronze and silver coats tend to be quite dense, while smoke-coloured coats are finer and more silky. The Egyptian Mau is the only naturally spotted cat.

Appearance

This cat is exceptionally elegant with a well-balanced, muscular body and long legs. It has a long, tapering tail and a rounded head. The large, pointed ears are set wide apart on the head, and the almond-shaped eyes are unusually large. Although they are usually green, they may be yellow or hazel, the intensity of colour diminishing as the cat matures.

Above: *The gentle Egyptian Mau has unusually large, almond-shaped eyes.*

Left: *The Mau's elegant muscular body is displayed by this Silver Tabby.*

Temperament

The Mau's gentle, affectionate nature makes it an ideal family pet but it does tend to be wary of strangers. It fits into a domestic environment well and is a good hunter. A lively cat, it loves to play and has a particularly melodious voice. It is also very intelligent and is one of the easiest cats to train. It will soon learn and adapt to walking beside you on a lead.

Daily care

Because it has quite a delicate constitution and reacts to sudden temperature changes, the Egyptian Mau is often kept indoors. The coat needs minimal grooming and it is an easy cat to look after.

Coat colours

◆ **Silver:** With charcoal markings
◆ **Bronze:** With dark markings
◆ **Smoke:** Grey and silver coat with black markings
The paw pads are brown or black.

Temperament

Intelligent, affectionate and gentle

Family suitability

Adapts well to family life

Grooming

Minimal grooming required

Indoors

Delicate so tends to be kept inside

Summary
An engagingly beautiful companion with a home-loving nature

Below: *The Mau is descended from the pharaonic cats of Ancient Egypt.*

Shorthair

Russian Blue

Temperament

Intelligent, tranquil and affectionate

Family suitability

Better suited to a family with older children

Grooming

Minimal grooming required

Outdoors/Indoors

Adapts well to outdoor or indoor life

Summary

A quiet cat which likes a peaceful life

These cats used to be known as Archangel Cats after the Russian port from which they embarked on their initial voyage to Britain several hundred years ago. Sometimes called the Maltese or Spanish Blue, similar cats are still found in Scandinavia and northern Russia. After a decline in their numbers during World War II, a Siamese strain was introduced and the Standard was subsequently rewritten in 1950. However, many breeders harked back to the original type of cat, and the modern Russian closely resembles the appearance of its original ancestors.

Coat

The plush coat texture is quite different from that of any other cat breed. The short, thick double coat has a dense, soft undercoat to protect the cat from cold Russian winters. Its distinctive characteristic is its silvery lustre and the way in which it stands out from the cat's body.

Appearance

This medium-sized cat has a powerful, muscular body and moves gracefully. Slenderly built and rangy, it has long legs, small, rounded feet and a long, tapering tail. The wedge-shaped head is set on

Right: *The Russian Blue is muscular and athletic looking with a distinctive plush coat unlike that of any other cat breed.*

Right: *The prominent whisker pads of the Russian Blue are a requirement in the UK but not in the United States.*

a long, sinuous neck. The erect, upright, pointed ears, which are set wide part on the head, are almost transparent. The short, wide head has a straight, medium-length nose and quite prominent whisker pads in the UK (the US standard does not require them). The large, almond-shaped eyes are a vivid emerald green.

Temperament

The elegant Russian Blue has a serene, sweet and affectionate nature. However, it likes to live in

a quiet household as it cannot tolerate a great deal of noise or boisterous young children. It has a tendency to be shy with strangers but is loyal and loving towards its owners. Although it likes to be outside, even in cold climates, it will adapt well to indoor life.

Daily care

A low-maintenance cat, the Russian Blue does not take long to groom and needs only a quick brush to keep the plush coat upright and to remove any dead hairs. It needs loving owners in a quiet household, preferably with grown-up children.

Coat colours

Blue is the only acceptable colour in the United States and Britain, including all shades of grey. However, other colours, such as Black, Red and White, are permissible in some countries, including Australia and New Zealand.

Korat

Shorthair

T his ancient breed originated in the Korat province of Thailand where it was reputed to bring good luck to its owners. Its original name was the Si Sawat, meaning 'good fortune', and it is mentioned in the early Thai book of cat poems. The first Korat actually arrived in Britain at the end of nineteenth century and was shown at the National Cat Show of 1896, although at the time it was believed to be a Siamese. In 1959, the US ambassador to Thailand imported a breeding pair into the United States, and the breed was recognised in 1966. The modern breed is identical to the ancient one and retains all the traditional characteristics, which breeders have striven to maintain.

Coat colours

The coat should be solid Silver-blue all over, tipped with silver to create a beautiful, lustrous sheen.

Coat

The Korat's short coat is thick, glossy and silky in texture. Flat and lying close to the body, it has no undercoat. Each hair is lighter at the root, darkening along the length with a silver tip.

Appearance

This medium-sized cat has a semi-cobby, muscular body with a slightly curved back and broad chest. The hind legs are slightly longer than the forelegs with oval paws, and the medium-length tail tapers to a rounded tip. The heart-shaped head has a tapering muzzle and erect, round-tipped ears. The Korat's large, prominent eyes are a luminous, brilliant green or amber-green.

Temperament

Intelligent and fearless, the Korat can be combative and defensive of

Left: *The Korat enjoys being outside and free to roam in a garden.*

its territory, especially males. It can also be very intolerant of strange cats. It dislikes sudden, loud noises and prefers to live in a calm, quiet domestic environment rather than a boisterous family. Ideally, it would suit a single owner or a quiet couple, as it has a tendency to get very attached to one person. Affectionate and sweet-natured towards its owners, it enjoys learning and performing tricks. It lives happily indoors but will enjoy some access to a garden or an outside terrace.

Daily care

Easy to groom, the Korat needs a quick daily combing session to remove any dead hairs. Hand stroking not only makes its coat shine but will also be an enjoyable experience for your cat. Lacking a full undercoat, it needs to be kept warm in cold winters.

Temperament

Intelligent, fearless, dislikes noise

Family suitability

One-person oriented

Grooming

Daily grooming required

Outdoors

Lives indoors but prefers outdoor access

Summary
Most suitable for a single owner or quiet household

Left: *The Korat has a heart-shaped head with luminous, large green eyes.*

Shorthair

Manx

Temperament

Intelligent, affectionate, a good hunter

Family suitability

Home-loving and family-oriented

Grooming

Requires daily, light grooming

Outdoors

Prefers to have access to outdoors

Summary

A brilliant mouser and great family pet

This historic breed of tailless cat is native to the Isle of Man, an island in the Irish Sea. Many theories abound to explain its origins, ranging from one view that it may have arrived 1,000 years ago on Phoenician trading ships to the more favoured explanation that it swam ashore from a wrecked vessel of the vanquished Spanish Armada in 1588. The truncated tail of the Manx is due to an incomplete dominant gene, which has been sustained by the breed's insularity. However, the distinctive lack of a tail also makes the cat susceptible to fused vertebrae. A Manx Club was founded in 1901 and the

Terminology

Manx cats may be known as:
◆ **Rumpies:** There is a small hollow where the tail should be
◆ **Stumpies and Stubbies:** The cat has a residual tail
◆ **Longies:** A small tail exists.

■ **Above:** *This young, classic Red Tabby Manx shows its truncated tail. The Manx is now a rare and unusual breed.*

future of the breed is ensured by the existence of a government cattery for this purpose.

Coat

The short, double coat of the Manx has a dense, thick undercoat and longer overcoat. The soft, shiny hair has a similar texture to that of a rabbit.

Appearance

With its solid, stocky body and broad chest, the medium-sized Manx is strong and muscular. The high, rounded rump, short back and hind legs, which are longer than the forelegs, create a curious, hopping-like gait. Where the tail should start, there is a natural hollow. The wide, round head has tall, wide-set ears with narrow, rounded tips. The colour of the round eyes should always match the coat colour.

Coat colours

Most recognised coat colours are acceptable, including solid, bi-colour, tabby, tortoiseshell and marbled colours and patterns, with the exception of the pointed Siamese pattern.

Temperament

The Manx is renowned for its hunting and mousing skills. It is an extremely agile cat – a fast runner and adept climber with good reflexes. It enjoys being outside although it will adapt to an indoor life. Naturally curious, intelligent and friendly, this cat gets on well with adults, children and dogs, and likes to take an active part in family life.

Daily care

To keep the dense coat in peak condition and looking healthy and shiny, it should be brushed daily. This will also remove any dead hairs. However, unlike a typical longhaired cat, the grooming session need not take long.

■ **Below:** *This Manx is Tortoiseshell and White in colour.*

Scottish Fold

Although stories exist of cats with falling ears being brought to Europe from China at the end of the nineteenth century, the modern Scottish Fold has been developed from a kitten born as a natural mutation in 1961 on the Perthshire farm of William Ross. From this cat, Ross started a new breed of cats with ears folded flat on the head. The breed subsequently became very popular in North America and it was recognised there in 1978. However, in the UK many doubts were raised about the breed's predisposition to deafness and ear mite infestations, and thus the Scottish Fold is quite rare and cannot be shown in Britain. The kittens are born with normal pointed ears and they start to fold down at two to three weeks.

Coat

This cat's short coat is thick and resilient with soft, dense, plush fur. In fact, it should be so thick that it stands away naturally from the animal's body.

Appearance

A unique and unusual cat, the medium-sized Scottish Fold has a powerful, cobby body set on short, sturdy legs with neat, round paws. The tail is thick at the base and it should be in proportion to the body length. The wide, round head is set on a short neck, and the large, round eyes are very expressive with an intense gaze. The ears, which are

Below: *This Black and White Scottish Fold has the classic folded over ears which are a breed characteristic.*

Coat colours

Any of the American Shorthair colours and almost all patterns are accepted, with the exception of Chocolate, Lavender and dark Siamese points.

the cat's distinctive feature, are small, neat and rounded at the tips. They are folded forwards, lying tightly against the head.

Temperament

This is an exceptionally good-natured cat: gentle, sweet and affectionate. It loves company and

is especially good with children, although it does have a tendency to attach itself to one person within a family. As well as being a very loving pet, it is an incredible hunter and makes a good working farm cat. Although it can adapt to living indoors most of the time, it enjoys the occasional foray into the outside world.

Daily care

The short, thick coat needs only minimal grooming. When you do groom your cat, it is a good idea to gently check the ears. It is generally a very healthy cat which is capable of withstanding cold winter temperatures.

Temperament

Placid, home-loving, affectionate

Family suitability

An excellent family pet

Grooming

Requires only minimal grooming

Outdoors

Prefers to have access to outdoors

Summary

An amazing hunter and good family pet

Left: *The thick coat of the Scottish Fold should stand away from its body.*

Shorthair

Rex: Cornish, Devon and Selkirk

Temperament

Intelligent, gentle, affectionate

Family suitability

A good pet for a quiet, gentle family

Grooming

Minimal grooming required

Indoors

A good indoor cat but enjoys going outside

Summary

An impish, playful cat with an independent streak

The original curly-coated Cornish Rex was born in 1950 on Bodmin Moor and was a male red tabby. A decade later, the Devon Rex was to evolve as a separate breed from a curly-coated kitten. However, attempts to combine the two lines proved to be unsuccessful as the resultant kittens did not have the distinctive curly coat of their parents. Thousands of miles away in 1987, a curly-coated kitten was born in Wyoming in the United States, and another new breed developed: the Selkirk Rex, which took its name from the local Selkirk Mountains. It seems that Rex-type cats do appear occasionally as spontaneous mutations around the world.

Coat

All three Rex breeds have a fine, short, curly coat which may be crimped or rippled. The Cornish Rex has the finest, shortest fur with less awn hairs. Plush and silky-textured, the coat is particularly wavy on the back and tail. The soft coat of the Devon Rex is harsher, and often appears rippled. The Selkirk Rex's coat may be short or long. Longhairs have longer, plume-like tail curls and a longer ruff.

Appearance

All the Rex breeds have a hard, muscular body but the Selkirk is more heavily boned and weighs

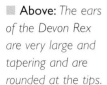

■ **Above:** *The ears of the Devon Rex are very large and tapering and are rounded at the tips.*

■ **Above:** *The fur of the Cornish Rex is very short and is silky in texture.*

more than the slender Cornish and Devon types. The Cornish has long legs with oval paws, and a long, flexible, tapering tail. The small, narrow head has oval eyes and large ears. The Devon has the same build but its head is wedge-shaped with a short nose. The rounded, tapering ears are wide-set on the head, and the eyes are large and oval shaped.

Temperament

Each of the breeds is intelligent, affectionate and playful, and will make a good family pet. Tranquil and home-loving by nature, these

Coat colours

◆ **Cornish and Devon:** All colours and patterns are acceptable.
◆ **Selkirk:** All colours and patterns are permissible, including Mink, Blue Mink, Champagne Mink and Platinum Mink.

cats are fast runners and agile jumpers and will adapt readily to an indoor existence although they love to play outside.

Daily care

Because they have so little hair, they need to live and sleep in a warm environment. They do not shed much hair so they are the perfect pets for cat-lovers who are allergic to cat hair. Grooming is obviously minimal, and because they have a faster metabolism than other breeds, owing to their higher body temperature, these cats have a big appetite. Therefore you must take great care not to overfeed them.

■ **Above:** *The coat of this Cornish Rex is slightly wavy, especially on its back.*

Ocicat

This exotic domestic cat with leopard-like spots has been bred selectively to emulate the spotted beauty of the wild big cats. The first Ocicat appeared in 1964 in the United States when Virginia Daly was trying to develop an Abyssinian pointed Siamese. A beautiful spotted, golden male kitten was born in a litter from a second-generation Siamese-Abyssinian cross. It was called an 'Ocicat' by Mrs Daly's daughter because it resembled a baby Ocelot. The American Shorthair was subsequently introduced to add size and a silver colour range, and outputting to Abyssinians is still allowed, thereby adding to the gene pool. The Ocicat was officially recognised in the United States in 1986.

■ **Below:** *A Chocolate Silver Spotted Ocicat shows the distinctive tabby 'M' marking on its forehead.*

Coat

The short, close-lying coat is smooth and sleek with a satiny texture and a lustrous sheen. It is agouti banded with the exception of the tip of the tail, and each hair must be long enough to carry the bands of colour. The spots lie in rows along the spine but are more randomly scattered on the body.

Coat colours

The following colours are permissible: Silver, Chocolate, Sorrel, Lilac, Blue, Fawn, Tawny, Chocolate Silver, Fawn Silver, Blue Silver, Lilac Silver and Sorrel Silver.

Appearance

This medium to large cat has a long, well-muscled body. It moves gracefully and fluently, keeping low to the ground like a big cat stalking its prey. The medium-length legs are muscular, ending in oval-shaped feet. The wedge-shaped head is slightly curved from muzzle to cheek. The round-tipped ears with vertical tufts are large. The almond-shaped eyes are rimmed with dark fur.

Temperament

In spite of its 'wild' appearance, the Ocicat is affectionate, friendly and good-tempered. It does not like being left alone and will complain loudly. It responds well to the human voice and is relatively easy to train. Like the Siamese from which they were bred, Ocicats are highly vocal, attention-seeking and companionable. Extrovert and friendly, some Ocicats do not like to live with other cats. They like access to outdoors and do not make very good indoor cats.

Daily care

Although it is an exotic breed, the Ocicat is usually very healthy and does not require special care. The coat needs only minimal grooming.

Temperament

Sweet-natured, friendly, attention-seeking

Family suitability

A sociable family pet

Grooming

Minimal grooming required

Outdoors

Needs access to outdoors

Summary
An exotic, graceful cat with an affectionate nature

■ **Below:** *The eyes of the Ocicat are prominent with dark rims.*

Shorthair

Bengal

Temperament

Intelligent, loving, playful

Family suitability

Adjusts well to family life

Grooming

Minimal grooming required

Outdoors

A cat that needs access to outside

Summary

A distinctive-looking cat with a playful nature

Owning a beautiful Bengal is like having a wild cat in miniature in your home, as far as the cat's appearance goes. This unusual cat was developed in the United States in the 1970s as a result of a special investigation into the natural immunity to feline leukaemia of the Asian Leopard Cat from southern Asia. It came from a hybrid derived by mating one of these cats with a domestic shorthair. The Bengal thus combines the temperament of a domestic cat with the striking markings and colouring of the wild Leopard Cat.

Coat

The medium-short coat is thick and plush with a distinctive luminous sheen. Whereas black

■ **Left:** *The Bengal resembles a miniature wild cat with its spotted, banded coat.*

■ **Right:** *Although it looks wild, the Bengal has a loving, playful nature and makes a good pet.*

and brown Bengals appear to have a gold dusting over their coat, the Snow coloured cats have a pearly sheen. The soft, dense fur on the underparts is paler than that on the remainder of the body, which may be marked with randomly placed spots, leopard-like rosettes and horizontal bands. The slender tail is ringed with a dark tip, and the legs are barred.

Appearance

This relatively large cat has a sleek, muscular body and strong legs with quite large, rounded feet. The medium-length tail is carried low to the ground. The small, narrow, wedge-shaped head has puffed whisker pads and rounded, wide-based ears. The almond-shaped eyes are usually green but may be gold or hazel in Brown Tabbies; blue-green or gold in Burmese- or Tonkinese-type cats; or sometimes even blue in Snow coloured cats.

Temperament

In spite of its recent part-wild ancestry, the Bengal is usually playful and loving and will adapt well to family life. Intelligent and responsive, it is a skilful hunter.

Daily care

Although it will live happily inside, the Bengal likes freedom and space to roam. Ideally, it needs access to a garden or outside run. Its coat requires only minimal grooming. It does enjoy playing games so you should put aside some time for play each day.

Coat colours

It may be Brown/Black Spotted or Brown/Black Marbled on an orange to play grey background; or its may be Snow Spotted or Snow Marbled with an ivory, creamy white or fawn background.

Useful addresses

British Veterinary Association
7 Mansfield Street
London W1M 0AT
Tel: 0207 636 6541

People's Dispensary for Sick
Animals (Head Office)
White Chapel Way
Priorslee
Telford
Shropshire TF2 9PQ
Tel: 01952 290999

Royal Society for the Prevention
of Cruelty to Animals
The Causeway
Horsham
West Sussex RH12 1HG
Tel: 01403 261181

Toxoplasmosis Trust
61 Collier Street
London N1 9BE
Helpline: 0207 713 0599

Wood Green Animal Shelters
Heydon
Royston
Herts SG8 8PN
Tel: 01763 838329

The Governing Council of the Cat
Fancy (GCCF)
4–7 Penel Orlieu
Bridgwater
Somerset TA6 3PG
Tel: 01278 427575
Fax: 01278 446627
Email:
GCCF_CATS@compuserve.com
Website:
http://ourworld.compuserve.
com/homepages/GCCF_CATS

The Feline Advisory Bureau
Taeselbury
High Street
Tisbury
Wiltshire SP3 6LZ

Tel: 01747 871872
Fax: 01747 871873
Email: fab.fab@ukonline.co.uk
Website: www.fabcats.org

Cats Protection
17 King's Road
Horsham
West Sussex RH13 5PN
Tel: 01403 221900
Fax: 01403 218414
Email: cpl@cats.org.uk
Website: www.cats.org.uk

The Association of Pet Behaviour
Counsellors (APBC)
PO Box 46
Worcester
WR8 9YS
Tel: 01386 751151
Fax: 01386 751151
Email:
apbc@petbcent.demon.co.uk
Website: www.apbc.org.uk

Acknowledgments

Fiona and Lee Adams, Mark and Sam Aldous, Clare Archer, Sally Backhouse, Jo Baldwin, Linda Blackburn, Claire Bridges, Mrs Brown and her Exotic Shorthair cats, Lisa Cameron, Sue Clarke, Rolf Clayton, Karen Cleyer, Gillian Crossley-Holland, Lindsy and Holly Dorrill, Daren Evans, Lisa Feacey, Chris and Lesley Fisk, Carole Florey, Jill Fyfe and her Bengal cats, Mel and Neil Gardner and their Norwegian Forest cats, Jan Lacy and her Korat cats, Linda and Paul Lewis, Deborah Love, Karen Lynn, Jill Macdonald, Louise Malone, Mr. and Mrs. Meekings, Mrs Miller, Colin and Joy Norfolk and their Abyssinian cats, Sarah Palmer, Wendy Raphael, Rebecca Reeve, Carol Reynolds, Laura Riches, Marion Rutherford, Peggy Schoeberl, Sylvia Smith and her Angora and Balinese cats, Tracy Stewart, Vivianne Turner, Jenny Thornton and Zena Ugolini.

Our special thanks go to Jim and Monica McLaren and their Egyptian Mau and Singapura cats, Kirsty Backhouse and her Tonkinese and Burmese cats, Mrs Barrell and her Persian cats and Nicky Palmer and her cats Theo and Suzie.

INDEX

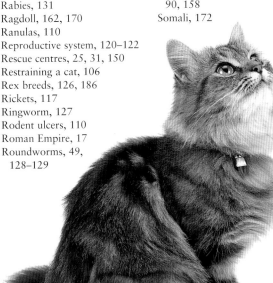